# BUILDINGS & LANDSCAPES

JOURNAL OF THE VERNACULAR ARCHITECTURE FORUM
VOLUME 30 | NUMBERS 1/2 | SPRING/FALL 2023

I0866278

*Buildings & Landscapes* (ISSN 1936-0886) is published twice a year in the spring and fall by the University of Minnesota Press, 111 Third Avenue South, Suite 290, Minneapolis, MN 55401-2520. http://www.upress.umn.edu.

Published in cooperation with the Vernacular Architecture Forum (VAF). Members of the VAF receive the journal as one of the benefits of membership. For further information about membership, go to https://vafweb.org/join.

Copyright 2023 by the Vernacular Architecture Forum

All rights reserved. With the exception of fair use, no part of this publication may be reproduced, stored in a retrieval system, or transmitted, in any form or by any means, electronic, mechanical, photocopying, recording, or otherwise, without a license or authorization from the Copyright Clearance Center (CCC) or the prior written permission of the Vernacular Architecture Forum.

Postmaster: Send address changes to *Buildings & Landscapes,* University of Minnesota Press, 111 Third Avenue South, Suite 290, Minneapolis, MN 55401-2520.

Manuscripts should be prepared to conform to the *Chicago Manual of Style*. Contributors agree that manuscripts submitted to *Buildings & Landscapes* will not be submitted for publication elsewhere while under review by the journal. Please feel free to direct any inquiries to either editor: Michael J. Chiarappa, Washington College, Center for Environment and Society, 485 South Cross Street, Chestertown, Maryland 21620, mchiarappa2@washcoll.edu; Margaret M. Grubiak, Department of Humanities, Villanova University, 800 E. Lancaster Avenue, Villanova, Pennsylvania 19085, margaret.grubiak@villanova.edu. Please send submissions to both editors, preferably in electronic form, illustrations included. Please see https://vafweb.org/buildingsandlandscapes for author guidelines.

Address subscription orders, changes of address, and business correspondence (including requests for permission and advertising orders) to *Buildings & Landscapes,* University of Minnesota Press, 111 Third Avenue South, Suite 290, Minneapolis, MN 55401–2520.

*Subscriptions:* For our current subscription rates please see our website: http://www.upress.umn.edu. For back issues, contact the Vernacular Architecture Forum. *Buildings & Landscapes* is a benefit of membership in the Vernacular Architecture Forum. Digital subscriptions to *Buildings & Landscapes* are available online through Project MUSE at https://muse.jhu.edu/.

The Vernacular Architecture Forum is the premier organization in the United States studying ordinary buildings and landscapes. Established in 1979–80 to promote the appreciation of and scholarship on vernacular structures, it is an interdisciplinary organization composed of scholars from many fields, including history, architectural history, geography, anthropology, sociology, landscape history, preservation, and material culture studies. Since its founding, the VAF has played a major role in the academic study and preservation of common buildings. The VAF holds an annual meeting, publishes an electronic newsletter and a journal, and maintains a website.

Copyright note for Figures 1, 3, 5, 7, 8, and 11 in Tania Gutiérrez-Monroy, "Bodies, Shawls, and Train Cars: Women and the Traveling Homes of the Mexican Revolution": the reproduction of images of archeological and historical monuments is regulated by the Ley Federal sobre Monumentos y Zonas Arqueologicos, Artisticos e Historicos and its Regulations, hence requiring approval of the Instituto Nacional de Antropologia e Historia.

Volume 30 is a double issue of *Buildings & Landscapes* and includes both issues 1 and 2.

EDITORS
Lydia Mattice Brandt
*University of South Carolina*
and
Michael J. Chiarappa
*Washington College*

EDITOR DESIGNATE
Margaret M. Grubiak
*Villanova University*

REVIEW EDITORS
Rachel Leibowitz
*SUNY College of Environmental Science and Forestry, Syracuse*
and
Amanda C. Roth Clark
*Whitworth University*

ILLUSTRATION EDITOR
Laura Kilcer VanHuss

EDITORIAL BOARD
Anna Vemer Andrzejewski
*University of Wisconsin–Madison*

Catherine W. Bishir, editorial advisor
*Preservation North Carolina*

James Michael Buckley
*University of Oregon*

Gretchen Buggeln
*Christ College, Valparaiso University*

Jennifer Cousineau
*Parks Canada*

Cynthia G. Falk
*Cooperstown Graduate Program, SUNY Oneonta*

Jeffrey E. Klee
*Classical American Homes Preservation Trust*

Matthew Gordon Lasner
*Hunter College, CUNY*

Richard Longstreth
*George Washington University*

Sarah Lynn Lopez
*University of Texas, Austin*

Carl Lounsbury
*College of William and Mary*

William Moore
*Boston University*

Louis P. Nelson
*University of Virginia*

Dell Upton
*University of California, Los Angeles*

# BUILDINGS & LANDSCAPES

JOURNAL OF THE VERNACULAR ARCHITECTURE FORUM

VOLUME 30 | NUMBERS 1/2 | SPRING/FALL 2023

MICHAEL J. CHIARAPPA

# Editor's Note

As most readers of *Buildings and Landscapes* (*B&L*) know, the Vernacular Architecture Forum (VAF) emerged in 1980 from a cohort of researchers committed to liberating the compelling stories of buildings that were not being given adequate attention, or in some cases were simply being ignored. So, in no small way, while VAF is about *buildings,* it is also, in equal measure, about *building* a paradigm that democratizes our considerations regarding what is experienced and meaningful in the widely conceived realms of architectural tradition and cultural landscape.

This double issue of *B&L* reflects these aspirations—both in its content and in the diversity of approaches taken by its authors. Throughout his career, longtime VAF member Joseph Sciorra has dedicated his energy to interpreting Italian American expressive culture, particularly as it has taken shape in the materiality of the group's vibrant devotional displays of vernacular religiosity. While some Italian American street feasts (*feste*) honoring the Madonna and other Catholic saints are recognized through their sheer cultural endurance or historical imprint in a community's collective memory, in other cases, they have gained wider public recognition through depictions in popular culture and cultural revitalization. But it is the "ephemeral constructions," what Sciorra describes as "decorative illuminations, elaborate sidewalk altars, freestanding multistoried chapels, and various ambulatory structures," that shape the contours of these ritualistic cultural landscapes. In the first exploration of its kind, Sciorra examines these fleeting material expressions and how they artistically imbue depth in devotions rooted in the Italian immigrant experience.

Similarly, the theme of ephemerality is paramount in Tania Gutiérrez-Monroy's article. She inverts the paradigm of architectural fixity, and instead, looks at place-making as a transient process inextricably connected to the bodies of women—*soldaderas*—who, while following soldiers, created fleeting domestic settings for them during the early twentieth-century Mexican Revolution. Central in constructing these settings were the improvised use of shawls that covered these women and the train cars that moved the troops. Shawls secured domestic items to women's bodies and then transitioned to being temporary walls or tents when needed in settings where soldiers camped or were temporarily housed in train cars.

The essays by Catherine Bishir and Alexander Wood take us into areas that have been a bedrock of vernacular architecture studies in the United States: the experience and occupational cultures of building artisans. Bishir's work on enslaved building artisans in antebellum North Carolina has been central in wider national conversations concerning the roles African Americans played in constructing some of the country's most well-known built environments. Along with illuminating the overlooked skill of enslaved artisans, Bishir provides vital methodological guidance for those investigating Black building artisans in other areas of the country and the tradition they established for themselves both before and following emancipation. Wood's research takes us into a new building tradition following the Civil

War, focusing on the structural ironworkers of New York City during the second half of the nineteenth century. Seemingly taking a cue from the sublime sheen that would later be cast by Lewis Hine's photographs of workers constructing the steel frame of the Empire State Building, Wood looks backward to the artisans who pioneered iron-framed structures, detailing the skill, tools, construction techniques, and unionization challenges they faced.

This volume of *B&L* is rounded out by two essays, one by James Kelleher, whose content will be readily recognizable by vernacular architecture researchers—the framed buildings of seventeenth- and eighteenth-century New England—and one by Robert Craig, whose material may be less familiar: the use of fire insurance records and the insights they provide on vernacular buildings and landscapes. Kelleher aims to present new perspectives on what are variously known as New England's "half houses" or end-chimney houses in southeastern Massachusetts, particularly the double-pile versions and how they structured interior organization. For Craig, the scarcity of documentary evidence that can sometimes accompany vernacular building and landscape patterns can be bolstered by the policy registers, daily reports, and graphic documents produced by insurance companies.

Finally, if VAF is about work that liberates our thinking about buildings and landscapes, then *B&L* strives to be a useful vehicle in advancing those aims. Such aspirations can only be achieved by the contributions of its editors, editorial board, peer reviewers, and VAF's wider membership. To this end, several acknowledgments are warranted. When I joined *B&L* as coeditor, I was honored to succeed Carl Lounsbury, whose scholarship, dedicated service, and humane temperament has advanced our field in countless ways. But added to this privilege was the opportunity to join Lydia Mattice Brandt as coeditor. Many in VAF are aware of Lydia's exemplary contributions as an architectural historian, historic preservationist, and public historian, as well as her wide-ranging leadership as president of the Southeast Chapter of the Society of Architectural Historians (SESAH) and vice-chair of South Carolina's State Board of Review for the National Register of Historic Places. But what most have not had the opportunity to see over the past four years in her role as *B&L* coeditor is the gracious intellect and mentoring that has accompanied her work in this role. Whether working with established scholars, graduate students aiming for their first publication, or independent researchers looking for an outlet for their work, Lydia's encouragement and commitment to this enterprise sets an admirable standard for how we should move our field forward. I will miss the good humor and positive spirit that Lydia brought to our work, and her contributions to *B&L* are just a prelude to the leadership she will provide for VAF in the years to come. She deserves heartfelt thanks from all of us and we wish her well in her continuing research and teaching at the University of South Carolina.

Additional thanks must also be extended to the other departing editors, A. Ian Stevenson (illustration editor) and Rachel Leibowitz (book review editor). We can scarcely underestimate the technical challenges that confront image preparation for *B&L*, and Ian's adroit handling of the process made the coeditors' tasks immeasurably more manageable and upheld the journal's capacity to provide compelling visual narrative. The same gratitude extends to Rachel for her efforts in consistently finding thoughtful book reviewers for *B&L*.

While we bid adieu to our outgoing editors, we are invigorated by the accomplished group of new editors that are joining *B&L*. Margaret M. Grubiak joins me as coeditor. She is Professor of Architectural History in the Department of Humanities at Villanova University. She completed her PhD and Master of Architectural History at the University of Virginia. Her research focuses on twentieth-century religious architecture in the United States, including her books *White Elephants on Campus: The Decline of the University Chapel in America, 1920–1960* (2014) and *Monumental Jesus: Landscapes of Faith and Doubt in Modern* America (2020). She has also published on American religious landscapes in *Winterthur Portfolio, Material Religion, Technology & Culture,* and *Buildings & Landscapes.* She received the Catherine W. Bishir Prize from the Vernacular Architecture Forum in 2017.

Amanda C. Roth Clark joins *B&L* as book review editor. Dean of the Library & Special Programs at Whitworth University in Spokane, Washington, she received her PhD from the University of Alabama. She holds a Master of Library and Information Studies degree, a Master of Arts in Theology, and an MA and BA from the University of Oregon in the fields of architectural history and Chinese art. She is coauthor of *Understanding Architecture: Its Elements, History, and Meaning* (2013), and *American Architecture: A History* (2016) with Leland M. Roth.

Laura Kilcer VanHuss joins *B&L* as illustration editor. She is a scholar and curatorial consultant whose work centers on the history, identity, and interpretation of historic houses, with a focus on those cultural landscapes with histories of trauma and/or enslavement. Having served as the curator at Oak Alley Foundation for eleven years, she now functions in a consulting capacity for the National Trust for Historic Preservation and other institutions. She has lectured as guest speaker at the University of New Orleans and Tulane University and is the editor of *Charting the Plantation Landscape from Natchez to New Orleans* (2021).

On behalf of *B&L* and the wider membership of VAF, I am delighted by the talented team—Margaret, Amanda, and Laura—that is joining me and I look forward to the working relationships we will collectively forge in shepherding the journal as an outlet for original research in vernacular architecture and landscapes.

JOSEPH SCIORRA

# "The Strange Artistic Genius of This People"

## *The Ephemeral Art and Impermanent Architecture of Italian Immigrant Catholic Feste*

ABSTRACT

During the late nineteenth and early twentieth centuries, Italian working-class immigrants in the United States staged religious *feste* (street feasts) in honor of the Madonna and other Catholic saints to express their beliefs in a socially acceptable, aesthetically pleasing, and recognizable manner. Impermanent edifices and other ephemeral constructions were integral parts of these cultural-religious extravaganzas. Hanging decorative illuminations, elaborate sidewalk altars, freestanding multistoried chapels, and various ambulatory structures were architectural wonders that boldly transformed, sacralized, and claimed American urban landscapes. A vernacular baroque aesthetic permeated the occupation and sacralization of the streets that engendered hallowed and convivial topographies that would have lasting ramifications for how people imagined their lives and neighborhoods. This article examines how these transient objects of devotion, predominantly in East Coast cities, enacted and proclaimed a diasporic community of believers that challenged hegemonic notions of artistry, religion, the built environment, and the public sphere. Ephemeral festival architecture captivated the attention of outsiders, including photographers, journalists, and visual artists, who depicted them in words and imagery. The article also contextualizes this source material as part of the Progressive era's xenophobic climate and, in particular, the picturesque gaze that racialized and othered Italian immigrants.

For his 1974 sequel *The Godfather: Part II*, director Francis Ford Coppola went to extraordinary lengths to recreate in mediated form a *festa*, or Italian Catholic street feast, in 1917 immigrant New York City. Bunting and flags hanging from tenement façades, decorative illuminations arching across the street, and an Italian-style processional band give the film's mise-en-scène a sense of authenticity. Coppola's cinematic ethnic realism includes using the statue of St. Roch (San Rocco) that belongs to a lay religious voluntary association active since 1889.[1] The centerpiece of this extravagant cinematic setting was an outdoor chapel where the processed figure was placed (Figure 1). What Coppola (and the production crew) must not have known was that his rendering of a festival structure, with its flat, marbleized surface studded with light bulbs, was a stylistic anachronism. It was based on models found at other New York City *feste* (the Italian plural for festa) during the early 1970s, when Coppola's immigrant saga was being filmed, and that were, by that time, greatly diminished examples of the architectural wonders created by Italian immigrant artisans from the 1890s up until the middle of the twentieth century.

The freestanding multitiered baroque-style shrines constructed by Italian immigrants consisted of recessed, arcuated niches where religious statues were housed, as well as pilasters and Corinthian columns, scrolls and volutes, medallions, triangular and pointed spires, and a pediment or a dome topping the structure (Figure 2). Stylistically these spectacular works referenced the fronts of baroque churches and cathedrals and exhibited an exceptional degree of detail and craft. Structurally, they were façade-like, with no significant depth beyond the alcove for the displayed effigy. These impermanent edifices were built with wood framing and their frontispieces made from molded papier-mâché or plaster, decorated with canvas, colored paper, tinsel, and gilded trimming. The sheer size of them was impressive—festa chapels were constructed up to five stories high, looming above the devotees gathered at their bases in the street below. Their artistry demonstrated a high level of design and expertise as they were the work of specialized artisans, the vast majority of whom remain unknown.

The street chapel was but one element in the festival complex that contributed to a holistic environment combining the sacred and the profane in a uniquely southern Italian social-religious aesthetic. The procession of the statue—the festa's raison d'être—consisted of devotees often walking barefoot as acts of penance and carrying large, heavy candles and wax ex-votos in the shape of body parts (objects offered in petition or in thanks for heavenly intercession), usually under the sweltering summer sun, moving through the narrow city streets where vendors with pushcarts or makeshift stalls hawked religious items and an assortment of foods. Musicians accompanied the ambulatory ritual and entertained people at nightly concerts. The "sacred theater of the festa" included the sounds of ardent prayers and hymns, brass bands performing symphonic marches, and the explosion of fireworks; the smells of burning candles, frying foods, and perspiration; and the visual spectacle of decorative illuminations, flags, and banners.[2] The vibrant and intense sensory overload was the driving pulse of Italian immigrants' enactment of faith and ethnic affinity in urban spaces.

Few scholars have sought to examine the artistic and architectural scenography of the Italian Catholic immigrant festa.[3] Denise Mangieri DiCarlo's 1990 dissertation on New York City feasts is one of the few studies to look at the various components that went into the making of the dense and dynamic public display events. Her work examines a broad range of elements, from fireworks to music, from processional formations to food vendors, by focusing on the feasts for Our

Figure 1. The St. Roch festa chapel from *The Godfather: Part II*. Still capture from digital file.

Figure 2. Street chapel for the Our Lady of Mt. Carmel festa located at East 112th Street, Harlem, Manhattan, reported to be fifty feet tall, depicted in "From Sunny Italy," *New-York Tribune Illustrated Supplement*, July 12, 1903, 5–6.

Lady of Mount Carmel, St. Anthony of Padua, and St. Januarius (San Gennaro) in Manhattan.[4] On the other hand, Robert Orsi's now seminal work *The Madonna of 115th Street* unpacks the feast of Our Lady of Mount Carmel in Harlem, Manhattan, to examine what he calls the "theology of the streets," that is, the ways in which the festa dramatized the fears and aspirations of the immigrant devotees, primarily women, and their children.[5] Orsi's nuanced analysis helps us understand the festa as an environment in which domestic family concerns played out in the sacralized public sphere, engendering a unique sense of place. His study above others provides an emic understanding of the historical festa from the perspective of immigrant participants.

The present essay builds on that research by focusing on the sacred artistic expression of the festa, the ways in which immigrant folk artists and craftspeople utilized, as I have written elsewhere, "ethnically infused aesthetic and religious choices, knowledge, and skills to give expression to individual creativity, shared values and spirituality, and a sense of community."[6] In this article, I am concerned with delving deeper into the topic of immigrant festa creativity to document and begin to categorize specific artistic objects and architectural structures that have not, until now, enjoyed the kind of scholarly analysis they deserve. In addition, my research leads me to organize these objects into four types of temporary festa art forms and architecture: 1) *decorative illuminations* that arched across streets to mark the festivalized urban space and outlined church façades; 2) *sidewalk altars* assembled by devotees in front of their home apartment buildings; 3) the above-mentioned *street chapels*; and 4) *ambulatory structures* such as carts and towers. The altars were made by individual devotees who assembled these works for a single feast as an expression of personal devotion to a specific aspect of the Virgin Mary or another Catholic saint. On the other hand, illuminations, chapels, and ambulatory structures were the work of professional artisans who were paid to construct these ceremonial objects for a variety of feasts with which they did not necessarily have a religious or personal affiliation. My study features a multitude of examples from New York City, where much photographic and textual documentation was produced, but also looks at impermanent festa structures in Gloucester, Massachusetts, and Chicago, Illinois.[7]

For Italian immigrants in the late nineteenth and early twentieth centuries, the aesthetics of the festa were bold artistic statements of religious and ethnic claims to urban space (Figure 3). These individuals took creative advantage of the possibilities of city life by adapting their religious artistry to the social-spatial conditions of vertical tenements, storefronts, and congested urban streets in the public feting of the pantheon of Catholic sacred personages. White American Protestants, who historically deemed religiosity a private matter, viewed such extravagant public displays of religion as inappropriate, tasteless, and superficial.[8] Locales of Italian migratory spatial practices such as these, according to Teresa Fiore, were both "pre-occupied," in that they were previously inhabited, and "preoccupied" with concern, thus constituting unstable realms of encounter, contestation, and negotiation.[9] The feste were dissonant sites for representatives and affiliates of institutional power like the police, the clergy, and journalists, as well as ethnic leaders, who all too often found these religious practices, their aesthetics, and in particular the use of city space, to be transgressive.[10] Nancy Fraser's notion of "subaltern counterpublics" is useful for understanding how "subordinated social groups" like working-class Italian immigrant and religious minority Catholics at the time established alternative settings that made manifest their beliefs in a socially accepted, aesthetically pleasing, and recognizable manner.[11] With these observations in mind, I am interested in exploring what Arjun Appadurai called "the constructed landscape of collective aspirations," which in the case of the feste constituted the vibrant and varied ways Italian immigrants used material culture, architecture, ritual behavior, and public ceremonial display to shape their sacred, artistic, and ethnic environments.[12] This essay sets out to rediscover the world of Italian Catholic immigrant placemaking through an examination of the mechanics and artistry of lived religious practice,

Figure 3. Street chapel erected for the feast of St. Mark the Evangelist, patron saint of Manocalzati (Avellino province), in Campania. Newark, New Jersey, ca. 1910. It is possible that this structure is the handiwork of the Suppa brothers (see Figure 6). Courtesy of the Newark Public Library/Michael Immerso.

especially through the material culture and built environment that visualizes and puts into action those practices. These aesthetic and devout acts of community engagement offered alternative notions of religious performance and urban involvement that fostered group identity through an enacted sense of place that would have long-lasting ramifications for how people imagined their lives and neighborhoods.

My article first looks at the nature of ephemeral objects and the difficulties of documenting their existence. I continue by examining how these festa art forms were represented in the English-language press within the anti-immigrant environment of the Progressive Era, and in particular the picturesque gaze that focused upon Italian immigrants. I then provide a brief history of and the contextual grounding for the creation and use of these structures and discuss these sacred arts in relationship to urban life and the immigrants' making of home, followed by an exploration of the four festa art forms—and their makers, when possible—that are the subject of my essay. By way of conclusion, I touch briefly on these vernacular sacred arts beyond the world of the immigrant neighborhood as memory culture for descendants and as sources of inspiration for visual artists in the work of particular painters.

## Creating a History of the Ephemeral through the Picturesque Gaze

How do we locate the ephemeral structures of past immigrant feste? What are the processes for tracking what José Esteban Muñoz calls the "traces, glimmers, residues, and specks of things" involving performances and fleeting objects long gone?[13] Kay Turner addresses the problematics of the ephemeral in her essay on spontaneous vernacular 9/11 memorials:

> Defined by the present, it [ephemerality] only exists in the present moment and its performance tense, even if it makes reference to the past or to the future, is a performative present. With reference to this over-determined present tense, ephemerality defines the vernacular workings of the phenomenological; it refers us to the fleeting moments in which sociality is *actual* occurring in experience and performance.[14]

As Coppola's cinematic simulacrum reveals in *The Godfather: Part II,* the full extent of the artistry from the immigrant past is felt but not fully known in contemporary Italian American Catholic feste. The persistence of this "material transience" in the twentieth-first century is a manifestation of lingering historical social forces and by extension a legacy of aesthetic predilections.[15] In some cases, local knowledge of past feast ephemera is conveyed through ongoing practice, oral history, vernacular documentation, and local collecting of artifacts. More often than not, present day feast participants acknowledge the significant loss of artistry and craftsmanship in the making of ceremonial festa objects, but the extent to which elements distinguish past works from their modern-day manifestations is at times difficult to measure and articulate. Uncovering the ephemeral structures of the immigrant past, we can begin to locate, as Muñoz suggests, "traces of lived experiences and performances of lived experience, maintaining experiential politics and urgencies long after these structures of feeling have been lived."[16]

What are we to make of the "ephemeral witnessing" of immigrant feste contained in the pages of the English-language press providing a wealth of textual and visual information about a wide variety of festa arts?[17] Descriptions found in the *New York Times*, the *Brooklyn Daily Eagle*, and other newspapers from the late nineteenth and early twentieth centuries often were part of reports on conflagrations, intra-ethnic rivalries, theft, violence, and other ascribed pathologies of sordid slum life. Headlines such as "Noisy Italians" (1889), "San Rocco Honored by Rival Factions" (1906), and "Fire Mars a Festival" (1903) describe—and to a large degree deride—Italian immigrants and their feste.[18] One telling example is a 1906 article that situates the Our Lady of Mt. Carmel festa in a squalid Harlem setting: "Little Italy was en fête yesterday, and its dark, dismal streets, with their towering tenements, many of which shelter thirty families of astonishing size, were transformed into a riot of color and gayety in honor of the feast of Our Lady of Mount Carmel, patron saint of the church."[19] The lead sentence for a *New York Daily Tribune* article on the 1906 feast for St. Roch in lower Manhattan consists of the following blanket statement: "Next to a religious festa, there is nothing Little Italy so enjoys as a red hot quarrel."[20] *New York Times* readers learned that during the 1889 St. Roch feast not only did devotees fete their spiritual patron in "exuberant fashion" to the consternation of firefighters and the police, but also that two musicians in the band went at each other with knives, drawing blood.[21] According to another uncredited journalist for the same newspaper, it took twenty-five police officers to maintain the peace between two rival groups of St. Roch devotees in lower Manhattan in 1906 who "went to bed toward morning, after many a Chianti bottle empty and with no new murder case for the Detective Bureau to work on."[22] The rhetoric of these accounts is in keeping with the racialized othering that became the dominant narrative and depiction of southern Italian immigrants at the time.[23] Journalists, politicians, social reformers, and others proclaimed or intimated in their various didactic discussions and writings that Italian immigrants were superstitious, disorderly, filthy, insular, philoprogenitive, volatile, vindictive, violent, and criminally inclined.[24]

Perhaps the most characteristic framing device English-language journalists used for reporting on the religious practices of Italian immigrants is that of the picturesque, a characterization of quaint primitives "untouched by modernity, arrested in their development, and bathed in pristine archaism."[25] The term and its associated referents are found repeatedly in English-language accounts of feste, as with the "oddly picturesque spectacle" that was the 1900 St. Rosa celebration in Brooklyn and "the Peculiarities, both Picturesque and Otherwise" of the 1903 Our Lady of Mt. Carmel feast in Harlem, thus exhibiting a fascination with the somewhat bewildering sights in the midst of American cities.[26] A description of St. Roch devotees during a Manhattan festa effectively stages a theatrical tableau of the immigrant Italian slum, complete with costume and lighting: "The women in their many-colored shawls, scores of them very old and feeble, prayed long and hard in the streets, while burly laborers, still in their working clothes, stood uncovered and gazed at the statue above upon which a calcium light played steadily."[27]

According to Carrie Tirado Bramen, White American Protestants strategically reconfigured southern Italians, as well as other European immigrants of the period, from quaint primitives into the "urban picturesque" in attempts to manage perceptions of drastically changing U.S. cities and their new foreign-born populations.[28] Written texts, paintings, photographs, and films framed the new urban poor as charming, nonthreatening, and depoliticized stereotypes and recast the American urban landscape from "the rubbish, congestion, and misery of the city into a source of rough and rugged pleasure" for a tantalizing aesthetic spectacle.[29] Thus reports and images of the feste—those "Quaint Italian Customs of Summer Festal Day"—made the religious environments and practices more comprehensible and manageable by being subjugated ultimately within the American urban picturesque.[30] In turn, accounts of the feste became sources, guidebooks so to speak, for "armchair slummers" and actual "slumming parties," those excursions of middle-class White American Protestants seeking to be entertained by the cities' squalid sections where poor immigrants resided, which included the "curiosity seekers" who attended the Brooklyn feast of St. Ann in the summer of 1902.[31] Such knowledge of the racialized context of text and imagery of Italian immigrant feste is essential for understanding and using this material as source information for contemporary analysis.

English-language journalists were often fascinated by the intensity and inventiveness of the religious productions Italians staged in the city's streets. They were torn between characterizing such celebrations as "gaudy" or "beautiful," sometimes doing both in the same article:

> Mott Street was gaudily decorated for several blocks on either side of the stands. American and Italian flags hung from the windows of almost every apartment in the front of the tall tenement buildings, festoons of bunting were suspended from one building to another across the narrow street, and there were huge, fantastic vari-colored designs, representing Italian religious and fraternal orders on many of the houses. At night the street presented a strange and beautiful spectacle.[32]

Despite the commonly articulated derision, many of those writing about feste could not help but concede that the immigrants exhibited inimitable yet bewildering artistry; photographer and social reformer Jacob Riis was one such author who, writing about one improvised sacred installation, marveled at "the strange artistic genius of this people."[33]

Conversely, the Italian-language press at the time did not publish accounts of actual feasts but provided announcements beforehand of featured activities.[34] However, one brief passage from a book is noteworthy because it reveals much about immigrant elites' views of the festa and its vernacular artistry. Immigrant *prominenti* (literally, prominent ones) compiled and published in New York City *Gli italiani negli Stati Uniti d'America,* a volume of essays and photographs to accompany the Italians Abroad pavilion at the 1906 Universal Exposition in Milan, and as such provided a self-aggrandized profile of their accomplishments in the United States.[35] In the collection, Ercole Cantelmo, editor of the newspaper *Il Giornale Italiano,* authored an article on Italian immigrants' "traditions, customs, and feasts," focusing primarily on secular celebrations. However, Cantelmo briefly mentions religious feasts by using the term *festicciole,* which applies a suffix that denotes the diminutive, not necessarily referencing the productions' size but more their perceived cultural insignificance. Illustrating the article with a close-up photograph detailing a street chapel, Cantelmo frets that American visitors characterized the feste as "*intermezzi di vita medioevale fra un atto e l'altro della vita più civilmente moderna*" (interludes of medieval life between one act and another in the midst of the most civilized modernity), a statement suggesting discontent, possible embarrassment, and a perspective that reduces working-class immigrants to passive players mindlessly adhering to ahistorical holdovers (Figure 4).[36] With over a century of hindsight, we can now situate the impermanent festa structures within the dynamic creative agency of individuals actively remaking their lives in a new land by affirming their shared values of religiosity and artistic expression in the creation of a unique ethnically keyed style and a place-centric sense of community identity.

### Establishing an Italian Catholic Festa Environment in the United States

During the late nineteenth and early twentieth centuries, Italian immigrants formed mutual aid societies (*società di mutuo soccorso*) organized around town and regional affiliations that offered members unemployment and burial insurance. These lay religious voluntary associations introduced Catholic devotions popular in Italy and raised money, at great sacrifice, for the purpose of commissioning wood or gesso statues from artisans in Italy, shipping them to the United States, and organizing the annual processions and feste for their respective spiritual patrons. Some devotions were for highly localized saints like St. Cono of Teggiano (introduced in 1888), St. Paulinus of Nola (introduced in 1903), and the Black Madonna of Tindari (introduced in 1905), originating in the regions of Campania and Sicily.[37] Other feste organized in honor of sacred personages like St. Roch, St. Donatus (San Donato),

UN ALTARE VIENE ERETTO SUL MARCIAPIEDI

Figure 4. Detail of a street chapel with lit candles and wax ex-votos for an unidentified saint, presumably in New York City, published in *Gli italiani negli Stati Uniti d'America* (1906). James J. Periconi Collection of Italian-Language American Imprints, Queens College Special Collections and Archives.

and Our Lady of Mt. Carmel were widely popular with a broad spectrum of southern Italians.[38]

Regardless of who was being feted, the festa complex staged by Italian immigrants was a dense commingling of sacred and secular elements that combined ardent prayer and intense votive acts with food vendors, nightly musical entertainment, and convivial, often boisterous, socializing, culminating in a colorful and thunderous display of fireworks (Figure 5).[39] This creative and religious expression dramatized participants' fears and tribulations, their hopes and desires, in a strange and estranging new world in a temporarily manifested embodiment of community. Sally M. Promey's observation on the public display of religion is useful in understanding the Italian immigrant festa as "a discursive space, a social and political arena, where cultural negotiations about identities both individual and collective take place."[40] The engendering of a sense of home and familiarity involved reimagining and reconfiguring a past place and its associated beliefs, feelings, behaviors, and objects in a constantly emerging new place in the United States.

Irish American and German American ecclesiastics on the East Coast, who had struggled to Americanize the Roman Catholic Church in the years before the great wave of Italian immigration began in the 1880s, found Italian immigrant religious practices inappropriate and unsettling.[41] Clergy often objected to a number of issues concerning the festa, ranging from who ultimately received the donated monies to matters

Figure 5. Devotees of Our Lady of Succor congregating around a festa chapel and flanking bandstand, Mott Street, Manhattan, 1908. (The photograph is misidentified as being in Brooklyn.) Courtesy of the Library of Congress Prints and Photographs Division.

surrounding religious comportment and visual style in the public sphere. For Italian immigrants, such targeted reproaches constituted "an existential rejection of their whole value system."[42]

The tensions between parish priests and lay festa organizers in turn led to ingenious methods for the latter to establish and maintain sacred spaces beyond clerical control. Ecclesiastical oversight of the feast often centered on the custody of the society's religious statue and ultimately the monies offered as donations. To subvert clerical claims to these effigies, resourceful society members housed their figures during the festa not in the church, as was the custom in Italy, but in several nonecclesiastical venues. In 1899, immigrants from the Campanian town of Auletta (Salerno province) celebrated their patron St. Donatus with a procession that made its way to the backyard of a saloon on Elizabeth Street in Manhattan's Little Italy. Riis's account is most instructive:

> Between birthdays [feast days] . . . the saint was left in the loft of the saloon, lest the priest get hold of him and get a corner on him, as it were. Once he got him into his possession, he would not let the people have him except upon payment of a fee that would grow with the years. But the saint belonged to the people, not to the church. He was their home patron, and they were not going to give him up. In the saloon they had him safe.[43]

The frictions concerning Catholic practice and cultural aesthetics directly contributed to the emergence and dominance of the immigrant festa street chapels as countervailing practices and commentary—quite simply, expressions contesting the prevailing and dominant understandings of Catholic public life in the United States. In Italy, the processed religious statues were (and continue to be) housed year round in churches, but the struggle for hegemony over immigrant Catholicism led Italian practitioners in the United States to reconfigure and reinterpret a rich patrimony of religious festival arts and material culture for the new contested and contentious environment.[44] Even as U.S. national parishes based on country of origin and language became the sites for Italian festa-based religiosity, Italian immigrant Catholics struggled to exert control over the public expressions of their faith by improvising from a body of deep-seated and culturally attuned knowledge, skills, beliefs, and practices as means of confronting and addressing emerging conditions.[45]

### The Vernacular Baroque of Southern Italian Feste

Immigrant festa aesthetics discussed herein were derived from the baroque period of the 1600s and 1700s.[46] The period's emergent style was the artistic and philosophic expression of the Catholic Church's vigorous and ardent Counter-Reformation initiatives that were amplified by Spain's dominance in this theological enterprise and its rule over parts of Italy, especially the south, until the early eighteenth century. The Church and the court displayed their monumental power in the style of the times in city streets and plazas through extravagant spectacles and pageants commemorating weddings, coronations, canonizations, and other events that functioned as "instruments of propaganda."[47] These massive religious and civic spectacles employed ephemeral architectural props such as towers, arches, fountains, and gigantic statuary, as well as illuminations and fireworks. In Italy at the time, and particularly in southern Italian cities like Naples and Palermo, these colossal and orchestrated urban public displays dominated.[48]

The baroque aesthetic continued to influence southern Italian religious and artistic practices well beyond the historical period, as it eventually became popularized, localized, and highly prized for Catholic life throughout the region and eventually in various parts of the diaspora.[49] It was the *paratore* (decorator) in southern Italy who was responsible for designing and building festa structures like decorative illuminations and bandstands.[50] Despite the fact that religious statuary was housed in churches year round, their public viewing during the festa could occur in ceremonial structures erected outdoors, as was the case with the so-called *tosello* housing the equestrian figure of St. Theodore in the city of Brindisi (Apulia region) in 1908 and the undated structure for St. Anthony of Padua in Montesano sulla Marcellana (Salerno province), Campania.[51]

With their emigration to the United States in the late nineteenth and early twentieth centuries, Italian craftspeople relied on this legacy of artistic philosophy, religious tenets, and artisanal competencies in their implementation of a festivalized and performed baroque architecture and landscape (Figure 6).[52] The Italian manifestations of diasporic baroque sensibilities and proclivities in the United States created a continuity in displacement as they altered the use and understanding of urban space. The ceremonial occupation and sacralization of city streets proclaimed and enacted an ethnic community of believers that challenged hegemonic notions of artistry, religion, and the public sphere.

In the following four sections I examine the textual and photographic traces of the specific artistic and architectural festa elements that are the subject of my research: *decorative illuminations, sidewalk altars, street chapels,* and *ambulatory structures.* I have highlighted this quartet of feast components above others (e.g., the saint statue, the processional line-up) because as transitory objects of religious artistry they were instrumental in altering the perception of the pre-existing built environment to establish a realm of Italian Catholic sensibilities. And as stated previously, this material culture and vernacular architecture have not been sufficiently studied.

**Decorative Illuminations**

Decorative illuminations were the crowning achievement of the festa's mise-en-scène, with temporary arches framing the night sky, forming an illuminated canopy for feast-goers strolling below (Figure 7).[53] In the early years of Italian immigration, thousands of small multihued glass jars containing candles or wicks floating in oil were attached to wooden lattice frames held up by poles planted along the sidewalk.[54] Occasionally these jars were lined up in sets of red-white-green to emulate the Italian tricolor flag, a public proclamation of national affiliation and ethnic sentiment. In some cases, gas jets were used and eventually electric lights. In addition, paper lanterns were strung from various sites, including

Figure 6. Several unidentified Suppa brothers working on a festa edifice component at their 36 Sheffield Street atelier, Newark, New Jersey, ca. 1928. Eight Suppa brothers—Angelo, Antonio, Francesco, Joseph, Luca, a second Luca, Michael, and Pellegrino—were each listed as "decorator" at three locations at 33, 36, and 37 Sheffield Street in the 1928 Newark city directory. Domenico B. Suppa of 114th Street was listed as a salesman. Courtesy of the Newark Public Library/Michael Immerso.

Figure 7. Installing decorative illuminations for the opening of the Italian national parish church St. Anthony of Padua, Albany, New York, 1908, unidentified photographer. Courtesy of Library Collections, Albany Institute of History and Art.

balconies, windows, and the rooftops of tenement buildings to create captivating "artistic effects."[55] According to journalistic accounts, the colors and patterns delighted the eye with their "brilliancy and elaborateness, and the curious designs" that included columns, floral patterns, "a series of scroll and spiral lines," and "bleeding hearts and other religious and semi-religious designs."[56] It was the illuminations that most often caught the fancy of American-born observers.[57]

Ultimately, decorative lighting served to mark the borders of festivalized space. According to Roger Abrahams, festivals "draw their own boundaries for the occasion and redraw the boundaries of the host community, ironically establishing themselves in the areas that, in the everyday world, have their own boundaries."[58] In Brooklyn's Red Hook area, a dozen illuminated arches lined four city blocks of President Street during the 1900 St. Rosa feast, delineating and highlighting the social topographies of place-making.[59] Decorations also included the illuminations, flags, and draperies added by individuals to their stores, stands, and buildings. The festa lights transformed the quotidian urban streets of industrial labor and poor housing into spaces of animated sacred playfulness and demarcated the Italian immigrants' collective realm of dynamic presence and imagination.

Lighting also became an important feature in framing and accentuating the façades of local Catholic churches for immigrant parishioners feting the Madonna and other saints with architectural elements echoing festa chapels (Figure 8). Church fronts were outlined in electric lights to indicate and accentuate their central place in devotional and votive practice, such as Brooklyn's Church of the Sacred Heart of Jesus and Mary, which was outfitted in 1896 with lights "hung in diamond clusters" and three tiers of "a flower pot of the colored lights," and four years later was "brilliantly lighted with a series of scroll and spiral lines made of gas jets."[60]

Family-run lighting companies emerged to meet the growing market for festa illuminations: Ralph Iacovacci in Harlem and Arnaldo Migliaccio on Mulberry Street, Manhattan; the Sica Maintenance Corporation of Ozone Park,

Queens; Michael Mangalardi in Chicago; and Emilio Matarazzo (discussed later) in Boston.[61] We know the names of some of these *paratori* (plural of paratore) but very little else, other than to assume that they were all men. How did they learn their skills and adapt them to the American urban environment? How were designs developed and implemented? How much did they charge? Is it safe to assume that festa lighting designers were electricians who engaged in quotidian electrical work beyond the ceremonial installations? Like so many artisans discussed in this essay, the complete record of their lives and creativity is yet to be uncovered and written.

**Sidewalk Altars**

As an integral component of these religious celebrations, devotees assembled altars on sidewalks in front of their tenement buildings in honor of the saints.[62] These altars were not the work of paid (most likely only male) artisans or sponsored by a religious society but were instead devotional objects and votive offerings made by individuals and their families. Given the documentation of women's involvement in home altars—what Kay Turner calls "a matrifocal legacy of religious custom"—and Italian American women's assemblage of sidewalk altars in New York City during the late twentieth and early twenty-first centuries, one can speculate that Italian immigrant women were a driving force in the design and creation of these religious objects and urban spaces, even when menfolk were involved in their physical construction.[63] Given the gendered aspect of domestic altars in Italian American life, I have chosen to use this term for outdoor festa assemblages even though the physical and structural components of horizontality, a common altar feature, are not always evident from the various historical descriptions (see below).

Sidewalk altars were located along the processional route and became reference points for the ambulant ensemble. As in Italy, devotees waited at their outdoor altars for the procession to arrive and when it stopped, they would proclaim their petition, make a monetary donation, and receive a blessing from the priest. As nodes in a network of devotion, sidewalk altars were personal demonstrations of a larger collective of believers and reference points on the urban grid where the devout met to pray and socialize.[64]

Figure 8. Decorative illuminations on the façade of the Our Lady of Mt. Carmel Church, Melrose Park, Illinois, 1944. Courtesy of Casa Italia Chicago.

During the 1906 festa of Our Lady of Mt. Carmel in East Harlem, according to the *New York Times*, "miniature" altars were found "every few feet," and some "were very elaborate, and were not only draped with silks and satins, but contained large wax figures of the saints."[65] Henri Cartier-Bresson's 1947 photograph of a sidewalk altar made for the St. Januarius feast in downtown Manhattan is a useful one because of its clarity and detailed visual information, although it may not be completely representative of earlier, perhaps simpler, works (Figure 9). This assembled street installation combines horizontality with the tiered altar section and verticality with the draped open-air canopy and parted curtains. The altar cloth is

Figure 9. Sidewalk altar for St. Januarius, Little Italy, Manhattan, 1947. Photograph by Henri Cartier-Bresson, courtesy of Magnum Photos.

a white-on-white embroidered material laid out on the tabletop on which rest candles and cut flowers below a framed image of the saint attached to the building wall.[66] Near the curb is a makeshift stand in which over a dozen approximately three-foot candles burn. More than twenty people sit and stand in proximity to the altar. In addition to sidewalk altars, devotees also created sacred space on fire escapes and in apartment windows. One reporter, comparing them with the multistoried street chapels, noted that they are "simple, but an extravagance nonetheless" with plaster statues surrounded by burning candles.[67]

At times the distinction between individual devotees' sidewalk altars and the street chapels erected by lay religious organizations is difficult to discern in a photograph because of the significant size of the former. Textual information can also be misleading, as accompanying captions in the New York Public Library's "Photographic Views of New York City: 1870s–1970s" collection refer to all festa art and architecture interchangeably as "altars" or "shrines." Thus, a relatively large (approximately fifteen feet tall), vertically oriented structure with visible architectural elements—flat, painted column shafts and a pediment trimmed with foil—appears to be a family-created shrine that houses a festa society's statue (Figure 10).

### Street Chapels

Descriptions of festa structures sponsored by either a collective of devotees or a formally state-registered lay religious society (as opposed to an individual's family-created sidewalk altar) began in the late nineteenth century with relatively small and modest creations. There are a few examples of outdoor shrines consisting of nothing more than an altar decorated with drapery or inside a tent, as was the case in these two examples from Manhattan in 1899 and 1900, respectively:

> A tent had been pitched in a vacant space on the street, and inside an altar was put up. Steps led up to the altar and along them were rows of candles. A band was stationed inside and short exercises were held. Then the crowd passed out and formed in the street.[68]

> There was a booth in front of 243 Elizabeth Street which was the great attraction. The booth was an

Figure 10. "The statue of St. Anthony in a temporary shrine at 323 East 106th Street," Harlem, Manhattan, 1930 (#731688F). Courtesy of the New York Public Library.

> ordinary red and white cloth affair no bigger than a sentinel's box. In front of it sat two men.[69]

And yet these tent shrines could be quite elaborate. In 1883, a group of eighty railroad workers who had recently moved from New York City to Palmyra, a town outside of Rochester, New York, constructed an altar for an unspecified aspect of the Virgin Mary. The lengthy description reveals intriguing details about the elements that went into creating this sacred space:

> An artistic altar in a tent covering not more than 60 square feet of ground was the center of attraction, in front of which the services for the most part were conducted. The tent was lined inside with a modern design of paneled paper or curtains with green background and vases of flowers pictured in startling colors at the base. From the top hung half a dozen Chinese lanterns, diamond-shaped and radiant with all the colors of the rain-bow. Canvas covered the floor of the tent in front, but in the rear a row of six shelves like steps formed the altar. The edges of the shelves were adorned with red and blue and yellow tissue paper of the filigree pattern, similar to that used some years ago to ornament the ceilings of shops. A plaster of Paris temple about a foot square and pictures of the crucified Christ, the Holy Virgin, and St. Joseph occupied the central places on the shelves, and about them on every side were lighted candles. Several triangles and circles covered with tissue paper were placed at the sides and before the altar. As there was a little wind stirring all day several attendants were kept busily employed in relighting the candles.

The anonymous *New York Times* correspondent informs the reader that the Italian immigrants took weeks erecting the altar after work and spent a sum of $40 for materials.[70]

Italian immigrants took advantage of the limited space available in the dense urban areas of Manhattan. Riis describes the sacralized space for St. Donatus assembled in 1899 in a saloon's backyard by what appears to be nonprofessional devotees in lower Manhattan (Figure 11):

Figure 11. Jay Hambidge's illustration—"The shrine in the saloon back yard"—accompanying Jacob Riis's 1899 article about the St. Donatus feast in Manhattan's Little Italy for *The Century*.

Figure 12. Jacob Riis's photograph of an outdoor altar to St. Roch in an alley off Mulberry Street, Manhattan, May 23, 1895. Courtesy of Collins for Jacob A. Riis, Museum of the City of New York.

> It was a yard no longer but a temple. All the sheets of the tenement had been stretched so as to cover the ugly sheds and outhouses. Against the dark rear tenement, the shrine of the saint had been erected, shutting it altogether out of sight with a wealth of scarlet and gold. Great candles and little ones, painted and beribboned, burned in a luminous grove before the altar. . . . The fire-escapes of the tenement had, with the aid of some cheap muslin draperies, a little tinsel, and the strange artistic genius of this people, been transformed into beautiful balconies, upon which the tenants of the front house had reserved seats.[71]

Riis's article makes evident the profound makeover of the backyard alley in order to establish, develop, and maintain vernacular sites of religiosity autonomous from priestly authority.

The examples cited thus far involve to a large degree the use of paper, tinsel, and cloth to create a sacred environment. As Italian immigrants became more acclimated to their new homes and neighborhoods, Italian festa organizers began using additional architectural elements such as columns and pediments referencing Catholic church façades with increasing monumental verticality. In this way, Italian immigrant festa architecture was in keeping with the Catholic precept of "replication" in which sacred sites are copied as new creations in different locations.[72] The art of duplication within Catholicism established its own form of authenticity in which a copy of an original object is imbued with significance through its myriad associations. Thus, the creation of religious simulacra, whether of church architecture or festa structures in Italy, was a means by which Italian immigrants established sacred space in alleyways, backyards, and the streets where they found themselves, reconfiguring how the built environment could be imagined and used.

There is no better example of the festivalized and sacred transformation of urban space than two Riis photographs of Bandits' Roost, off Mulberry Street in lower Manhattan. His 1888 image shows ten people, the majority men, who confront the viewer in a portrait of immigrant urban life conveying a "hint of menace" and a "fascinating promise of danger."[73] Seven years later, the area had been converted into sacred space with the presence of an evidently nonprofessionally made altar that is a few feet taller than a man standing in front of it (Figure 12). The structure is made up of a tiered altar, laid out horizontally and covered in embroidered white cloth, on which stands a vertical structure. This handmade object consists of a rectangular alcove in which the sacred image resides, flanked by two panels decorated with triangles, which in turn are each edged by rectangular sheets of drapery. The structure has a pediment (it is not visibly evident that the tympanum contains any decorative elements) and oval acroteria resting at the apex and on both flanking sides.

Over the years, the festa chapels' architectonics remained fundamentally the same but were augmented in scale and decoration with the involvement of paid and skilled paratori. One need only compare the St. Roch object that Riis photographed in 1895 with the undated festa chapel to Our Lady of Succor in Manhattan (Figure 13). The form remains constant with the two structures—verticality, alcove, flanking columns, triangular pediment—but the superior detailing and craftsmanship of the latter are visibly evident. In 1902, a mere three years after Riis described and Jay Hambidge depicted the shrine to St. Donatus created by immigrants from Auletta in the courtyard behind the saloon, this community of devout townspeople feted their spiritual patron with a "large beautifully decorated archway" complete with "pillars" and an "immense canopy" in front of 272 Mott Street.[74] Newspaper accounts of the time would report that festa chapels in New York City were being erected as high as fifty feet, or five stories, tall (Figure 14).[75]

Very little textual information exists regarding the design and construction of festa chapels. One newspaper account offered this observation of street chapels in New York City: "Generally they are of wood, enameled or covered with bunting, with some attempt at fancy carving. The top pieces are most elaborate and follow various designs, generally allowing for floral decoration."[76] The wood balloon framing of these structures is evident in the image from the 1932 Feast of the Assumption at 121 Mott Street, Manhattan, which instead of being decorated with a façade of architectural elements is simply highlighted with electric lightbulbs.[77] Repeatedly reporters state that the structures' façades are made from canvas, paper, and tinsel, and yet the breadth of visual evidence indicates that the detailed ornamentation of these monumental structures was made from more substantial materials such as pasteboard, papier-mâché, plaster, and/or stucco, as some sources indicate (Figure 15).[78] Given the prodigious involvement of Italian artisans in both small-scale and monumental plaster work,

Figure 13. Street chapel for Our Lady of Succor, 504 East 12th Street, Lower East Side, Manhattan, undated. Courtesy of the John D. Calandra Italian American Institute, Queens College, The City University of New York.

Figure 14. Newspaper article featuring two street chapels for Our Lady of Grace, South Brooklyn, New York, *Brooklyn Daily Eagle*, 1902. Courtesy of the Brooklyn Public Library.

it is likely that these chapels were also crafted from such molded material.[79]

The lacuna regarding information about building techniques is compounded by the paucity of biographical documentation of individual paratori (see Figure 6). One of the few artisans to be documented to any degree is Emilio Matarazzo of Boston. Matarazzo, along with his family company, constructed some of the largest festa chapels in the United States—monumental edifices that combined chapel and bandstand.[80] A report conducted in 1988 for the Smithsonian Folklife Festival stated that Matarazzo was born in 1900 in "Quisana (or Quisano)" in Avellino province, Campania.[81] Given that no such town exists in either that province or region, it is quite possible he was born instead in the Campanian town of Chiusano di San Domenico. The family company consisted of his four sons and a daughter and subsequently grandchildren, as well as an apprentice.[82] After Matarazzo died in 1964, the company continued until 1980, closing with the death of his son Anthony, who had run the business for sixteen years.[83]

Matarazzo and his company constructed several chapels over the years, before and after the death of the "master," for the St. Peter's feast in Gloucester, Massachusetts, that have been visu-

Figure 15. Detail of the street chapel to Our Lady of the Immaculate Conception, Little Italy, Manhattan, 1929. Courtesy of the New York Public Library.

ally documented with fifteen photographs in the 2001 book *St. Peter's Fiesta through the Years* (Figure 16).[84] These structures begin to approach the scale of nineteenth-century world's fair pavilions. Gloucester resident Joseph Palmisano, one of the book's editors, gleaned information from Matarazzo's son Sonny when the company came to town to erect the structures for the feast: Maestro Emilio worked out of a warehouse in Boston's Chinatown where his children would join him after school and on the weekends. Palmisano said that the open area of the town's Fort section overlooking Gloucester Harbor provided Matarazzo with significantly more space than could be found in the crowded, narrow streets of Boston's North End, thus allowing for structures that were larger, wider, and deeper than anything constructed in the state's capital city. With the maestro's death, according to Palmisano, only four (undefined) types of structures were being built during the 1970s and 1980s, a noteworthy difference from the diversity of festa structures designed by Matarazzo.[85]

The market for these elaborate impermanent structures was particularly intense in New York City, a situation underscored by a 1906 newspaper story about two societies dedicated to St. Roch holding their respective celebrations at the same time on the same street in lower Manhattan. According to the *New York Times*, a newly formed organization erected a three-story chapel on Mott Street close to Hester Street.[86] Members of an older association, in turn, commissioned a chapel that stood five stories high several blocks north (quite possibly at 272 Mott Street, where a shrine was built in 1902). The reporter does not describe the actual shrines in detail (instead recounting the rivalry and the heavy police

Figure 16. Street chapel and pavilion for St. Peter, designed by Emilio Matarazzo, Gloucester, Massachusetts, 1935. Courtesy of the Gloucester Coalition for Youth.

presence to prevent violence), but the fact that two chapels were erected at the same time suggests the significant presence of trained craftspeople in New York City. Only one report, from 1903, mentions the cost of these monumental impermanent structures: "It is a poor shrine, indeed, that does not cost $1,000, and sometimes they are much more expensive."[87] An individual street chapel could also be used by multiple societies, as occurred in 1902 when devotees of St. Roch and St. Donatus shared the same edifice, one on Saturday followed by the other on Sunday, at 272 Mott Street, or when the same festa chapel was used for three saints at three different locations in Little Italy during August and September of 1929 (Figure 17).[88] The existence of photographic documentation of a vast number of unique and individual festa chapels (a fact that the selected images herein can only hint at) suggests a complicated economic and religious system that scholars have not begun to properly explore and fully comprehend.

The temporary festa chapels were sites of Catholic devotional and votive practices, including offerings of flowers, candles, ex-votos, and money, accompanied by prayer and genuflection. The 1905 shrine to Our Lady of Succor in Manhattan held "more than a dozen candles, varying in size from twelve-inch canon size to that of a stick of candy."[89] The Sicilian-led Società San Rocco constructed a five-story shrine where "200 huge candles planted in spaghetti boxes flared in front of it."[90] Candles presented a constant problem as the cloth, canvas, and paper used in the chapels' decoration were prone to burning.[91] This was the case in New York City on the morning of August 15, 1903, when a devotee apparently dropped a lit match while praying to Our Lady of Succor, thus setting the three-story structure ablaze. The society's response was immediate and creative:

> Around the singed and hastily repaired altar in the afternoon was a changing crowd of old and young, aged women, swarthy men, dark-eyed children. In a tray at the Virgin's feet were piles of coin—mostly coppers—and dollar bills were pinned to the votive candles. Upon one painted and gilded candle of immense size hung a photograph of the altar as it had been in the morning, and beside the photograph a notice in Italian that the picture was for sale for 15 cents for the benefit of a restoration fund.[92]

The feast organizers felt it necessary to rapidly raise funds to rebuild a chapel even though it would only temporarily occupy the streets.

In addition to candles and coins, devotees deposited ex-votos, some in the form of personal items such as "jewelry, rings, earrings, quaint Italian brooches, shirt studs, and collar buttons" or "the poor garments" of a woman's epileptic son placed near the housed statue "in the hope that

Figure 17. Street chapel for St. Augustine, Little Italy, Manhattan, 1929. This same chapel was also used for the 1929 feasts of St. Januarius and St. Fortunata. Courtesy of the New York Public Library.

Figure 18. Priests from the Church of the Sacred Hearts of Jesus and Mary at a street chapel for Our Lady of Consolation, South Brooklyn, New York, ca. 1935. Courtesy of Sacred Hearts of Jesus and Mary–St. Stephen Parish Archives, Brooklyn.

[in doing] so he might be healed."[93] Visitors placed wax ex-votos of various anatomical shapes—hands, arms, legs, feet, heads—at street shrines in request or in thanks for heavenly intervention of physical healing (see Figure 4). An anonymous *New York Times* reporter opined in 1906, "Some of the waxen figures were not attractive, but others were of the heads of children, skillfully molded and fashioned after the figures of Raphael's cherubs, which smile from the lower edge of his canvas in the famous Sistine Madonna."[94] In the streets of New York City, Italian Catholics knelt before the festa shrine to pray, often vocally and quite ardently, for help with matters concerning health, work, safety, and the family. In time, Catholic priests, especially Italian immigrant clergy, would take to the streets to officiate at the festa chapels, as occurred in 1930s Brooklyn (Figure 18).

### Ambulatory Structures

In addition to constructing majestic feste chapels, paratori also created elaborate ceremonial objects that were paraded through the streets as the central focus of various celebrations. Immigrant artisans designed and constructed these ornate ambulatory structures, which were rooted in the festival *apparati* (literally, apparatuses) of the baroque period, to cut spectacular paths through the streets of urban America. While the common Catholic procession transported a religious statue on a litter or carved baldachin circuitously through neighborhood streets, these larger festa structures tended to be paraded down a thoroughfare without much deviation. In both cases, the perambulatory movement of ceremonial objects sacralized the quotidian streets and extended the realm of the holy to believers' physical spaces of home and work.

Perhaps the best documentation of these ceremonial objects is the *giglio* tower, historically constructed annually with a wood frame and papier-mâché façade and transported on the shoulders of men in three New York City neighborhoods (Williamsburg, Brooklyn; Ravenswood, Queens;

and Harlem, Manhattan) and in the New Jersey townships of Fairview and Cliffside in honor of either St. Paulinus of Nola or St. Anthony of Padua. Dating back to the early 1500s in the Campanian city of Nola (Naples province), the feast is a dramatization of the manumitted Bishop Paulinus's return by ship and the townspeople greeting him waving lilies. In contemporary Brooklyn, the "flower" used to welcome home the bishop saint is a multistory, tapering spire known as the *giglio* (lily). The giglio, along with a singer and brass band, is lifted and carried on the shoulders of approximately 125 able-bodied men. The giglio feast's rich historical past with its commanding impermanent construction remains a powerfully galvanizing symbolic presence for festa participants, as the celebration honors not only a Catholic saint but also the community's more than one-hundred-year presence in the area.[95]

Brothers Giuseppe and Pasquale Villani left Nola in 1902 for New York City, where they constructed the first ceremonial spire in the United States, in Williamsburg, Brooklyn, the following year (Figure 19).[96] In 1918, a giglio was built, presumably by the Villanis, and carried in honor of St. Anthony of Padua by immigrants from Brusciano (Naples province), Campania, living in Harlem.[97] Pasquale repatriated in 1923 apparently leaving Giuseppe in New York City.[98]

In 1920, seventeen-year-old Romualdo Martello (1903–88) immigrated from Nola and went on to spend the next forty-one years designing and building ceremonial giglio spires out of wood balloon framing and papier-mâché panels. He was known within his community as maestro for his technical innovations and the sheer beauty of his designs. In 1981, I interviewed Martello as he recounted his life story, his methods of construction, and his ideas about design and technical innovations.[99] Before emigrating he had worked with his father building the giglio's wood frames and went on to work as a carpenter in the United States. After the death of New York City's resident giglio builder—presumably Giuseppe Villani—Martello was commissioned to create his first giglio in 1927.[100] He hired local sculptors to craft statues of saints from which he in turn created plaster molds to be used with papier-mâché pieces. He also recycled discarded objects into design elements, such as broken dolls for angels, pie pans for halos, and architectural detritus for columns and cornices. Over time, Martello made significant changes in the construction of the giglio's wood lattice frame. In Italy, the structure was nailed together and then destroyed at the feast's end. In order to save time and money,

Figure 19. The carrying of the *giglio* spire for St. Paulinus of Nola, Williamsburg, Brooklyn, ca. 1903. Courtesy of the Brooklyn Public Library.

Martello created a system of numbered pieces of wood that could be assembled with bolts anew each year: "I made up my own idea to make the frame, all screws and numbered and everything, and then I would assemble it up, I used to put it together, bolts and nuts and everything, and then after the feast, I used to take it down pieces by pieces. I used to use the same lumber all the time, four or five years."[101] This developed strategy of disassembly and reuse resulted in the giglio's becoming less ephemeral over time.

Another example of a festa ambulatory structure with origins in baroque Italy is the Sicilian *vara*, which can take the form of towers, boats, carts, and portable baldachins.[102] As with the giglio in New York City, these structures appear to have lost much of their ephemeral quality over time, but they are no less impressive. One example is Chicago's *carro trionfale* (triumphal chariot) of the Near North Side neighborhood, a work that has been crafted and processed in honor of the Madonna of Milicia by immigrants from Altavilla Milicia (Palermo province) (Figure 20). The hometown society was founded in 1900, and soon afterward the boat-shaped cart was built with its four-square tiered tower rising from the stern. A group of men dressed in matching outfits pulled the carro while a full brass band rode on board. The cart, according to the society's former president Giuseppe Camarda, would be reassembled annually and repaired as needed. It lasted until the mid-1940s when a fire consumed the warehouse where the *vara* was stored.[103]

Figure 20. The *carro trionfale*, Chicago, ca. 1920. Courtesy of the Maria SS. Lauretana Society of Altavilla Milicia in Chicago.

## Conclusion: The Vernacular Baroque as Artistic Inspiration

In the early twentieth century, Italian American festa artisans fashioned architectural wonders that stupefied the beholder even as they humanized urban space and its immigrant residents. The artistry of religious public display and the ephemeral monumental edifices transformed space into place by instilling feelings of intimacy and identification with one's immediate surroundings, thus rendering the city more familiar and cherished over time. As part of the larger festa complex, these temporary structures had an impact on establishing and maintaining a sense of home for urban residents by staking claims to sidewalks, apartment buildings, and blocks of city streets. They helped reconstitute a sense of community annually by dramatizing the bonds between individuals and place. The festa, with all its accoutrements, was a sacred and artistic template through which people reproduced everyday notions of self-identity and collective memory. The religiously charged and ethnically keyed edifices refashioned how the city could and would be imagined and used.

These immigrant artisans' aesthetic valence inspired a host of coeval visual artists, especially those associated with the Ashcan school. For example, painters such as Joan Sloan, with his two canvases titled *Italian Procession* (1913–25), and others were fascinated with the vitality and color of Italian immigrants' enactment of a new vision of urban life. Jerome Myers was particularly inspired by festa aesthetics, painting no fewer than six works depicting processions and, in particular, street chapels.[104] His *Street Shrine* (1931), for which he won the prestigious Altman Prize, depicts an ensemble of predominantly women and girls standing before a festa chapel

Figure 21. Jerome Myers, *Street Shrine* (1931), oil on canvas. Courtesy of the Smithsonian American Art Museum, bequest of Henry Ward Ranger through the National Academy of Design.

for the Madonna, as tiered groupings of women peer down from apartment balconies festooned with bunting and images of the Virgin Mary (Figure 21). The painting depicts a dense and crowded urban space with the Madonna's chapel connecting the streets below with the heavens above. For many studio-trained artists the festa's allure involved, as Margarita Karasoulous has observed, "pictorial strategies [and] racial dynamics" that created picturesque and othering depictions of Italian immigrants, especially women, in the New York City urban landscapes.[105]

After World War II, second-generation Italian American painters sought to capture on canvas the treasured festa at the very moment the children of immigrants were leaving the urban neighborhoods for suburbia in a flight into American middle-class whiteness. Painters like Vincent La Gambina (*Mott Street Festival,* 1954) and John Costanza (*Festa D'Santa Lucia,* 1960) tapped childhood memories and lived experiences to capture the vivacious visuals of Italian American Catholic festivities. One of self-taught artist Ralph Fasanella's greatest works is *Festa,* (1957), an oil painting that places the statue of the feted Madonna on a raised platform at the canvas's center highlighted by decorative illuminations that recede into a glowing canopy of arches (Figure 22). Feast attendees fill the street in a convivial atmosphere of balloons, games of chance, and food stands. The iconic power of Fasanella's festa painting is evident from its use as the cover

Figure 22. Ralph Fasanella, *Festa* (1957), oil on canvas. Courtesy of the Estate of Ralph Fasanella.

image for at least five scholarly books on Catholicism and/or Italian Americans.[106]

Immigrant artisans continued their work well into the middle of the twentieth century and, in the cases of Martello and Matarazzo, until the 1960s. In some cases, paratori passed on their technical knowledge and aesthetic appreciation to a new generation of American-born apprentices, as was the case with the Brooklyn giglio structure.[107] But for one reason or the other the craftsmanship diminished in the post–World War II era, and the labor-intensive and detailed baroque flourishes were increasingly simplified and flattened. In fact, there is pictorial evidence that the reduction of visual and material festa chapel elements began in the 1930s. The reasons for this change may be attributed to a number of interrelated factors, including shifts in economics, taste, and skills. The imposition of restrictive immigration laws in the early 1920s that targeted southern and eastern European immigrants with a racialized quota system certainly may have impacted the arrival of new, younger paratori. Another significant aspect was the waning of the hometown lay societies that sponsored the feasts and commissioned chapels as local Catholic churches increasingly took possession of the religious statues to stage and manage the feste. This tapering of previous immigrant artistry can be witnessed not only with the replica in *The Godfather: Part II*, but also in numerous photographs from the postwar period. In the end, the decorative lights and the chapels, while still erected in some Italian American communities, pale in comparison to those created by the *paratori* working in the first half of the twentieth century (Figure 23).

The baroque-style festa artistry of Italian-trained craftspeople is a former practice that haunts the periphery of collective memory. The historic context of such artistic magnificence from the historical past is known to but a few in local communities, and even then, only in regard to their specifically beloved feasts. And yet the fleeting environments created out of a shared religious aesthetic shaped how Italian immigrants and their children established and navigated new social sacred spaces while dramatically reconfiguring how American cities were imagined and experienced, to bequeath an expressive legacy lasting long after the fireworks ended and the illuminations dimmed.

Figure 23. Street chapel to Our Lady of Succor and St. Pio of Pietrelcina, Ridgewood, Queens, 2022. Photograph by Joseph Sciorra.

## AUTHOR BIOGRAPHY

**Joseph Sciorra** is the director for academic and cultural programs at the John D. Calandra Italian American Institute, Queens College, a City University of New York research institute. He is the author of *Built with Faith: Italian American Imagination and Catholic Material Culture in New York City* (University of Tennessee Press, 2015).

## ACKNOWLEDGMENTS

I dedicate this article to folkloristics and religious studies scholar Leonard Norman Primiano, who encouraged me to undertake this study of what he would call vernacular Catholic material culture. This essay would not have been possible without the assistance of Stephanie Romeo, a photo researcher and dear friend, who helped locate and organize multiple images used for my study. A 2014 Bard Graduate Center research fellowship allowed me much-needed time to assemble old and new research on ephemeral festa architecture. I am indebted to Stefano Albertini, Paul Basile,

Ben Camarda, Giuseppe Camarda, Salvatore Camarda, Robert Cascella, Domenic Candeloro, Paul D'Ambrosio, Marc Fasanella, John Heyer, Maggie Holtzberg, Joseph Palmisano, James Periconi, and Mark Pezzano, who provided me with invaluable materials pertaining to my study, and to the librarians and archivists Alice Griffen (Center for Brooklyn History, Brooklyn Public Library), Laura Morrill (Albany Institute of History and Art), Riche Sorensen (Smithsonian American Art Museum), and Beth Zak-Cohen (Charles F. Cummings New Jersey Information Center, Newark Public Library). I want to thank Augusto Ferraiuolo, Siân Gibby, Stefano Luconi, Laura E. Ruberto, Kay Turner, and Dell Upton for their astute reading of a previous draft of this article.

## NOTES

1. Interview with Stephen La Rocca, May 31, 2011.

2. Robert A. Orsi, *The Madonna of 115th Street: Faith and Community in Italian Harlem, 1880–1950* (New Haven: Yale University Press, 1985), xvii.

3. Brooks McNamara, "Scenography of Popular Entertainment," *The Drama Review* 18, no. 1 (March 1974): 16–24.

4. Denise Mangieri DiCarlo, "The History of the Italian Festa in New York City: 1880s to the Present" (PhD diss., New York University, 1990). For more on festa artistry, see George E. Pozzetta, "The Italians of New York City, 1890–1914" (PhD diss., University of North Carolina, 1971), 290–95; Bogdana Simina Frunza, "Streetscape and Ethnicity: New York's Mulberry Street and the Redefinition of the Italian American Ethnic Identity" (MS thesis, University of North Carolina Greensboro, 2008), 65–72; and Augusto Ferraiuolo, *Religious Festive Practices in Boston's North End: Ephemeral Identities in an Italian American Community* (Albany: State University of New York Press, 2009).

5. Orsi, *The Madonna of 115th Street*, 219.

6. Joseph Sciorra, *Built with Faith: Italian American Imagination and Catholic Material Culture in New York City* (Knoxville: University of Tennessee Press, 2015), xix.

7. The New York Public Library's "Photographic Views of New York City: 1870s–1970s" collection includes a panoply of baroque festa chapels that has provided invaluable visual information needed to fully appreciate the prodigiousness of these impermanent edifices. Many images found in this collection were taken by little-known photographer Percy Loomis Sperr, whom the library commissioned to document the city's changing landscape. See "Photography Collection: A Research Guide," https://www.nypl.org/node/5651; and Todd Berken, "The Unknown Person on the Other Side of the Lens, PL Sperr," April 3, 2013, https://placesnomore.wordpress.com/tag/pl-sperr/.

8. Sally M. Promey, "The Public Display of Religion," in *The Visual Culture of American Religions*, ed. David Morgan and Sally M. Promey (Berkeley: University of California Press, 2001), 27–31.

9. Teresa Fiore, *Pre-Occupied Spaces: Remapping Italy's Transnational Migrations and Colonial Legacies* (New York: Fordham University Press, 2017), 12–14.

10. For example, Jacob Riis characterized Italian immigrants' religious feste and patriotic parades by pointing to their "insane passion for pomp and display." Jacob Riis, *The Children of the Poor* (New York: Charles Scribner and Sons, 1905), 24.

11. Nancy Fraser, "Rethinking the Public Sphere: A Contribution to the Critique of Actually Existing Democracy," *Social Text* 25–26 (1990): 67.

12. Arjun Appadurai, *Modernity at Large: Cultural Dimensions of Globalization* (Minneapolis: University of Minnesota Press, 2003), 31.

13. José Esteban Muñoz, "Ephemera as Evidence: Introductory Notes to Queer Acts," *Women & Performance: A Journal of Feminist Theory* 8, no. 2 (1996): 10.

14. Kay Turner, "September 11: The Burden of the Ephemeral," *Western Folklore* 68, no. 2/3 (Spring/Summer 2009): 158.

15. Gabrielle Berlinger, *Framing Sukkot: Tradition and Transformation in Jewish Vernacular Architecture* (Bloomington: Indiana University Press, 2017), 212.

16. Muñoz, "Ephemera as Evidence," 10–11.

17. Muñoz, "Ephemera as Evidence," 9.

18. "Noisy Italians," *New York Times*, August 18, 1889, 6; "San Rocco Honored by Rival Factions," *New York Times*, August 17, 1906, 7; "Fire Mars a Festival," *New York Times*, August 16, 1903, 11.

19. "Little Italy Honors Lady of Mt. Carmel," *New York Times*, July 17, 1906, 2.

20. "A Religious Festa," *New York Daily Tribune*, August 17, 1906, 12.

21. "Noisy Italians," *Times*, 6.

22. "San Rocco Honored," *Times*, 7.

23. Giorgio Bertellini, *Italy in Early American Cinema: Race, Language, and the Picturesque* (Bloomington: Indiana University Press, 2010), 165–204; Gian Antonio Stella and Emilio Franzina, "Brutta gente: Il razzismo anti-italiano," in *Storia dell'emigrazione italiana,* ed. Piero Bevilacqua, Andreina De Clementi, and Emilio Franzina (Rome: Donzelli Editore, 2009), 283–311; William J. Connell and Fred Gardaphé, *Anti-Italianism: Essays on a Prejudice* (New York: Palgrave Macmillan, 2010).

24. Ethnic leaders, in particular newspaper editors, were attuned to verbal slights as well as injurious discrimination and physical attacks against Italian immigrants and challenged them in print. See Peter G. Vellon, *A Great Conspiracy against Our Race: Italian Immigrant Newspapers and the Construction of Whiteness in the Early 20th Century* (New York: New York University Press, 2014).

25. Bertellini, *Italy in Early American Cinema,* 6. For depictions by landscape and genre painters inspired by Italy's cultural heritage and in particular lighting, see Paul A. Manoguerra, *Classic Ground: Mid-Nineteenth-Century American Painting and the Italian Encounter* (Athens: Georgia Museum of Art, 2004); and William L. Vance, Mary McGuigan, John Fuller McGuigan, and Paul S. D'Ambrosio, *America's Rome: Artists in the Eternal City, 1800–1900* (Cooperstown, N.Y.: Fenimore Art Museum, 2009).

26. "Italian Celebration in Honor of St. Rosa," *Brooklyn Daily Eagle,* September 2, 1900, 36; "From Sunny Italy," *New-York Tribune Illustrated Supplement,* July 12, 1903, 5–6.

27. "San Rocco Honored," *Times,* 7. The dramatization of immigrant neighborhood life in theatrical plays on Broadway stages was prevalent in this period and was part and parcel of the larger voyeuristic practice and industry of slumming. See J. Chris Westgate, *Staging the Slums, Slumming the Stage: Class, Poverty, Ethnicity, and Sexuality in American Theatre, 1890–1916* (New York: Palgrave Macmillan, 2014), in particular 115–44.

28. Carrie Tirado Bramen, "The Urban Picturesque and the Spectacle of Americanization," *American Quarterly* 52, no. 3 (September 2000): 444–47; Carrie Tirado Bramen, "William Dean Howells and the Failure of the Urban Picturesque," *New England Quarterly* 73, no. 1 (March 2000): 82–99. See also Bertellini, *Italy in Early American Cinema,* 134–64.

29. Bramen, "William Dean Howells," 87. As Bramen demonstrates, the urban picturesque was highly racialized, with African Americans excluded from the category of the quaint and harmless members of modern U.S. urban life, a legacy she traces to the European origins of the picturesque. "The Urban Picturesque," 444–77.

30. "Quaint Italian Customs of Summer Festal Day," *New York Times,* July 12, 1903, 30.

31. Chad Heap, *Slumming: Sexual and Racial Encounters in American Nightlife, 1885–1940* (Chicago: University of Chicago Press, 2000), 18, 24; "Honor Patron Saint," *Brooklyn Daily Eagle,* July 27, 1902, 5. Comic performer Aristide Sigismondi's 1919 song "Lu mastu de festa 'e Mulberry Stritto," about a fictional festa with its musical bands and fireworks, proclaims that "*Gli mericane della fift'evene verranno tutti quanti da qua abbasso e quanto sentiranno stu fracasse ma come si vorranno divertì!*" (The Americans from Fifth Avenue will go downtown and they will enjoy themselves when they hear this din). Paquito Del Bosco, *Cartoline da Little Italy II* (Fonit Cetra CDFO 3642, 1997).

32. "Festival of San Donato," *New York Times,* August 18, 1902, 7.

33. Jacob A. Riis, "Feast-Days in Little Italy," *The Century Magazine* 58, no. 4 (August 1899): 493.

34. Italian-language newspapers, particularly the long-lasting and influential *Il Progresso Italo-Americano,* have not been completely digitized, thus making them a more difficult resource to explore easily. I conducted a cursory search of festa-related articles from *Il Progresso* available on microfilm from the 1910s to 1950s and did not find any firsthand coverage of these religious practices nor advertisements for the craftspeople involved in festa arts.

35. For more on this publication, see Robert Viscusi, "The Universal Exposition" in *Strangers in a Strange Land: A Survey of Italian-Language American Books (1830–1945),* ed. James J. Periconi (New York: Bordighera Press, 2013), 30–41.

36. Ercole Cantelmo, "Usi, costume e feste degli italiani negli Stati Uniti" in *Gli italiani negli Stati Uniti,* ed. Luigi Aldrovandi (New York: Italian American Directory Co., 1906), 161. The Italian immigrant anarchist and socialist press repeatedly depicted vernacular Catholicism as "medieval" and/or akin to "uncivilized" practices found in sub-Saharan Africa in its relentless attacks on Catholic clergy and its perceived

exploitation of the devout. See Vellon, *A Great Conspiracy*, 27, 39, 42–43, 50, 142n51, 146n24.

37. Sciorra, *Built with Faith*, 160–63; Joseph Sciorra, "The Black Madonna of East Thirteenth Street," *Voices: The Journal of New York Folklore* 30, nos. 1–2 (Spring–Summer 2004): 14–17.

38. Michael P. Carrol, *American Catholics in the Protestant Imagination: Rethinking the Academic Study of Religion* (Baltimore: Johns Hopkins University Press), 68–71.

39. It is beyond the scope of this article to explore properly the art and history of fireworks created for Italian immigrant feste. Fireworks artisans, or *fuochisti*, and their pyrotechnic displays are often mentioned in early accounts in the Italian-language press. See "La Festa Di San Rocco a East New York," *Il Progresso Italo-Americano*, August 24, 1912, 2; and "Su e giù per la Colonia," *Il Progresso Italo-Americano*, July 16, 1912, 2. For more on Italian immigrant fireworks and, in particular, the Italian American Grucci family's company, see George Plimpton, *Fireworks: A History and Celebration* (New York: Doubleday, 1984).

40. Promey, "The Public Display of Religion," 38.

41. Silvano M. Tomasi, *Piety and Power: The Role of the Italian Parishes in the New York Metropolitan Area, 1889–1930* (New York: Center for Migration Studies, 1975), 33; Peter R. D'Agostino, "'Utterly Faithless Specimens': Italians in the Catholic Church in America" in *Anti-Italianism*, 33–39; Richard Juliani, "Italian Americans and Their Religious Experience," in *The Routledge History of Italian Americans*, ed. William J. Connell and Stanislao G. Pugliese (New York: Routledge, 2018), 193–211.

42. Orsi, *The Madonna of 115th Street*, 190.

43. Riis, "Feast-Days in Little Italy," 493.

44. Ferraiuolo, *Religious Festive Practices*, 141–42.

45. Tomasi, *Piety and Power*, 127.

46. See the special issue of *Revista de História da Arte* 10 (2021), "Baroque Festivals between the Sacred and the Profane: Europe and the Atlantic," edited by Maria João Pereira Coutinho and Sílvia Ferreira.

47. Franco Mancini, "Piazze, feste ed apparati." *Campo* 18, no. 1 (April-September 1984): 24; Alan J. Plattus, "Emblems of the City: Civic Pageantry and the Rhetoric of Urbanism," *Artforum* 20, no. 1 (September 1981): 48–52.

48. Luisa Del Giudice, "Mountains of Cheese and Rivers of Wine: Paesi di Cuccagna and Other Gastronomic Utopias," in *Imagined States Nationalism: Utopia and Longing in Oral Cultures*, ed. Luisa Del Giudice and Gerald Porter (Logan: Utah State University Press, 2001), 11–63; Maurizio Fagiolo Dell'Arco and Silvia Carandini, *L'effimero barocco: Strutture della festa nella Roma del '600*, vol. 1 and 2 (Rome: Bulzoni Editore, 1978); Guido Bertolotti and Renata Meazza, "La macchina rituale: I Gigli di Nola al Lorenteggio," *Mondo Popolare in Lombardia: Milano e il suo territorio* 13 (1985): 487–552.

49. Bertolotti and Meazza, "La macchina rituale," 516–23. In contemporary times, it is with the ephemeral ambulatory structures such as the spires in the Campanian cities of Fontanarosa, Mirabella Eclano, and Nola and the Sicilian *vare* in Palermo and Altavilla Milicia that we see the baroque aesthetic in its full glory at Italian Catholic feste. In 2013 several Italian "celebrations of big shoulder-borne processional structures" were inscribed in UNESCO's Representative List of Intangible Cultural Heritage of Humanity. See https://ich.unesco.org/en/RL/celebrations-of-big-shoulder-borne-processional-structures-00721. On the continuance of the baroque style in Italian American art practices see Luisa Del Giudice, "Folklore, Folklife," in *The Italian American Experience: An Encyclopedia*, ed. Salvatore J. LaGumina, Frank J. Cavaioli, Salvatore Primeggia, and Joseph A. Varacalli (New York: Gardland Publishing, 2000), 237–45.

50. Ferraiuolo, *Religious Festive Practices*, 142. The 1863 Italian dictionary definition of paratore refers to *"quegli Artefici che, in occasioni di feste o sacre o profane, adornano con festoni, drappi, arazzi, ed altro, o le chiese o i luoghi dove, si fa la festa"* (those craftsmen, who for sacred and profane feasts, adorn with garlands, draperies, tapestries, and other things, churches or other places where the feast is held). Pietro Fanfani, *Vocabolario dell'uso Toscano* (Florence: G. Barbera, 1863), 674.

51. Teodoro De Giorgio, "La festa patronale," April 24, 2012, https://sites.google.com/site/centrostuditeodoriani/la-traslazione-delle-reliquie-a-brindisi/la-festa-patronale-brindisina. I found the festa chapel for St. Anthony on the now defunct website http://www.prolocomontesanoterme.it/montesano-ieri-e-oggi.html. I have not received replies to my repeated email queries to the respective sites' webmasters concerning these two structures.

52. A cinematic depiction of Italian artisans emigrating to the United States is found in Paolo Taviani

and Vittorio Taviani's 1987 film *Good Morning, Babylon,* which tells the story of two Italian brothers who immigrate to California and end up designing and building the elaborate sets for D. W. Griffith's 1916 film *Intolerance.* In addition to the understudied Italian immigrant iteration of the style, the baroque found its strongest foothold in Latin America. See Monika Kaup, *Neobaroque in the Americas: Alternative Modernities in Literature, Visual Art, and Film* (Charlottesville: University of Virginia Press, 2012).

53. McNamara, "Scenography of Popular Entertainment," 23. Travel writers often made note of Italian festa lighting. With their "love of tinkling decoration and illuminations," in the words of Maurice Vaussard, the residents of eighteenth-century Palermo celebrated the feast of their patroness, St. Rosalia, by adorning the city's cathedral with lights. Maurice Vaussard, *Daily Life in Eighteenth-Century Italy* (New York: Macmillan, 1963), 142. See also Gabriele Tardio, *Le luci, le luminarie, gli apparati effimeri, gli archi* (San Marco in Lamis, Italy: Edizioni SMiL, 2008).

54. "An Italian Fete," *Brooklyn Daily Eagle,* September 13, 1896, 24.

55. "An Italian Fete," *Eagle,* 24.

56. "Italian Celebration in Honor of St. Rosa," *Eagle,* 36; "Noisy Italians," *Times,* 6.

57. "Italian Celebration in Honor of St. Rosa," *Eagle,* 36.

58. Roger D. Abrahams, "An American Vocabulary of Celebrations," in *Time Out of Time: Essays on the Festival,* ed. Alessandro Falassi (Albuquerque: University of New Mexico Press, 1987), 178.

59. "Italian Celebration in Honor of St. Rosa," *Brooklyn Daily Eagle,* September 2, 1900, 36.

60. "An Italian Fete," 1896, 24; "Italian Celebration in Honor of St. Rosa," *Eagle,* 36.

61. Marty Caliendo, "Enthusiasm Dimming for Feast Fireworks." *Fra Noi,* June 25, 1987, 13–14; DiCarlo, "The History of the Italian Festa," 155, 200–202.

62. Descriptions of southern Italian devotional altars placed in front of the home for the passing procession witnessed during the 1930s are found in Carlo Levi, *Christ Stopped at Eboli* (New York: Farrar, Straus and Giroux, 1977), 119; and Charlotte Gower Chapman, *Milocca: A Sicilian Village* (Cambridge, Mass.: Schenkman Publishing, 1971), 173.

63. Kay Turner, *Beautiful Necessities: The Art and Meaning of Women's Altars* (New York: Thames & Hudson, 1999), 44; Sciorra, *Built with Faith,* 1–60; Joseph Sciorra, "Yard Shrines and Sidewalk Altars of New York's Italian-Americans," *Perspectives in Vernacular Architecture, III,* ed. Thomas Carter and Bernard L. Herman (University of Missouri Press, 1989), 185–98.

64. "Thousands Do Homage to Our Lady of Carmel," *New York Times,* July 17, 1904, 7.

65. "Little Italy Honors Lady of Mt. Carmel," *Times,* 2.

66. On the close relationship between embroidered cloth and Catholicism in Italy and among Italian Americans see Edvige Giunta and Joseph Sciorra, eds., *Embroidered Stories: Interpreting Women's Domestic Needlework from the Italian Diaspora* (Jackson: University of Mississippi Press, 2014).

67. "From Sunny Italy," *Times,* 6; see also "Thousand Do Homage," *Times,* 7.

68. "Noisy Italians," *Times,* 6.

69. "Sicilians Honor Fortuna," *New York Times,* September 11, 1900, 14.

70. "An Altar in a Tent," *New York Times,* August 4, 1883, 2.

71. Riis, "Feast-Days in Little Italy," 491, 493.

72. Colleen McDannell, *Material Christianity: Religion and Popular Culture in America* (New Haven: Yale University Press, 1995), 154–62.

73. Joseph P. Cosco, *Imagining Italians: The Clash of Romance and Race in American Perceptions, 1880–1910* (Albany: State University of New York Press, 2003), 46, Figure 1.3.

74. "Festival of San Donato," *Times,* 7.

75. "From Sunny Italy," *Times,* 6; "San Rocco Honored," *Times,* 7.

76. "From Sunny Italy," *Times,* 6.

77. Photographic Views of New York City, #731587F. During the 1930s lightbulbs were introduced as decorative elements to a few festa chapels.

78. "Two Great Festivals Keep Italians Busy," *New York Times,* August 16, 1905, 7; "Italians Celebrating Saint Roque's Day," *Times,* 6; "Peaceful San Rocco Day," *Evening Post,* August 16, 1907, 5.

79. Laura E. Ruberto and Joseph Sciorra, "Italian American Stuff: A Survey of Material Culture, Migration, and Ethnicity," *SOAR: The Society of Americanists Review* 3 (2021–2022): 40–41.

80. Paratori-crafted bandstands figure prominently in immigrant feste, as in this example from 1902 Brooklyn: "By far the most gorgeous part of the

decorations are the three music stands, two of which are erected over the sidewalk. The principal one of these stands is combined with an altar, surmounted with a cross, and such splendor as is shown here would have attracted especial notice on Dewey day. The brightest colors have been lavished on these stands, and not wholly without artistic effect." "Italians Celebrating Saint Roque's Day," *Brooklyn Daily Eagle,* August 26, 1902, 6.

81. Mary Jo Sanna, "Miracles of the Heart: A Report on the Feasts of St. Anthony and Madonna del Soccorso," unpublished report, 1988. Maggie Holtzberg of the Massachusetts Cultural Council emailed me excerpts from this unpublished manuscript on May 23, 2014.

82. Ferraiuolo, *Religious Festive Practices,* 142.

83. Maggie Holtzberg, email to author, 2014.

84. The Young Men's Coalition, *St. Peter's Fiesta Through the Years* (Gloucester, Mass.: The Young Men's Coalition, 2001), 56.

85. Interview with Joseph Palmisano, March 3, 2016.

86. "San Rocco Honored," *Times,* 7.

87. "From Sunny Italy," *Times,* 6.

88. "Festival of San Donato," *Times,* 7; Photographic Views of New York City: St. Augustine at 89 Elizabeth Street, #731697F, https://digitalcollections.nypl.org/items/510d47dd-982a-a3d9-e040-e00a18064a99; St. Januarius on Mulberry Street at the corner of Hester Street, #721806F, https://digitalcollections.nypl.org/items/510d47dd-4af3-a3d9-e040-e00a18064a99; St. Fortunata at 248 Elizabeth Street, #731741F, https://digitalcollections.nypl.org/items/510d47dd-9882-a3d9-e040-e00a18064a99.

89. "Two Great Festivals," *Times,* 7.

90. "San Rocco Honored," *Times,* 7.

91. "Altar Ablaze in the Street," *The World,* August 18, 1904, 8; "Fire Mars a Festival," *Times,* 11.

92. "Fire Mars a Festival," *Times,* 11.

93. "Sicilians Honor Fortuna," *Times,* 14; Riis, "Feast-Days in Little Italy," 493. For more on Italian American ex-votos, see Joseph Sciorra, "Miracles in a Land of Promise: Transmigratory Experiences and Italian-American Ex-votos," in *Graces Received: Painted and Metal Ex-votos from Italy (from the Collection of Leonard Norman Primiano),* ed. Rosangela Briscese and Joseph Sciorra (New York: John D. Calandra Italian American Institute, 2012), 38–51.

94. "San Rocco Honored," *Times,* 7. See also "Festival of St. Rocco," *Times,* 20.

95. For discussion of the feast in Italy and among contemporary Italian Americans see Bertolotti and Meazza, "La macchina rituale"; Katia Ballacchino, *Etnografia di una passione: I Gigli di Nola tra patrimonializzazione e mutamento ai tempi dell'UNESCO* (Rome: Armando Editire, 2015); and Alyssa Maldonado-Estrada, *Lifeblood of the Parish: Men and Catholic Devotion in Williamsburg, Brooklyn* (New York: New York University Press, 2020).

96. Leonardo Avella, *Documenti-Cronaca: Nola 1896–1906* (Naples: Liberia Editrice Redenzione, 1978), 166, 166n85. The image in the Brooklyn Public Library's Center for Brooklyn History is dated "ca. 19—?," but Benjamin Blum in his book *New York Photographs, 1850–1950* (New York: E.P. Dutton, Inc., 1982, 376) dates the same photograph from the Culver Picture Services as 1903.

97. See Photographic Views of New York City, # 731679F, https://digitalcollections.nypl.org/items/510d47dd-9806-a3d9-e040-e00a18064a99.

98. Leonardo Avella, *Documenti-Cronaca: Nola 1920–1926* (Naples: Liberia Editrice Redenzione, 1980), 555.

99. For more on Martello see I. Sheldon Posen, "Storing Contexts: The Brooklyn Giglio as Folk Art," in *Folk Art and Art Worlds,* ed. John Michael Vlach and Simon J. Bronner (Ann Arbor, Mich.: UMI Research Press, 1986), 171–91; I. Sheldon Posen and Daniel Franklin Ward, "Watts Towers and the Giglio Tradition," *Folklife Annual 1985,* ed. Alan Jabbour Alan and James Hardin (Washington, D.C.: Library of Congress, American Folklife Center, 1985), 142–57; and Joseph Sciorra, "Romualdo Martello: Giglio Builder," *Made by Hand—Played by Heart: A Guide to Traditional Arts in Queens,* ed. Kathleen Condon (New York: Queens Council on the Arts, 1991), 32–33.

100. That same year a ceremonial tower was constructed for St. Philomena at the corner of Sullivan and West Houston Streets, Manhattan, presumably by Martello. Photographic Views of New York City, # 731699F, https://digitalcollections.nypl.org/items/510d47dd-982e-a3d9-e040-e00a18064a99.

101. Interview with Romualdo Martello, June 5, 1981.

102. While not impermanent structures, the multihued baldachins, Sicilian in origin, that continue to

be used to transport statues of St. Sebastian in Montclair, New Jersey, and St. Lucy in Omaha, Nebraska, are noteworthy for their beauty and craftsmanship of carved Corinthian columns, arches, cherubim, and gilded swags of foliage.

103. Interview with Giuseppe Camarda, March 5, 2016. In 2000, Rosario Abinante, an immigrant who arrived after World War II, constructed a new *carro.*

104. *Street Shrine* (1915), *Italian Procession* (1925), *Street Shrine* (1931), *Catholic Festival* (n.d.),"*Italian Procession* (n.d.), and *The Italian Procession* (n.d.).

105. Margarita Karasoulous, "The 'American Ward'? Italian Immigration and the Ashcan School's Greenwich Village," in *The Ashcan School and the Eight: "Creating a National Art,"* ed. Brandon Ruud (Milwaukee: Milwaukee Art Museum, 2022), 41.

106. Orsi, *The Madonna of 115th Street,* 1985; Pellegrino D'Acierno, *The Italian American Heritage: A Companion to Literature and Arts* (New York: Garland Publishing, 1999); James T. Fisher, *Catholics in America* (New York: Oxford University Press, 2000); Paul S. D'Ambrosio, *Ralph Fasanella's America* (Cooperstown, N.Y.: Fenimore Arts Museum, 2001); Jennifer Gillan, Maria Mazziotti Gillan, and Edvige Giunta, eds., *Italian American Writers on New Jersey: An Anthology of Poetry and Prose* (New Brunswick, N.J.: Rutgers University Press, 2003).

107. See Posen, "Storing Contexts" 1986, 183–85; Maldonado-Estrada, *Lifeblood of the Parish,* 2020, 75–104.

TANIA GUTIÉRREZ-MONROY

# Bodies, Shawls, and Train Cars

## *Women and the Traveling Homes of the Mexican Revolution*

ABSTRACT

This article examines the ephemeral architectures and the place-making practices of the women in charge of building the mobile dwellings of military columns during the early twentieth-century Mexican Revolution. During this decade-long civil war, federal and rebel armies mobilized throughout Mexico and were heavily dependent on the services provided by the crowds of working-class women who traveled with them. Better known as *soldaderas,* these camp followers cared for the daily necessities of cooking, laundry, and health care for soldiers, while also creating ephemeral dwellings for the military columns. These domestic settings developed cyclically in a process of building, using, dismantling, transporting, and building anew. Two different artifacts remained constant and central to the building and rebuilding work of soldaderas: the train car and the shawl. This article analyzes how they worked in tandem with the bodies of soldaderas to produce a domestic architecture in need of constant rebuilding, a domestic architecture whose contingent transformation meaningfully fused the fabrication process and its material malleability. Losing its unity and fixity, this architecture unfolded in a series of domestic and material practices that were no longer contained in a single site and moment.

---

The Mexican Revolution to overthrow dictator Porfirio Díaz started on November 20, 1910. During the three decades of his presidency, a period known in Mexico as the Porfiriato, politicians, leaders in the Roman Catholic Church, aristocrats, foreign investors, and landowners held great power in a society in which the poor majority lived under conditions akin to slavery. Dispossession of peasant lands and the misery of the general population, in combination with discontent with Díaz's fake democracy, initiated an armed mobilization.[1] The decade-long revolution slowly shifted from a fairly unified effort to depose Díaz to a series of power struggles among factions.

Throughout this civil war, federal and rebel armies mobilized throughout Mexico and heavily relied on the services provided by the crowds of working-class and peasant women who traveled with them. This article examines the ephemeral architectures and the place-making practices of these camp followers, who are better known as *soldaderas.*[2] These women cared for the daily necessities of cooking, laundry, and health care for soldiers, while also configuring temporary dwellings for the military columns. Through a process of building, dismantling, and transporting the home elsewhere, the architectural practices of soldaderas situated domesticity in a continuum between place-making and the fleeting conditions of travel. This article observes the building processes of these mobile homes while drawing attention to two different artifacts that remained somewhat constant and central to the work of soldaderas: the train car and the shawl.

Continuously adapted to changing landscapes and supplemented by the resources of those landscapes, the train car and the shawl were key elements of a domestic architecture in need of constant rebuilding, a process that punctuated the malleable (or endlessly adaptable) possibilities of domestic architecture. No longer defined by fixed sites but simultaneously maintained and recreated in the form of space-events, the temporary wartime home was configured by these two artifacts. Along with their original function of carrying and caring, the bodies of the soldaderas also became key organizers of these domestic spaces.

Soldaderas played a vital role in the war by preparing camps, carrying weapons, and often fighting alongside the men they accompanied.[3] They left their own homes and assumed the task of creating a mobile domesticity that no longer relied on the walls of a building. In this process, the home of armies was dematerialized and remained a moving, practiced architecture.[4] The fluid spatial practices of soldaderas reshaped the limits between the geographies of home and war, and their labor afforded them a place on the male-dominated battlefield.[5]

To observe these ephemeral architectural forms, this article gathers evidence from print and oral histories, which I read in parallel with photographic materials (Figure 1). The latter require a careful analysis that moves beyond literal readings of their content, and a section of the article discusses their use and framing in relation to dominant narratives of space and gender during the revolution. The ensuing method provides a model for the analysis of ephemeral architectures.

**Bodies and Shawls**

Throughout the revolution, soldaderas marched alongside cavalries or traveled by train with troops while carrying children, food baskets, blankets, kitchenware, and basic first-aid kits.[6] Upon arrival at villages and campsites, they would forage and utilize any material they found to cook, to assemble shelter, and to wash clothes.[7] Numerous period images and testimonies depict the ways in which women transformed fields, pathways, buildings, streets, and even train cars and tracks into dwellings.

Seeing these space-events as more than shelters, this article advances them as homes. An important part of the traveling home was its cyclical life in relation to its users or enablers: the mobile home left behind the anchoring qualities of a regular home but was still installed, operated, occupied, and dismantled by a group traveling together. Here, individuals not necessarily united by kinship built a form of community that resembled one or many families, or even a "domestic group."[8] As this article explores, the woman was at the center not only of the domestic labor sustaining the war landscapes, but also of the connection and collaboration whereby the "domestic group" made the sites of travel inhabitable.

Figure 1. *Rurales comen en compañía de mujeres y niños en el exterior de una casa* (Troopers eat in the company of women and children outside a house), Mexico City, ca. 1911. Unknown photographer. Reproduction authorized by the Instituto Nacional de Antropología e Historia, Secretaría de Cultura-INAH-SINAFO F.N.-Mex.

While leisure camping might seem similar in its cyclic creation and in its existence along a series of space-events, such a camp does not necessarily seek the domestic qualities pursued by the war encampments that engaged soldaderas. In other words, when camping recreationally, any participant can set up the tent, build a fire, and cook, whereas, in revolutionary camps, the women "had to" carry out these activities.[9] A former member of an army states: "If you wanted to have soldiers, you needed to have soldaderas," and another recalls the contradictory attitudes of renowned General Francisco Villa, who wanted women away from the battle site, but eventually allowed them in, conceding that their presence was key to the survival of armies. This army member elaborates on what a woman means to a soldier on campaign: "She gives him food, offers him a clean shirt, sews his breeches, and brightens up with her songs those merciless nights of rain and cold wind, spent on the top of cars."[10] These examples evoke the need for a "domestic feeling" (attributed to the gendered work of women) that would prevent soldiers from abandoning the years-long, perilous war travel.

Leisure camping arguably relies on a home to return to, even if the intention is a temporary escape from it.[11] War camps seldom offer the same certainty: their undefined duration and hardship foreshadow the possibility of never returning home. One of the sources used in this essay describes a war camp: "No one speaks of heading back. . . . No sad eyes look back. The encampment is all. Therein one lives, thrives, falls ills, recovers, dies."[12]

Hotplates, brazier fans, baskets, pots, and pans were (and still are) traditionally hung in kitchens, visually becoming part of the walls of a popular Mexican house. Troops needed these items as part of their mobile domestic settings and soldaderas carried them, transferring them from the surfaces of dwellings to the surface of their own bodies. The soldadera's shawl secured these objects onto the traveling body it wrapped, supplementing baskets and bags.[13] Layered onto the mobile bodies of camp followers, elements of the Mexican home left the fixed walls of the house.

Transported through the space of war, these layers became part of an architecture no longer defined by enclosing walls. Delineating a traditional view of domestic space, Michel de Certeau states that the home is "constituted on the basis of the wall," as its sheltering qualities separate the inhabitants from the outside.[14] Soldaderas shifted this definition by enabling parts of domestic architecture (the objects that were part of walls) to take up a form that left behind the fixity and enclosure of walls; in other words, layers of the home clad mobile bodies during travel only to re-establish their architectural, space-defining function upon installation and "unfolding" at camping sites.[15]

Not only did the shawl play a crucial role in the creation of temporary architectures; it also became a key mediator between bodies and spaces. Its use as a mobile wall for "hanging" objects transported by the body of the soldadera is only one example of this role of connection—specifically as it related the site of departure, the site of travel, and the site of arrival. In the latter, a new domesticity emerged as the shawl and its packed contents unfolded in space. Upon arrival, the shawl could also be removed from the body that it wrapped to become a tent itself. It took the enveloping function of a wall or roof to shelter other bodies. This use of the shawl comes forth in the recollections of Brondo Whitt, a doctor whose published memoirs narrate his days serving with the Villista army.[16] At an encampment in the city of Saltillo, Whitt describes a camp follower improvising a dwelling by hanging a shawl in a tent-like shape on short trees: "By our train car a family arrives: a man, a woman, a boy . . . and a donkey. The woman extends over the many branches of the *gobernadora* [. . .] a protecting textile (the rag) and, under the exiguous shade enhanced by the textile, the family settles, like gypsies."[17]

As the shawl wrapped objects onto traveling bodies and later unfolded as a definer of space, corporeal and architectural layers interacted in a way that sets in motion the proposition of architecture scholar and artist Katarina Bonnevier regarding buildings as dressing the body.[18] In her exploration of queer architecture, Bonnevier advances the idea of clothes as links between architecture and its occupants, drawing special attention to tents (and their textile constitution) as "direct examples of buildings dressing the body."[19] The spatial practices of soldaderas bring mobility and continuous change to this view of tents and textiles as spatial definers, as the shawls-cum-tents performed their connecting function (connecting bodies and architecture) through travel.

The shawl's relationship with domesticity changed dramatically during the revolution. Before mass-production and long before the war, the tradition of making shawls linked this garment to the domestic setting through women's labor. At home, working-class and peasant mestiza or Indigenous women would weave shawls both for their own use and for sale.[20] Transformed by the practices of soldaderas during the revolution, the shawl was a product *from* the home that became a tool *to produce* the home.[21]

Camp dwellings also depended on the contingent use of household items carried and obtained by soldaderas along the way.[22] During travel, braziers, grinding stones, cookware, and blankets constituted a packaged domesticity that then unfolded when the women spread the items at stopovers. The story that former soldadera Josefina Bórquez shared with writer Elena Poniatowska exemplifies these spatial practices. As part of her experiences serving in the Carrancista forces, Bórquez recalled:

> My dad travelled by foot and I would follow alongside the infantry. I carried a basket with kitchenware and walked in high heels; not those bayonets people use these days and that just pierce the ground, but good heels. My dad had my footwear made with shoemakers from Acapulco: black shoe, brown shoe, and tights. . . . I walked only with a basket on my arm: plate, cup, jug, a pot for making coffee or frying something that he would eat.[23]

This folded domestic space was constituted by the objects that soldaderas carried in a basket, shawl, or in the *impedimenta* carts that they kept safe during travel.[24] At a Maderista camp in Bustillo (Chihuahua), a reporter from the newspaper *El Tiempo* writes about the heaps of serapes, clothes, and other items lying at a military campsite.[25] American journalist Edith O'Shaughnessy, who traveled with her diplomat husband through revolutionary Mexico between 1913 and 1914, describes the camp followers: "Having no homes, these women are wont to take all their possessions with them."[26] In the course of travel or at stopovers, the clustered, layered objects simultaneously held mobility and stasis. That soldaderas spread these objects on the ground determined the condition of the space around the packages: either as a site of passage or a site of settlement. The folded, mobile home connected domestic spaces and the landscapes of travel. So did the woman carrying, organizing, and operating this home.

To configure, operate, and maintain the mobile dwellings, camp followers needed to buy, find, and steal additional supplies.[27] In her recollections, Bórquez narrated how she and other women would comb through the sites where armies arrived in search of materials and food that would supplement their transported gear and goods.[28] Newspapers of the time also describe the foraging mission of soldaderas.[29] As the mobile home unfolded, the traveling layers merged with those of the landscape. By leaving behind objects and picking up new ones, the women set off an ever-changing practice of home building.[30] This action destabilized domesticity as a construct once believed fixed and anchoring.

Initially serving as carriers and then becoming spatial organizers, soldaderas became elements of connection: on the one hand, between permanent and mobile homes; and on the other, between these mobile homes and the geographies that armies inhabited. Brondo Whitt describes an episode on the way to Paredón when General Francisco Villa, claiming that women slowed his troops, ordered them to stay behind, expelling them from the train with their packages and pots. After much protestation, the soldaderas realized that they could walk alongside the train, which was slowed down by the need to repair detonated tracks. At some point, the women went ahead of the army and set up camp at the destination: the camp followers were now the followed. They gave form to the home at the station before the arrival of the train, which later assumed its place in the readily shaped domestic landscape.[31]

Soldaderas not only arranged domestic settings, but also transformed their own bodies into architectural elements. When a camp follower organized space at a stopover, her body and the artifacts that clad it during travel worked in tandem to shape ephemeral architectures within contingent contexts. But unlike the role of a wall in conventional architecture, this shaping "moved away" from the function of enclosing.[32] Overcoming their traditional stasis, domestic settings became living performances as women created diverse layouts in which they turned their own bodies into functional and physical parts of architecture.

Becoming pivots of ephemeral living sites, the bodies of women merged with the environment that they reshaped. Illustrations of this appear in the testimonies of revolutionary veterans recorded in the Programa de Historia Oral (PHO), a project by the Instituto Nacional de Antropología e Historia (INAH). Among its collection of interviews is the account of veteran Justino López Estrada, who recalls: "Women placed braziers on the tracks. There, they prepared food for their 'Juanes.' I would often eat with them."[33] Both López Estrada and Brondo Whitt described women arranging spaces for meals. Whitt's account offers a sense of the axial position of the women and how their materials gave shape to the site:

> Soldiers gather in groups or families to eat. Every soldadera feeds several men. . . . A young woman makes flour tortillas using a bottle to flatten the dough on a plank. The bottle comes and goes, it rolls and presses; the dough gets thinned, rounded, and outspread. . . . Thereon, it goes on the "comal" [hotplate] to get fire-cooked, and then comes another. At a distance, a girl watches over a pan splashing hot oil, where pieces of meat and potatoes emit Olympic smells. A third woman cuts a hen into pieces with a double-edged bayonet, helped by a fourth one who prepares a chili *molcajete*. The three-legged molcajete is a mortar made in raw clay. The chili is a red-colored pepper of visible fire-like spiciness. The soldadera beats and shreds the pepper in water inside the molcajete, takes it and squeezes it with the fingers. . . . In this way she detaches the tasty pulp of the *capsicum* [genus of pepper] and separates the skin and the seeds, which she discards towards the ground.[34]

**Reading Fragments**

Literary scholar Tabea Linhard notes that, marginalized from official and popular narratives, women's stories "come to us in fragments."[35] Observing the architectures created by soldaderas calls for reading the invisible space between those fragments. In the method presented below, I contend that the existing materials necessitate a tandem reading in which textual descriptions testify to the central, organizing role of women that images suggest. This parallel reading allows the pieces of evidence to speak from their sites of absence, from the negative space amid the visual and the textual.

The Mediateca INAH archive holds photographic materials that help to illustrate the narratives by Whitt, Bórquez, and the PHO interviewees. Recent criticism on the use of images as proof of historical events rightfully points out that the production, handling, and framing of these images inevitably carry meaning and intention, for which they cannot be read as "neutral" evidence.[36] Investigating the relationship between war and photography, Caroline Brothers states:

> The contents of a photograph can offer only two-dimensional information about the past, what its surface looked like, the faces perhaps of its actors. Its focus is selective, its vision is blinkered, its opinion always subjective. . . . Never evidence of history in terms of providing incontrovertible proof of what they literally depict, photographs *are* yet evidence precisely of the interplay of historically rooted power relations which generate such images and make use of them. The conditions of their production and the context in which they are used determine the meaning they transmit.[37]

While agreeing with arguments that regard visual materials as insufficient proof of historical and spatial events, I suggest we consider literary scholar Christine Arce's warning: "To dismiss the photographs would be to neglect that they nevertheless reveal a presence, a reality that existed, and which permits these women to constitute themselves in the many roles they incarnated [in the Mexican Revolution]."[38] Throughout the years, the meanings of the labor of soldaderas have changed. Even in the midst of morphing interpretations, the images remain a somewhat stable referent.[39] Read as a collection rather than individually, the photographs reveal the indelible female presence in the war. As Arce argues, some images are evidently staged, but others candidly caught camp followers in the background, "underscoring the diverse ways in which they participated, and in which their presence was to be interpreted by those who observed them—both in real life and as a photographic image."[40] Altogether, these visual materials confirm the presence of women in the revolution, a presence long obscured by academic research and popular texts.[41]

The use of photographs from the Mediateca INAH calls for caution against their reading as direct evidence, as well as for acknowledgment of the ways in which their content, edition, and message can be manipulated by producers.[42] Yet this plausible manipulation can actually become part of our reading of the pieces of evidence. How does the visual material help us read the textual and how does the textual help us read the visual? Here, each reading can be seen as supporting the other. Considering that the scene could be contrived or spontaneous, we can start by scrutinizing its visual elements while remaining attentive to the descriptions by Whitt, Bórquez, and the PHO protagonists. For example, many Mediateca images show groups of revolutionaries installed next to buildings. In Figure 1, women face a group of men and a child who consume a meal conceivably prepared by the women. If we start rearranging the elements, including bodies, which give form to the depicted space, we know that they can all be in different positions, but always organized around the soldadera and her cooking arrangements: the textual descriptions testify to this central, organizing role of women.

The series of plans constructed here rearrange the elements of the images and textual accounts (Figure 2). Keeping women at the center of the spatial arrangement and activity, the plans explore different possibilities whereby subjects and items organize space. These architectural representations start from what the texts and the photographs have in common: women as pivot-points and their dispersed items as definers of space. These representations depart from the "faithful" depiction of the photograph, making clear that the position and relation of elements can have multiple variations, but that women remain the key organizers of the domestic site. Unlike architectural drawings, these diagrams forego the intention of grounding *one* single reading—one spatial arrangement suggested by the photograph. Instead, they play with multiple possibilities, and their variations attest to an open-endedness that further reinforces the argument of women as space producers: the woman is an organizer of space in its multiple forms. She both arranges space and becomes a part of the arrangement, while her objects help shape

Figure 2. Plans that disarrange and rearrange subjects and elements from descriptions and images of the revolution. They show the role of women as pivots of the temporary architecture. Drawing by Tania Gutiérrez-Monroy.

the limits and distribution of the temporary architecture.

The architectural function of the body of a camp follower becomes evident in the interlocking and mutual disarrangement of the textual and visual materials. In them, we see soldiers sit or stand around a woman and the kitchen-diner that she has arranged. Men define the perimeter of the eating space while the woman's body becomes the pivot-point. Her body thus becomes the wall (or column) that organizes the unbounded site—and later disassembles it. It is possible to see here the corporeality of soldaderas at the center of spatial production. To borrow the words of Susana Torre, "bodies produce space by introducing direction, rotation, orientation, and occupation, and by organizing a *topos* through gestures, traces, and marks."[43]

As testimonies from the PHO reveal, the homemaking role of women often went beyond the physical arrangement and extended into a social task in the places where they arrived with their troops. To improve their fleeting domestic setting, soldaderas negotiated with town dwellers so that the traveling group could eat next to houses.[44] The space inside the walls provided food, water, or utensils to cook. The village inhabitants opened up their homes, which not only supported the improvised outdoor site but also became physically and functionally connected to it. Both domesticities—the ephemeral and the permanent—became a temporarily expanded dwelling. This sociospatial configuration showed an additional change: homes now accommodated individuals not necessarily sharing family ties. The lived space in the permanent building thus exceeded its definition as a monolithic, intimate, familial venue.

The existing architecture often supplemented these ephemeral settings. Whitt narrates an episode in which his army unit and its impedimenta occupied Avenida Juárez in Chihuahua. It resembles a setting described by veteran Juan Arellano Aguilar, where he grouped with his fellow soldiers to eat outside the houses of villagers: "They willingly gave us food: one or two tortillas. [Villagers would say] 'Here, this is what I have left. The rest is for my children.' "[45] A similar scene in San Diego, later a borough of Mexico City, illustrates a group of soldiers and soldaderas encamped on a street, leaning against continuous walls of buildings to rest and eat (Figure 3). Again, I propose reading the image and descriptions while considering the disarrangement previously described. Gathered around the woman, the travelers use the vertical surfaces to define an outdoor space. In this case, the walls originally built to enclose a traditional domestic space have their function turned outwards. Mirrored by other walls across the street, they all "contain" the space of the temporary outdoor home inhabited by revolutionary travelers.

Throughout the war, the integration of artifacts, bodies, and site paradoxically happened in the dismantling of the construct of the home as a monolithic space—believed to be unified immaterially by sociofamiliar practices and materially by brick and mortar or wood, *bahareque* (a building technique using bamboo and soil), and other materials. The cycle in which women arrived at the site, manipulated its layers, built the dwelling, occupied it alongside soldiers, dismantled it, moved elsewhere, and built anew turned domestic architecture into an aggregate of events. Through these spatial practices and settings, the home extended along fragments instead of being defined by fixed spaces. The events (activities) of cooking and eating, resting, setting up, and sleeping unfolded serially along time and space: morning at a certain place, afternoon at another, and evening elsewhere. These events no longer took place, they created *places*. Traced as an itinerary, such places altogether formed home. The home was one (the one lived at a specific "present"), but also multiple (its many versions along the timeline of an advancing troop). Domestic space became fragments, consisting of spatial and material practices no longer contained in a single space and time.

**Train Cars**

Often during the revolution, the home transported and built by soldaderas switched from its original containment inside the house to containment inside a train. As shown in Figure 5, the soldaderas dislocated components of the home upon arrival at stops, extending domestic practices

Figure 3. *Revolucionarios descansan en el callejón de la rinconada de San Diego, Ciudad de México* (Revolutionary group rests on alley of San Diego Ranch, Mexico City), Mexico City, 1910. Photograph by Agustín V. Casasola. Reproduction authorized by the Instituto Nacional de Antropología e Historia, Secretaría de Cultura-INAH-SINAFO F.N.-Mex.

from the carriages to the surrounding landscape. Soldaderas' inventive use of the train hardware, often in combination with found materials, was key to the emergence of the domestic spaces of the revolution.

With a network of tracks built prior to the revolution, the railroad played a fundamental role in the uprising.[46] The federal and some rebel military columns relied on it to cover more territory and to quickly gather strength in numbers.[47] The most powerful armies were those that firmly secured the railroad as an essential piece of their territorial "equipment." Visual culture historian John Mraz states that the train was a weapon itself.[48] As an essential part of most armies' travel, train cars became the sheltering hardware of encampments and a considerably stable component of the cyclic revolutionary home.

Long travels to reach battle sites and occupied areas required revolutionary crowds to spend days and nights inside or even on top of speeding boxcars.[49] These carriages took on domestic functions and, at stops, the work of soldaderas connected them to the broader landscape that provided material and spatial resources. The cars offered a coveted, ephemeral domesticity to the traveling military columns and became mobile fragments of the homes that were fleetingly completed at every site of arrival.

The actions of soldaderas transformed the seemingly rigid architectures of train cars into more plastic, dislocated dwelling sites. Whereas the rigid commands of military authorities would limit the spatial affordances of camp followers, the actual occupation by these women often exceeded (functionally or symbolically) the domestic space envisioned as ordered and hierarchical—mainly by the authorities but also by society at large. The frequent movement and accommodation of crowds allowed for the women builders/homemakers to configure dwellings that gave distinct uses to existing surfaces, envelopes, openings, and interiors.

Armies experienced a domestic life that depended on the material conditions of the different boxcars that formed a military convoy. At the time, most of the locomotives used in Mexico were manufactured in the United States and Germany and were acquired in the late nineteenth century.[50] Platform cars and gondolas (open-topped wagons with low side planking for transporting bulk materials) were solid wrought-iron structures usually attached behind the engine.[51] During an offensive, however, platforms carrying artillery were attached to the front and pushed by the engine.[52] Freight boxes were designed some years after the gondolas to provide additional protection from the weather that some transported materials required. Wood was the most common material used in early freight box construction but was gradually replaced by metal (both for the frame and paneling) around 1875.[53] American- and European-made carriages running in Mexico were made of both wood and steel. In the case of stock cars, louvered wooden walls that allowed ventilation for horses and mules wrapped a metal framework—although the oldest models featured a wooden skeleton.[54] The first- and second-class passenger wagons, mostly fabricated by the U.S. Pullman Company, had a metal frame with wood or iron cladding, pierced by windows. Many of them were armored. These carriages had built-in seats, washroom areas, and upper railings for luggage.[55] The caboose at the end of the train accommodated members of the crew. Built of iron and wood, it featured sleeping, washing, cooking, and office spaces.[56]

Contrasting with these trains were those in which generals and chiefs of staff traveled—usually with sleeping and dining cars—as well as wagons with offices and telegraphic equipment, armament, and munitions (Figure 4).[57] War conditions forced traveling armies to combine different types of carriages in the same convoy; Brondo Whitt recalls that the army in which he served (División del Norte) would reorganize and switch the wagons of different trains arriving at its occupied sites.[58]

Newspapers of the time offer a glimpse of the linear array of the convoy. In general, first-class coaches for officers and second-class wagons (which occasionally accommodated soldaderas) were at the end of the train, preceded by freight wagons and stock cars. These last two were the most usual space for women. When the space inside was insufficient, soldiers and camp fol-

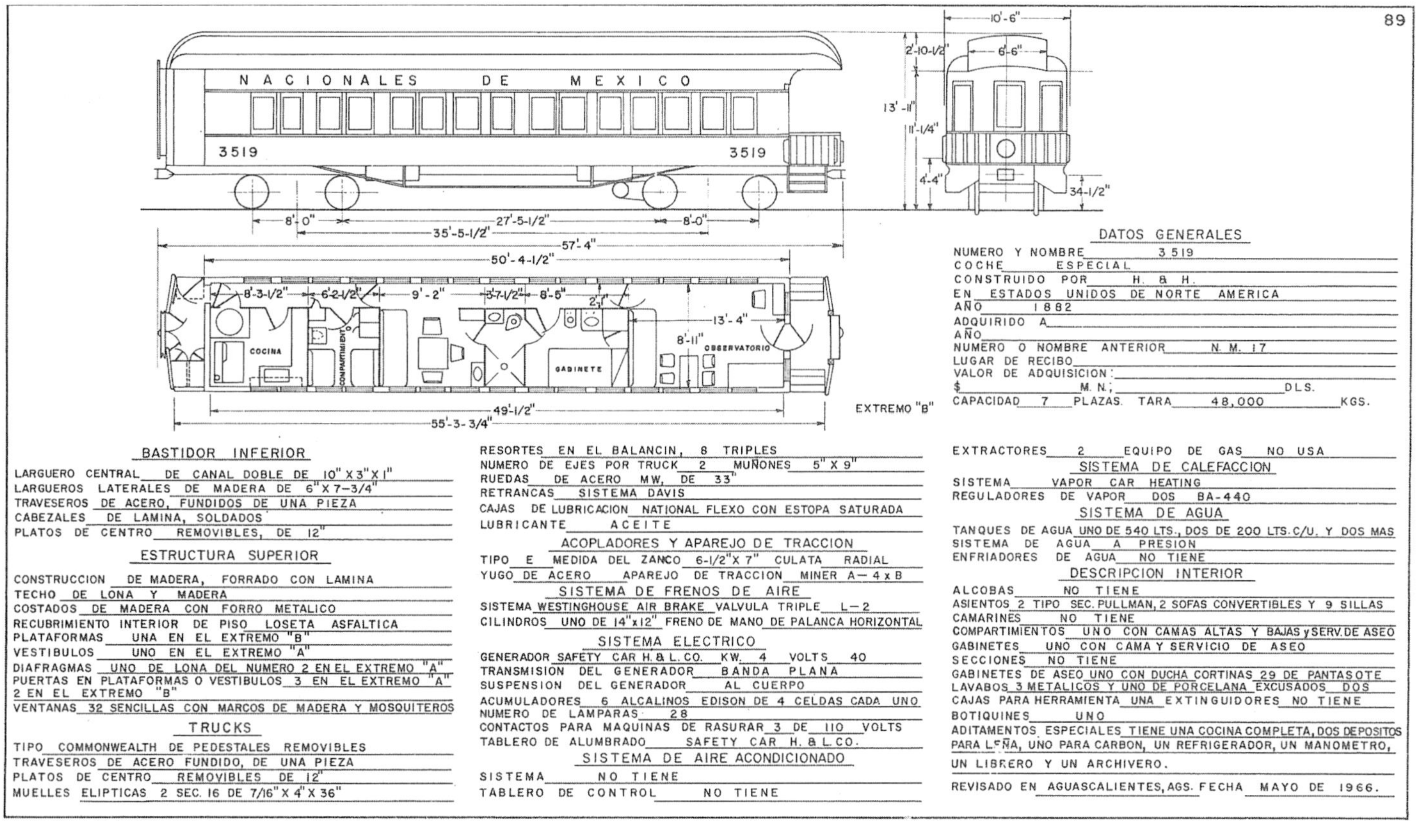


Figure 4. Plans and data sheet of wagon property, published by Ferrocarriles Nacionales de México during revolutionary times (built 1882). See *Sección de coches y carros, Libro de datos de coches dormitorios, dormitorio-buffet, observatorios, comedores, comedor-observatorios, bar-observatorios, bar-salón, especiales y autovías* (Mexico: Ferrocarriles Nacionales de México, 1970), 89. Reproduction authorized by the Centro de Documentación e Investigación Ferroviarias, Centro Nacional para la Preservación del Patrimonio Cultural Ferrocarrilero, Museo Nacional de los Ferrocarriles Mexicanos/Secretaría de Cultura.

lowers traveled on top of the trains.[59] A March 1912 train traveled to Orizaba with a stock car and three second-class wagons, two with 152 soldiers and one with thirty soldaderas.[60] A few days later, another convoy left Buenavista station (Mexico City) with a water tank, six freight cars (three of them fully occupied by soldaderas), four second-class and two first-class coaches (occupied by infantry and officials, respectively), and a caboose.[61] A few months later, a ten-car train also took off northbound. Six of its boxcars accommodated soldaderas, provisions, and equipment. The troop also took two stock cars and a platform carrying two machine guns.[62] Another news report describes a collision in the municipality of Jiménez in June 1912. Two camp followers died as the engine of one train impacted the stock car at the end of another, where the women traveled.[63]

At first sight, the solid structures of the carriages shown in photographs offer little evidence of their reshaping into a home. The agency and experience of women in the revolution seem invisible when looking solely at the railway hardware. Closer observation into the patterns of use legible in other sources reveals the transient material and immaterial conditions that enabled soldaderas to turn these spaces into ephemeral homes. Camp followers traced their revolutionary actions on the apparently solid, hardly negotiable surfaces of boxcars, even if impermanently. Christine Arce states: "Soldaderas had no official texts: the trains were one of their texts, their 'practiced places.' . . . [They] turned the *primum mobile* [traveling machine] into a home."[64]

The occupation of trains during long journeys domesticated these vehicles, with camp followers, soldiers, and high-ranking officers finding accommodation in strictly differentiated places in the cars.[65] In some, the domestic function is underscored by the layout and décor. For instance, the coaches commercialized as "palace cars," used by chiefs of staff, featured a design evoking the interior of a luxurious house.[66] In contrast, soldaderas occupied the crowded stock and freight wagons, which lacked furniture and décor.

In the traveling boxcar, soldaderas transported the "folded home" previously described—the home compressed into layers and packages to be unfolded at train stops. Upon arrival, the train connected its own spaces and surfaces to those existing at the stopovers. A new set of relations evolved as the wagons opened up, with the outdoor sites connecting to the once enclosed spaces of the train by means of both the touching surfaces and the dynamics of people. Brondo Whitt describes women getting off at the stations to immediately set up their open-air kitchens. He calls these setups "mandatory": the kitchens were *de rigueur* features at a camp. About a scene at a station, he states: "On the rails there is a cluster of train cars, an entire, fickle, portable city: constituted by soldiers, soldaderas, vendors, suppliers."[67]

Photographic evidence offers a view of the process by which women transferred the traveling items from the boxcar to the landscape (Figure 5). Read in parallel with Whitt's descriptions of outdoor kitchens at train stops created by soldaderas, these images make legible the path of the home: the open wagon appears as the container that transported the objects now spread on the ground beside it. The possibility that the photograph is staged raises the question of how exactly arrangements such as the one(s) described by Whitt worked, since he provides little information about the position of the kitchens with respect to the convoy. But even if the proximity depicted between the tent and the train is inaccurate, the image makes clear the "path" of the home, from its folded state inside the train car to being spread out on the ground. The transfer of these items from the walls of a regular house to the changing surfaces of travel brought about a mobile, refigured domesticity that spilled toward the cradling landscape.

Figure 5. *Revolucionarios en un campamento a las órdenes de Lucio Blanco* (Revolutionary people at a camp under the command of Lucio Blanco), Monterrey, Mexico, 1913. Photograph by Agustín V. Casasola. Reproduction authorized by the Instituto Nacional de Antropología e Historia, Secretaría de Cultura-INAH-SINAFO F.N.-Mex.

The spaces that flowed between the interior and the exterior of trains unfolded under diverse conditions depending on the place, the timing, and the weather. These sites acquired a flexibility that contrasts sharply with the contained and unchangeable layout of the sitting areas in the passenger wagons, used on very rare occasions by soldaderas. The side opening of freight and stock cars allowed for efficient expansion of the "living" spaces to the grounds of the station. The sliding door depicted in the photographed train car was a threshold that proved to be crucial in this fluid spatial connection.

Connected through doors and walls, the home was both inside and outside the train car. The interior space created by the wall of a wagon, clearly defined when closed off, was negotiated and expanded by the homebuilders and inhabitants during stops. The inner and outer surfaces of the cars were at that moment hardly distinguishable and gave form to a home that flowed past this division. A description by Whitt illustrates such a situation: a bedroom was improvised in a boxcar and expanded toward the surrounding grounds as a group of women took over both the indoor and outdoor space to sleep.[68] In spatial uses like this, the grounds on which soldiers and camp followers settled were not set apart from the interior of the coaches, but rather continued reaching back inside through the openings, always in use by the people coming in and out while the train was idle.

Soldaderas shaped domestic life by using existing architectural elements (grounds, floors, walls, roofs, openings, layers) to profoundly link home and landscape—as well as the public and the private. As described by veteran Justino López Estrada, an example of such configurations saw soldaderas prepare food for their "Juanes" at a site that took place by an idle train.[69] In one of Whitt's memoirs, a social setting arranged next to the boxcars acted as a living room where men and women enjoyed taking turns to sing *corridos* (folk songs). Shortly after, most of them fell asleep and spent the night therein. Days later, at a stop ahead, Whitt recalled that the passengers disembarked and

> spread out to form an encampment. Some soldiers have lit a huge fire out of a *gobernadora* (a high-resin plant that is very flammable, even when green) and, by the flame or smoke, they dry the blankets drenched in the rain [of the day before]. Women have set up their open-air, *de rigueur* kitchens and prepare coffee.[70]

The home that the soldaderas carried, having switched from its original containment inside a building (the regular dwelling) to containment inside a train, had its components dislocated when arriving at the station: the practices of cooking, sleeping, and resting were more randomly distributed in a space that flowed between the train cars and the station. Using the same qualifier that he used with the "portable city," Whitt calls the train car a "fickle dwelling."[71]

Soldaderas also made use of existing hardware to redefine the architectural, material, and functional terms of domesticity. Justino López Estrada recalls that, when the train stopped, these women improvised cradles for their babies by placing planks on the lower "ironwork" of train cars.[72] By ironwork he refers specifically to the tensor cables that gave rigidity to the bottom frame of the carriages. As these cables hung from the longitudinal edge of these carriages, they were suitable supports for the planks that soldaderas placed across them (Figure 6; see also Figure 4). Babies would lie on them, hanging under the boxcars.[73] Whitt describes having encountered a couple installed on the ground by a train and using the tracks as a headrest, "cushioned" by a blanket and a rifle.[74] Other photographs show similar scenes of the appropriation of surfaces, with people on the ground using packages and baskets to configure the areas that they claimed for rest (Figures 7 and 8).

At a campsite within proximity of the renowned Battle of Torreón, Whitt narrates having seen a group of camp followers "transform a gondola into a dwelling."[75] On one end, some of them cooked on small, smoking braziers, while the rest built a toilet area covered by branches and shawls on the other end. One of the women leaned on a wall close to an inner corner of the gondola and fell asleep in that position while stroking a

Figure 6. *Coche especial pagador* (Paymaster's car) *FCM-604*, built 1918, Puebla, Mexico, 2022. Photograph courtesy of Ana Karina Silveti Ortega, Área de resguardo de equipo rodante histórico, Museo Nacional de los Ferrocarriles Mexicanos.

Figure 7. *Soldado acompañado de su familia en la estación Buenavista* (Soldier in company of his family at Buenavista station), Mexico City, 1914. Unknown photographer. Reproduction authorized by the Instituto Nacional de Antropología e Historia, Secretaría de Cultura-INAH-SINAFO F.N.-Mex.

Figure 8. *Tropas federales en la estación Buenavista antes de salir a combate* (Federal troops at Buenavista station before heading to battle), Mexico City, 1913. Photograph by Agustín V. Casasola. Reproduction authorized by the Instituto Nacional de Antropología e Historia, Secretaría de Cultura-INAH-SINAFO F.N.-Mex.

weapon.[76] The plan provided follows Whitt's account (Figure 9). The gondola's rectangular space and the multiple uses given to it by the soldaderas resembles working-class dwellings of the time, which, for the most part, remained undivided by walls and accommodated different activities.[77]

*Vecindades* constitute a type of urban complex featuring these working-class dwellings. These blocks for collective housing had accommodated the underprivileged urban majority since the seventeenth century (Figure 10). Many of these buildings were first erected and owned by the Roman Catholic Church, which generated revenue from leasing the living units.[78] In its basic form, a *vecindad* was structured around or aligned by a patio. Other vecindades were manors left by bourgeois families who moved from city centers to residential areas on the outskirts. The new owners subdivided these sixteenth- and seventeenth-century buildings into dwelling units for rent.[79] Both in repurposed manors and in purpose-built vecindades, the bathrooms and washing areas were located in the patio or the roof terraces to be shared by the numerous apartments of the cluster. The humblest but most common living units had no ventilation, and their only opening was the doorway. Their continuous blind walls evoked a ring, which gave these quarters the name *cuartos redondos* (round rooms).[80]

The repurposed walls, rooftops, and spaces of train cars gave shape to the ephemeral homes yet were contingent on the dynamics of the train. An example of this dependence is the changing form of a "bedroom" in the testimony of Josefina Bórquez. As she describes, horses had priority within a boxcar's space, which forced soldiers and soldaderas to sleep on the rooftops. When the train stopped, however, these travelers made a bedroom for themselves in the boxcar after the horses were removed. Enclosing themselves in these spaces, occupants created some moments of couple intimacy.[81] During these stopovers, the very public "bedroom" area that people had shared on the top of trains was transferred below, now using the vertical surfaces of the cars to offer privacy to its occupants. When the train was speeding along the tracks, these vertical surfaces

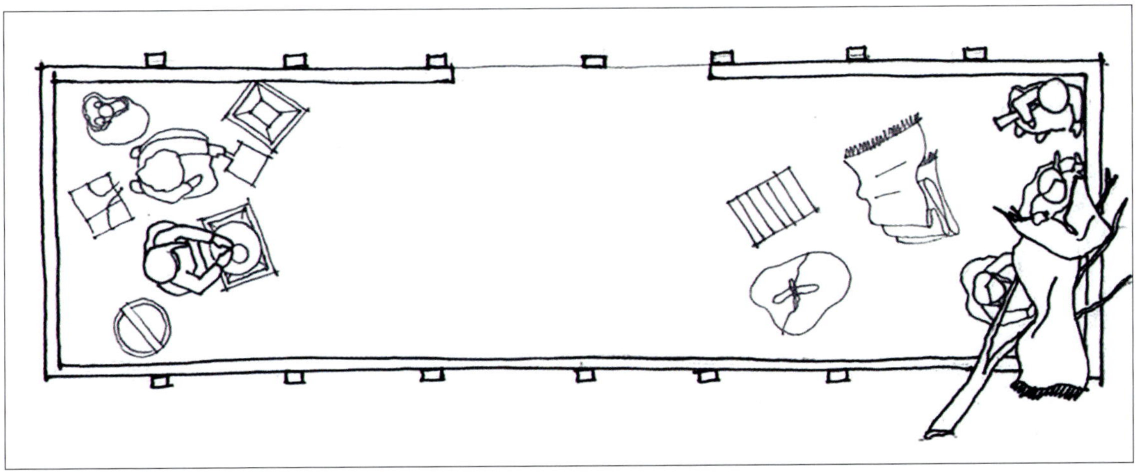

Figure 9. Women transform a gondola into a dwelling. Drawing by Tania Gutiérrez-Monroy.

were meant to physically protect those inside (in this case, the horses) from falling out of the car. When the train stopped at the station, the same surfaces took on the function of visually protecting the new dwellers in the space: those who had traveled on top now appropriated the space for having sex.

Women's repurposing of surfaces included other domestic uses as well. Bórquez narrates what happened after a battle in which she fought:

> A downpour made us return to the station where we had left the impedimenta. We were all covered in mud. . . . The following day, at the station, I just saw that the women had hung our clothes to dry on cables.[82]

This particular example leaves unclear whether the soldaderas used the hardware of the trains or the hardware of the stations to hang clothes to dry. Regardless, the objects that these women hung, spread, and prepared on these surfaces functioned as built-in cues for the type of activity required—laundry, cooking, or sleeping.[83]

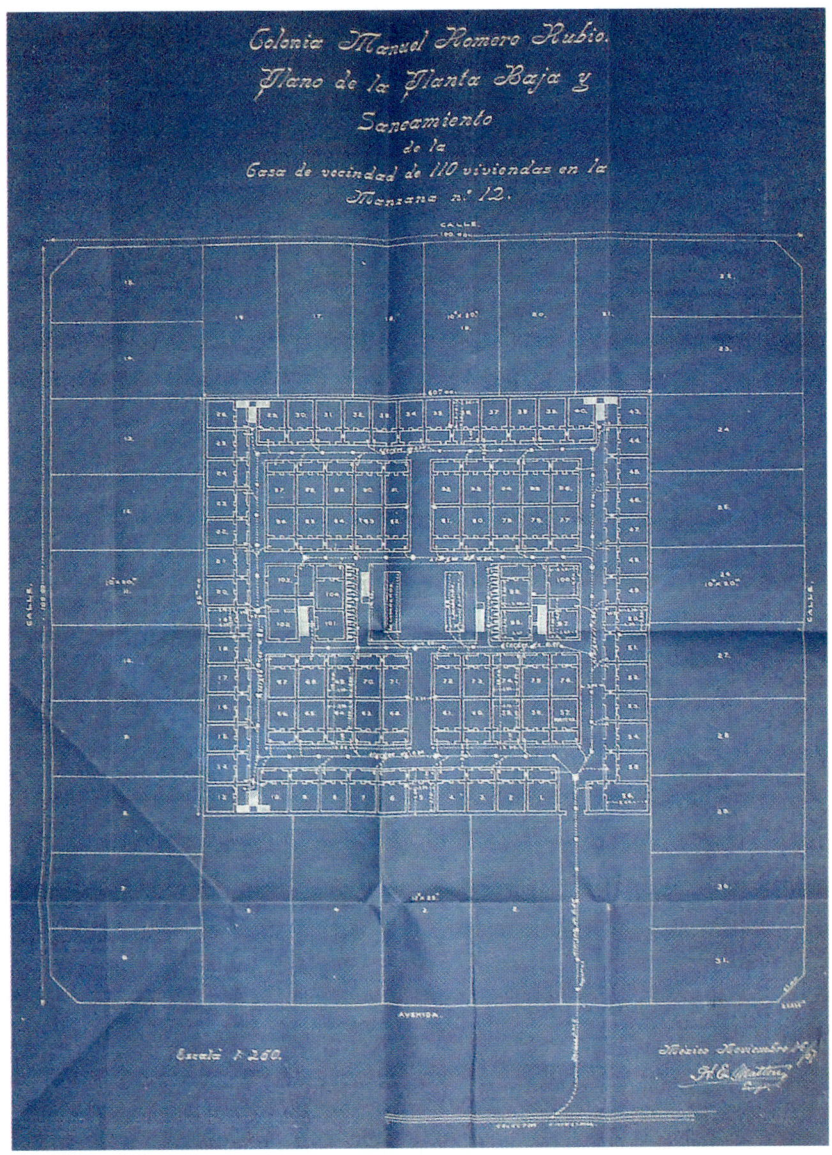


Figure 10. *Plano de la planta baja y saneamiento de la casa vecindad de 110 viviendas en la manzana no. 12, Colonia Manuel Romero Rubio* (Ground floor and sewer plan of 110 housing-unit *vecindad* in block no. 12, Manuel Romero Rubio neighborhood), Mexico City, 1907. Item 2.32, file 3, box 35, Fondo Planos y Proyectos 1861–1992, Planoteca, Archivo de la Coordinación de Monumentos Históricos, INAH.

The use of the rooftops of train cars by soldiers and soldaderas also merits attention, especially with regards to appropriating unused spaces in a way that strengthened the traveling community. It is difficult to imagine the hardship of this accommodation as the free choice of army members. Walking along the speeding line of train cars was dangerous, and many soldaderas fell to their deaths.[84] And yet these "top-floor residents" claimed such spaces as collective homes and used them for everyday collaboration in subtle ways.

Bórquez describes the inclement weather through which she traveled alongside other women and men. All of them had to sit or squat to avoid falling. She says that they used *mangas de hule* (also called *jorongos*, ponchos for horse riders made of oilcloth) to protect their belongings from the rain. Bórquez and her companions cooked as the train moved along the railway: "We would eat up there, on top of the train. We brought a brazier that we kept lit as we covered its opening, preventing air from entering underneath and from making the sparks jump above."[85]

Some of the most widely circulated images of women in the revolution depict these rooftop kitchens. Suggesting some of the forms that the kitchens could take, they often parallel the scenes from Bórquez's recollections (Figure 11).[86] Similarly, Brondo Whitt's memoirs reveal that soldaderas often appropriated the tops of boxcars as social spaces during halts in their journeys.[87] His description of the ease with which they climbed up and down the challenging ladders reminds us of the owner of a home who can run up or down its staircase with a familiarity and speed that outsiders cannot match. Women also stood together on cars to watch battles or events nearby. They even gave birth on this top space claimed as a home.[88] Whitt recalls:

> Walking along a military train prior to departure, one can see the cars crowned by masses: men and women spend the night "à la belle étoile," sleeping rough, wrapped in their serapes. . . . On these men's way to battle, a car's interior is full of officers, and its top is crowded with privates who defy the weather, sleeping on the wet surface and covering themselves with a *four-thread* [frayed] blanket. And there they go, undaunted and still cheerful, with their *vieja* [pejorative for woman] alongside, so that she softens the cold-air nights with her presence and songs.[89]

Figure 11. *Soldaderas preparan comida en el techo de vagón de ferrocarril* (Soldaderas prepare food on train top), Mexico City, 1914. Unknown photographer. Reproduction authorized by the Instituto Nacional de Antropología e Historia, Secretaría de Cultura-INAH-SINAFO F.N.-Mex.

While the spatial adaptation of trains was comparable to the vecindad, perhaps more important was the manner in which these changes accommodated collective living—specifically, the shared livelihoods of vecindad dwellers as shaped by the use of public bathrooms and laundry areas. The domestic groups that constituted an army shared daily practices in ways that transformed the train into a moving vecindad. The domestic architectures that emerged within boxcars were ephemeral, yet the togetherness of the group in the months- or years-long journey fostered lasting sociospatial dynamics like those of a vecindad. Throughout their journeying and settling, revolutionaries remained neighbors, a livelihood that evokes the literal meaning of the word vecindad: vicinity.

The empty boxcar of a train, with its single opening and multiple uses, behaved like a mobile cuarto redondo or round room. Aligned in the same fashion as the units of vecindades, the boxcars allowed domestic life to expand to the station's grounds. The central role of the patio in a vecindad included not only circulation, but also collective activities and common services. The grounds adjacent to the revolutionary train resemble the patio or the common spaces of a vecindad in the shared use for laundering and cooking by women.[90]

The spatial strategies of soldaderas allowed them to create a measure of community privacy. Despite being an unwalled domestic space, the rooftop allowed its occupants to regulate the connection with the space of the camp while positioned at an elevated vantage point. This site was visually connected to the surrounding landscape, while keeping some level of privacy. From above, the landscape where the train stopped was visible, but not all that was happening on the tops of trains could be seen from the ground. Such visibility depended on the angle but was certainly more advantageous from above: the height difference regulated visual access in the same fashion as the walls of a closed-off car (Figure 12). It was as though the walls folded invisibly upwards to continue providing a privacy now negotiated through the position of subjects. Thus, privacy would no longer depend on an interior being closed off, but on an exterior in which elevation and angle served to control visual and physical access. Constantino Caldero complains about soldaderas appropriating the space of rooftops with their children: "A real headache! . . . What a drag, handling women. They were so unruly!"[91] As a deputy chief of staff of the Villista army, Práxedes Gíner Durán found out that camp followers used the train tops to hide weapons from the very eyes of their troop leaders.[92]

In a famous episode in Camargo, Chihuahua, General Francisco Villa was barely missed by a gunshot from the rooftop of a train where a group of soldaderas stood.[93] The higher position allowed the sniper to watch Villa on the ground without being noticed; being among this crowd on the boxcar granted her anonymity. Willing to face collective punishment, the women never revealed who among them had fired at the rebel leader. José María Jaurrieta, secretary to Francisco Villa at the time, wrote in his *Memorias de Campaña* that the general ordered the execution of all the women.[94] Elsewhere, Villa's chief of staff, Práxedes Gíner Durán, recalls a safe retreat of his military corps from Aguascalientes, made possible by the women who shot from the rooftops against enemies who attempted to block the advance of the train.[95]

Combining controlled spatial strategies and contingent unpredictable conditions, the cyclic home of the war led soldaderas to improvise settings that were strongly linked to the landscape. Whitt describes geographies in Rincón de Romos connected along diverse sites on which women created eating, resting, and washing or bathing spaces. This series of makeshift domestic settings extended all the way from the train station to a river and illustrate how multiple, sequential places constituted homes with undefined boundaries.[96]

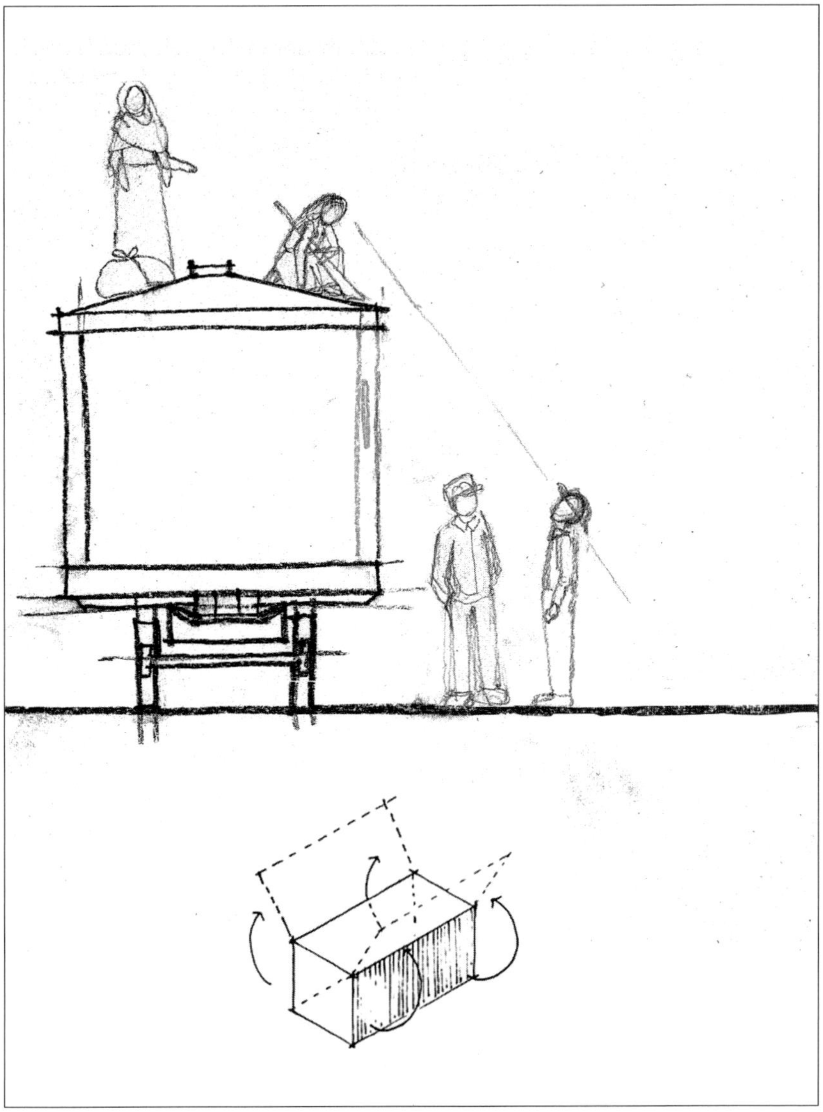

Figure 12. Rooftops were often appropriated by soldaderas. The section shows the vantage point of people positioned on top of a train car with respect to subjects on the ground. Drawing by Tania Gutiérrez-Monroy.

### The Home as a Space-Event: Place-Making and Places That Happened

Soldaderas established connections to place that ran deeper than mere passage through space.[97] As exemplified earlier, leaders such as Villa considered the crowd of camp followers an encumbrance because of its slow pace. However, I contend that this slowness, coupled with women's constant engagement with sites to set up camp, resulted in a deep knowledge of and attachment to place. If men directing a contingent had to know a landscape for successful military moves, women connected with it through ways of *being* in that landscape. The sites and events referred to in this essay show that soldaderas had to build homes where contingents could afford a restful—even if short-lived—dwelling in space.

Acting as articulators of home and landscape, soldaderas reinforced their own connections with both. This is visible in the war experience of former camp follower Alberta Galindo (from the Programa de Historia Oral). At her encampment outside of Tenango del Aire in central Mexico, one of her duties was to provide food. She acquired a thorough knowledge of the types of edible plants available and where they grew, as well as the animals that they could hunt: "In the wild you won't starve: there are mushrooms, amaranth, pigweed and other edible weed, . . . rabbits, deer. There, on the mountain, one finds anything to eat."[98]

Women's fundamental role of building and maintaining mobile homes called for inventive and discerning use of the resources and features of the landscapes they traversed. They did the legwork that would transform ever-changing surroundings into familiar sites, deepening their knowledge of places all the while. As soldaderas (perhaps unwittingly) strengthened the relationship between dwellings and geographies, they turned the action of homemaking into *place-making*. Here, "place" is understood: a) in its more traditional definition that involves a subject who experiences it or appropriates it by dwelling in it;[99] and b) in the sense that considers the complex, outreaching relations that constitute the site and the multiple forms of apprehending it.[100] Whereas soldaderas interacted with wild and human-altered spaces seeking to create conditions of appropriation and dwelling, their place-making actions also align with Doreen Massey's definition of place: with a specificity not so much fixed into an unchanging shape and inward-looking history, but "constructed out of a particular constellation of social relations, meeting and weaving together at a particular locus."[101] During the Mexican Revolution, the travels of women connected and transformed places through movement.

Soldaderas built a revolutionary home that kept at its center elements such as the train car and the shawl, which these women continuously adapted to changing landscapes. This home building involved fleeting place-making practices. The train car and the shawl worked alongside the bodies of soldaderas, which shifted from transporting to anchoring roles in space. Together, they created a domestic architecture in need of constant rebuilding—an architecture that they transformed into a process.[102]

The accounts that inform this essay offer examples of domesticity during the revolution that existed outside notions of fixity and unity. Attending to the cyclical creation of these dwellings (constructed, used, dismantled, transported, and reconstructed) reveals the home's fragmentary existence. As revolutionaries traveled, their practices of spatial occupation transformed events—such as cooking, sleeping, laundering—into components of a dwelling. Shaped as events, the spaces of this dwelling *happened*. Reading Whitt's itinerary between Fresnillo and Calera, we can observe how an army's (one-)day home unfolded beyond a single space or time: in it, the morning kitchen *happened* at a train car before departure; the afternoon kitchen and laundry *happened* outdoors at a stop a few hours later; even some form of patio or play area *happened* farther ahead when a group of soldiers playfully captured a snake; the evening kitchen(s) *happened* at empty houses that women occupied in a village at the next stop; here, the living room and bedroom also *happened* at the end of the day of travel.[103]

What was the role of bodies, shawls, and train cars along and across these places that happened?

Whereas the mobile home of the revolution was defined by change, a few elements needed to remain somewhat constant for this architectural process to take place. Elements like the shawl and the train car provided certain stable and reliable forms that enabled the cyclical existence of the dwelling of armies. Combined with bodies that became architectural components themselves, these key elements sustained a mobile domesticity that can hopefully inform new understandings of the home and the forms we consider reliable in it.


AUTHOR BIOGRAPHY

**Tania Gutiérrez-Monroy**, assistant professor at the School of Architecture and Landscape Architecture at the University of British Columbia, studies architecture as a material and signifying practice that spatializes colonial and patriarchal forces as well as resistance mechanisms. Prior to her UBC appointment, she was assistant professor of architecture at the University of Wisconsin–Milwaukee.



ACKNOWLEDGMENTS

I extend my gratitude to Annmarie Adams, Kristin Norget, and Cynthia Hammond for their comments on earlier versions of this text, part of my PhD dissertation (McGill University). Lydia Mattice Brandt and Michael J. Chiarappa, as well as two anonymous reviewers, provided invaluable feedback to improve the final version of this essay. I am also thankful to Maria Agnes Olaguera and Steven Yuvan for their editorial suggestions.


NOTES

Copyright note for Figures 1, 3, 5, 7, 8, and 11: The reproduction of images of archeological and historical monuments is regulated by the Ley Federal sobre Monumentos y Zonas Arqueologicos, Artisticos e Historicos and its Regulations, hence requiring approval of the Instituto Nacional de Antropologia e Historia.

1. Juan Gómez-Quiñones, *Teorizando sobre la revolución mexicana: Interpretaciones de sus historiadores y cronistas*, trans. María Rosa García (Mexico City: INEHRM, 2015), 51–61.

2. All quotations from sources in Spanish, including image credits, were translated by Tania Gutiérrez-Monroy.

3. Andrés Reséndez Fuentes argues for the differentiation between camp followers and women fighters. Elizabeth Salas, however, points to the porosity of both identities in the actions of soldaderas. This essay aligns itself with the broader understanding of Salas. Soldaderas took part in the revolution for various reasons. They traveled with military groups motivated by either interest in the promise of social change, the desire to follow a family member, or the remuneration for their services to soldiers. As Elizabeth Salas shows, many of these women were unattached to one man and charged various members of an army for cooking and laundry services, as well as for the provision of goods. Andrés Reséndez Fuentes, "Battleground Women: Soldaderas and Female Soldiers in the Mexican Revolution," *The Americas* 51, no. 4 (1995): 525–53; Elizabeth Salas, *Soldaderas in the Mexican Military: Myth and History* (Austin: University of Texas Press, 1990), 33–36, 44.

4. The home was dematerialized in terms of building materials, although it relied on other materials like the shawl and the train car.

5. The highest rank women attained was *coronela*. It was uncommon for women to officially hold these leadership positions. Martha Eva Rocha, *Los rostros de la rebeldía. Veteranas de la Revolución mexicana, 1910–1939* (México D.F.: INEHRM / INAH, 2016), 103–4. The renowned General Francisco Villa strove to keep camp followers away from battle. Like him, other generals stated this gendered "unbelonging." Brondo Whitt, *La División Del Norte, 1914: Por Un Testigo Presencial*, 2nd ed. (Mexico City: Lumen, [1940] 1984), 222. See testimony of Jesús Arias Sánchez, Programa de Historia Oral, interview by Eugenia Meyer, January 1973, PHO/1/33, Biblioteca Manuel Orozco y Berra, Instituto Nacional de Antropología e Historia, Mexico City [hereafter PHO].

6. Women brought offspring along or gave birth at some point during the long periods in which they served, so the landscapes of the Mexican Revolution were largely populated by families.

7. See personal chronicle of Rosa E. King, English owner of a hotel in Cuernavaca, Mexico. Rosa E. King, *Tempest over Mexico: A Personal Chronicle* (Boston: Little, Brown, 1935), chapter 7.

8. This term is proposed by anthropologists and sociologists as an alternative to existing notions for the term family, which has so far remained patrilocally based. See Heather Fowler-Salamini and Mary K. Vaughan, *Mujeres del campo mexicano, 1850–1990* (Mexico: El Colegio de Michoacán, 2003); and "Las Soldaderas," *La Opinión,* January 1, 1913, 3, Hemeroteca Nacional de México (National Newspaper Library of Mexico), hereafter HNM.

9. Abigail Van Slyck shows, however, that American modern summer camps had strict prescriptions for the roles of participants in camp-building. These roles were often gendered, but I see them more as means to instruct children into social models of adulthood and citizenship than as prosthetic homes (because they were seen as escapes from the home, as explained in a later note). Abigail Van Slyck, "Connecting with the Landscape: Campfires and Youth Culture at American Summer Camps, 1890–1950," in *Designing Modern Childhoods: History, Space, and the Material Culture of Children,* ed. Marta Gutman and Ning De Coninck-Smith (New Brunswick, N.J.: Rutgers University Press, 2008).

10. Whitt, *La División Del Norte,* 222.

11. Even if hardly mentioning a home to return to, architect and scholar Charlie Hailey's description of "breaking camp" implies the same certainty in his analysis of encampments. *Campsite: Architectures of Duration and Place* (Baton Rouge: Louisiana State University Press, 2008). Abigail Van Slyck examines the intentions behind temporarily removing children from the family home in early twentieth-century North American summer camps in order to shape childhood according to modern principles. Whereas such removal was often aimed at "protecting" the youth from the perceived dangers of home and city raising, there was indeed a home where they would return and put to practice the values learned. Abigail Van Slyck, *A Manufactured Wilderness: Summer Camps and the Shaping of American Youth, 1890–1960* (Minneapolis: University of Minnesota Press, 2006). See also Jonathan Clark and Hyman Kempler, "Therapeutic Family Camping: A Rationale," *The Family Coordinator* 22, no. 3 (October 1973): 438, 440.

12. Whitt, *La División Del Norte,* 221. Arguably, refugee camps are more similar in their pursued domesticity.

13. Christine Arce, *México's Nobodies: The Cultural Legacy of the Soldadera and Afro-Mexican Women* (Albany: State University of New York Press, 2017), 74; Elena Poniatowska, *Hasta no verte, Jesús mío* (Mexico City: Ediciones Era, 1994), 65–66.

14. Michel de Certeau, *The Practice of Everyday Life* (Berkeley: University of California Press, 1988), 123.

15. Later in the article I describe how objects became parts of architecture by taking up the function of defining space, like the setting for a meal that a soldadera organized around the objects.

16. It is important to point out that Whitt held the sexist, classist, racist views on women (and Mexicans in general) prevalent in his privileged stratum. Hence, stereotyping, objectifying, and moralizing annotations taint his daily entries.

17. Whitt, *La División Del Norte,* 248–49. Not without some classicist scorn, Whitt often calls women's shawls "rags."

18. Specifically, Bonnevier speaks about masks, costumes, and disguises as connections between architecture and performing subjects. Her analysis expands Gottfried Semper's theory of architectural cladding to advance buildings as dressing the body. Katarina Bonnevier, *Behind Straight Curtains: Towards a Queer Feminist Theory of Architecture* (Stockholm: Axl Books, 2007), 375; Gottfried Semper, *The Four Elements of Architecture and Other Writings* (Cambridge: Cambridge University Press, 1989).

19. Bonnevier, *Behind Straight Curtains,* 375.

20. Julia Tuñón, *Women in Mexico: A Past Unveiled* (Austin: University of Texas Press, Institute of Latin American Studies, 1999), 77. Soledad González Montes and Pilar Iracheta Cenegorta describe the role of peasant women providing income to the family by weaving and making handcrafts at home during the Porfiriato. Soledad González Montes and Pilar Iracheta Cenegorta, "La violencia en la vida de las mujeres campesinas: el Distrito de Tenango, 1880–1910," in *Presencia y transparencia: La mujer en la historia de México,* ed. Carmen Ramos Escandón, 2nd ed. (Mexico City: El Colegio de Mexico, 1987), 123. Neither the shawl (*rebozo, ruana, jorongo*) nor this use for carrying are unique to Mexico. Women in many Latin American countries have worn the garment, arguably a variant of the Arabic veil brought by the Spanish conquest. See Martha Alfaro, "Utilización del rebozo y el mecapal para el transporte de objetos durante el período virreinal. Estudio de caso de cuatro mujeres de la colec-

ción de San José de los Naturales," in *Memoria del VII Congreso de la Asociación Latinoamericana de Antropología Biológica,* ed. P. Hernández, C. Serrano, and F. Ortiz, vol. 507, Colección científica (Mexico City: INAH, 2006), 56–64.

21. Christine Arce describes the shawl's function during the revolution: "This humble article of clothing cum domestic tool is transformed into a weapon, and not just a symbol of resistance in the metaphoric sense, but rather as another manifestation of resistance, an actualization of struggle and war. The rebozo carries that which will nourish the soldiers, that which transforms products into sustenance, and the progeny who represent both the soldadera and the soldier's immortality, as they in turn, will continue the fight." Arce, *México's Nobodies,* 75–76.

22. For descriptions, see Ignacio Herrerías, "Desde el campo revolucionario," *El Tiempo,* April 17, 1911 (HNM); and Josefina Bórquez's testimony in Poniatowska, *Hasta no verte, Jesús mío,* 66.

23. Poniatowska, *Hasta no verte, Jesús mío,* 65–66. Authorship is attributed to Poniatowska alone, but Jean Franco convincingly argues that it is a compositely authored book. Jean Franco, *Plotting Women: Gender and Representation in Mexico* (New York: Columbia University Press, 1989), 177–78.

24. The part of a moving army where equipment and women traveled was often called impedimenta ("luggage" or "baggage": literally "that by which one is impeded"). See Jean Meyer, "Grandes compañías, ejércitos populares y ejército estatal en la revolución mexicana (1910–1930)," *Anuario de Estudios Americanos* 31 (1974): 1010; and "Las tropas federales se proponen asestar un golpe terrible," *El Imparcial,* May 19, 1912 (HNM).

25. Herrerías, "Desde el campo revolucionario," *El Tiempo,* 1911 (HNM).

26. Edith O'Shaughnessy, *A Diplomat's Wife in Mexico: Letters from the American Embassy at Mexico City* (New York: Harper & Brothers, 1916), 245.

27. See examples in "Federales envían a sus soldaderas antes a saquear," *El País,* August 16, 1912 (HNM); "El General Angeles ordena que salgan las tropas," *El País,* September 3, 1912 (HNM); and Irene Copado, Programa de Historia Oral, interview by Alicia Olvera de Bonfil, print interview, 1975, PHO-Z/1/10 (PHO).

28. Poniatowska, *Hasta no verte, Jesús mío,* 66–67.

29. "El General Angeles ordena que salgan las tropas," *El País,* 1912 (HNM); "Unos infelices indios piden justicia y piedad," *El País,* August 16, 1913 (HNM).

30. Brondo Whitt describes a landscape covered by shawls ("rags") and items abandoned by a passing army. Whitt, *La División Del Norte,* 248.

31. Whitt, *La División Del Norte,* 245.

32. Especially the perimetral wall described by de Certeau, 123.

33. Male soldiers from the revolution were called "Juanes," from the common Spanish name "Juan." The gendered pseudonym worked specifically to refer to the men that soldaderas supposedly followed, as in "a soldadera and her Juan." I use the word "supposedly" because it was not always the case that women entered the war in an attempt to accompany a male relative, even if hegemonic accounts reduce their revolutionary labor to such gendered role. Justino López Estrada, Programa de Historia Oral, interview by América T. Briseño, print interview, March 29, 1973, PHO/1/49 (PHO).

34. Whitt, *La División Del Norte,* 79.

35. Tabea A. Linhard, *Fearless Women in the Mexican Revolution and the Spanish Civil War* (Columbia: University of Missouri Press, 2005), 9.

36. Informed by Roland Barthes, Andrea Noble analyzes images from the revolution in this light; see for instance Andrea Noble, "Gender in the Archive: Maria Zavala and the Drama of (Not) Looking," in *Phototextualities: Intersections of Photography and Narrative,* ed. Andrea Noble and Alex Hughes (Albuquerque: University of New Mexico Press, 2003), 136–64; Roland. Barthes, *Camera Lucida: Reflections on Photography* (New York: Hill and Wang, 1980).

37. Caroline Brothers, *War and Photography: A Cultural History* (London: Routledge, 1997), 17.

38. Christine Arce, *México's Nobodies,* 68. See also Caroline Brothers, *War and Photography,* 17.

39. Interpretations morphed from self-abnegating followers to sexualized warriors to key revolutionaries. See Delia Fernández, "From Soldadera to Adelita: The Depiction of Women in the Mexican Revolution," *McNair Scholars Journal* 13, no. 1 (2009): 53–62.

40. Arce, *México's Nobodies,* 69.

41. Renowned historians like Alan Knight, Werner Tobler, Luis González y González, James Cockroft, Friedrich Katz, and Lorenzo Meyer have analyzed the revolutionary decade mostly through masculinist

narratives. These historians, while doing revisionist work at length, reproduced the masculine-centered perspectives of the very first accounts, written by participants in the struggle like Jorge Vera Estañol, Manuel Bonilla Gaxiola, Manuel Calero y Sierra, Alfonso Taracena, and Francisco Bulnes. See Alan Knight, *La Revolución Mexicana* (Mexico City: Fondo de Cultura Económica, 2010); Luis González y González, *Así Fue La Revolución Mexicana* (Mexico City: Consejo Nacional de Fomento Educativo, 1985); James Cockcroft, *Intellectual Precursors of the Mexican Revolution, 1900–1913* (Austin: University of Texas Press, Institute of Latin American Studies, 1968); Friedrich Katz, *The Secret War in Mexico: Europe, the United States, and the Mexican Revolution* (Chicago: University of Chicago Press, 1981); Lorenzo Meyer, *La Segunda Muerte de La Revolución Mexicana* (Mexico City: Aguilar, León y Cal Editores, 1992); Jorge Vera Estañol, *Historia de la Revolución Mexicana: Orígenes y Resultados* (Mexico City: Porrúa, 1976); Manuel Bonilla, *Diez años de guerra: Sinopsis de la historia verdadera de la Revolución Mexicana* (Mexico City: Impr. Avendaño, 1992); Manuel Calero y Sierra, *Un decenio de politica mexicana* (Ann Arbor: University of Michigan Library, 2009); Alfonso Taracena, *La verdadera Revolución Mexicana* (Mexico City: Editorial Jus, 1963); and Francisco Bulnes, *El verdadero Díaz y la revolución de México* (Mexico City: Instituto de Investigaciones Dr. José María Luis Mora, 2008).

42. In the case of the Mexican Revolution, this manipulation tended to reinforce the feminization of the domestic work of soldaderas in ways that othered them as war participants and that strengthened the imagined division between the home and war fronts.

43. Susana Torre, "Claiming the Public Space: The Mothers of Plaza de Mayo," in *The Sex of Architecture*, ed. Patricia Conway, Leslie Weisman, and Diana Agrest (New York: Harry N. Abrams, 1996), 429. Here Torre paraphrases Henri Lefebvre.

44. See Jesús Chávez, Programa de Historia Oral, interview by María Alba Pastor, print interview, August 31, 1973, PHO/1/99 (PHO); Domingo Yedra Islas, Programa de Historia Oral, interview by Laura Espejel, print interview, August 31, 1973, PHO-Z-1–15 (PHO); and Whitt, *La División del Norte*, 265.

45. Juan Arellano Aguilar, Programa de Historia Oral, interview by Alicia Olivera de Bonfil, print interview, August 7, 1973, PHO-Z/1/7 (PHO).

46. John Mraz, *Photographing the Mexican Revolution: Commitments, Testimonies, Icons* (Austin: University of Texas Press, 2012), 144.

47. More reliant on guerrilla strategies in the thick landscapes they occupied, armies such as the Zapatista would hardly use the railroad.

48. Mraz, *Photographing the Mexican Revolution*, 148.

49. Francisco Gorostiza Pérez, *Los ferrocarriles en la Revolución Mexicana* (Mexico City: Siglo XXI, 2010), 10.

50. Jorge Gómez Pérez, "Catálogo de Equipo Rodante de IMNFM Locomotoras," *Mirada Ferroviaria, Revista Digital* no. 6 (2008): 81–84.

51. Anthony Bianculli, *Trains and Technology*, vol. 2, *Cars* (Newark: University of Delaware Press, 2002), 98–99.

52. Gorostiza Pérez, *Los ferrocarriles*, 651.

53. Bianculli, *Trains and Technology: Cars*, 101–2.

54. Bianculli, *Trains and Technology: Cars*, 102.

55. Departamento de Curaduría de Colecciones, "Coches de pasajeros," *Mirada Ferroviaria, Revista Digital*, no. 8 (2009): 80. Brondo Whitt describes this type of wagon on a train operated by the División del Norte army. Whitt, *La División del Norte*, 86.

56. Departamento de Curaduría de Colecciones, "Coches de pasajeros," 75.

57. Gorostiza Pérez, *Los ferrocarriles*, 10.

58. Whitt, *La División del Norte*, 374.

59. Constantino Caldero, Programa de Historia Oral, interview by María Isabel Souza, print interview, October 27, 1973, PHO/1/110 (PHO); Poniatowska, *Hasta no verte, Jesús mío*, 94.

60. "Fuerzas Federales Rumbo a Orizaba," *La Opinión*, March 30, 1912 (HNM), 2.

61. "Con El Ánimo Muy Levantado Salió Para El Norte La Brillante Columna Del Gral. Victoriano Huerta," *El Diario*, April 11, 1912 (HNM).

62. "Marchó Blanquet al. Norte," *El Imparcial*, June 3, 1912 (HNM).

63. "Hasta El Último Momento," *El Imparcial*, June 3, 1912 (HNM), 5.

64. Arce borrows the term *primum mobile* from Michel de Certeau. Arce, *México's Nobodies*, 43, 45; de Certeau, *The Practice of Everyday Life*, 113.

65. In their military travels, trains differed from regular overnight trains in the need for the encampment and its members to create a domestic feeling. Unlike regular travel, the long and dangerous war jour-

neys offered little certainty of returning home. The traveling dwellings accommodated kinship-related families as well as other communities for which the term "domestic group" is suitable (as explained earlier in the text). This group includes members who may or may not be related by kinship either sharing a dwelling or dispersed in different geographies but with a social connection of some kind. Bórquez, for instance, belonged to different family nuclei, some connected by kinship and some not. Heather Fowler-Salamini and Mary K. Vaughan, *Mujeres del campo mexicano, 1850–1990* (Zamora: El Colegio de Michoacán, 2003).

66. Brondo Whitt describes the charming draped beds, dining table, sinks, storage of culinary delights, and cutting-edge water closet. Whitt, *La División del Norte,* 86.

67. Whitt, *La División del Norte,* 269.

68. Whitt, *La División del Norte,* 397.

69. Justino López Estrada, Programa de Historia Oral, interview by América T. Briseño, print interview, March 29, 1973, PHO/1/49 (PHO).

70. Whitt, *La División del Norte,* 234–45, 269.

71. Whitt, *La División del Norte,* 244–45.

72. López Estrada, PHO/1/49 (PHO).

73. I am thankful to Ana Karina Silveti Ortega (Head of the Department of General Services and Material Resources) and Bruno Sebastián Wilson Ebergengyi (Subdirector of Preservation and Restoration, Mobile Equipment) at the National Museum of the Mexican Railway, who explained in detail the hardware of the train cars and the use to which Justino López Estrada referred. Personal communication, July 9, 2022.

74. Whitt, *La División del Norte,* 213.

75. Whitt, *La División del Norte,* 121.

76. Whitt, *La División del Norte,* 121.

77. Even across the vast differences of urban and rural dwellings in Mexico, the described single space that accommodated multiple activities was a very common feature at the time, especially when little influenced by European forms. Guillermo Boils, *Las casas campesinas en el Porfiriato* (Mexico City: Martín Casillas, 1982), 26; Vicente Martín Hernández, *Arquitectura doméstica de la Ciudad de México, 1890–1925* (Mexico City: Universidad Nacional Autónoma de México, Escuela Nacional de Arquitectura, 1981), 99–100.

78. Hernández, *Arquitectura doméstica,* 99–100.

79. María Teresa Esquivel, "El uso cotidiano de los espacios habitacionales: de la vecindad a la vivienda de interés social en la Ciudad de México," *Scripta Nova: Revista Electrónica de Geografía y Ciencias Sociales* 7, no. 146 (August 2003).

80. The vecindad provides only one of many examples of working-class living units. Both in urban and rural areas, single-family dwellings shared the feature of an undivided space and were often self-built, which produced few architectural plans.

81. Poniatowska, *Hasta no verte, Jesús mío,* 94–96.

82. Poniatowska, *Hasta no verte, Jesús mío,* 111.

83. See also Whitt, *La División del Norte,* 428.

84. Salas, *Soldaderas in the Mexican Military,* 43.

85. Poniatowska, *Hasta no verte, Jesús mío,* 94. Bórquez clarifies that a convoy with numerous cars moved slowly.

86. Whitt, *La División del Norte,* 223.

87. Whitt, *La División del Norte,* 306.

88. Whitt, *La División del Norte,* 108, 317.

89. Whitt, *La División del Norte,* 222–23.

90. Whitt, *La División del Norte,* 219, 428.

91. Caldero, PHO/1/110 (PHO).

92. Práxedes Gíner Durán, Programa de Historia Oral, interview by María Isabel Souza, print interview, July 21, 1973, PHO/1/75 (PHO).

93. While rebelling against the federal government and fighting its army throughout the war, revolutionary armies such as the Villista, Carrancista, and Zapatista often confronted each other. One of the most visible schisms came about after the 1914 *Convención de Aguascalientes.* Soldaderas often infiltrated rival columns to work as informants (or to smuggle weaponry) for the army they served in. Working undercover or a vendetta after one of the massacres ordered by Villa could be reasons for the woman to have attempted to kill the general.

94. José María Jaurrieta, *Con Villa (1916–1920), memorias de campaña* (Mexico City: Consejo Nacional para la Cultura y las Artes, 1997), 76. See also Durán, PHO/1/75 (PHO); Silvestre Cadena Jaramillo, Programa de Historia Oral, interview by María Alba Pastor, print interview, 1973, PHO/1/98 (PHO). Jaurrieta describes the event as having taken place in December 1916. Interestingly enough, a newspaper narrates a very similar incident in 1920 (also in Chihuahua), which supposedly ended with Villa granting a pardon to the group of women. "Una Soldadera a Punto de Matar a Villa," *El Informador,* June 18, 1920 (HNM).

95. Durán, PHO/1/75 (PHO).

96. Whitt, *La División del Norte,* 397.

97. Here I have no intention to embrace the idea that there is a clear-cut difference between the notions of space and place. I understand them as existing in a continuum and propose that the spatial practices of soldaderas are one of many examples bringing together these notions. Michel de Certeau differentiates them by stating, "Space is a practiced place," where a certain fixity in the term *place* seems opposed to the mobility and change of the term *space.* As suggested in the following lines, soldaderas both profited from the changing spatial conditions that war travel offered (or imposed) and shaped homes connected to their landscapes, configured to have users be or dwell in those landscapes. De Certeau, *The Practice of Everyday Life,* 117.

98. Alberta Galindo Mantilla, Programa de Historia Oral, interview by Alicia Olvera de Bonfil, print interview, 1975, PHO-Z/1/69 (PHO).

99. Edward Casey, "Between Geography and Philosophy: What Does It Mean to Be in the Place-World?" *Annals of the Association of American Geographers* 91, no. 4 (December 2001): 683–93; Jeff Malpas, *Place and Experience: A Philosophical Topography* (Cambridge: Cambridge University Press, 1999); Edward Relph, *Place and Placelessness* (London: Pion, 1976); Yi-fu Tuan, *Space and Place: The Perspective of Experience* (Minneapolis: University of Minnesota Press, 1977).

100. Doreen Massey, *Space, Place, and Gender* (Minneapolis: University of Minnesota Press, 1944), 3–4.

101. Massey, *Space, Place, and Gender,* 15.

102. My focus on domestic architecture as a process relates both to the process of its construction as well as to the process of its occupation. Recent scholarly attention to the process of building has decentered traditional understandings of architecture as an end product, but my point in this essay is that such "end product" was in constant rebuilding. Key to my understanding of space as a process are the ideas of Susana Torre, Elizabeth Grosz, and Jane Rendell: Torre, "Claiming the Public Space"; Elizabeth Grosz, *Architecture from the Outside: Essays on Virtual and Real Space* (Cambridge, Mass.: MIT Press, 2001), 119; Jane Rendell, *The Pursuit of Pleasure: Gender, Space & Architecture in Regency London* (New Brunswick, N.J.: Rutgers University Press, 2002), 136–38.

103. Whitt, *La División del Norte,* 268–74.

ALEXANDER WOOD

# The Structural Ironworkers of New York City, 1845–1895

ABSTRACT

This article examines the life and work of New York City's ironworkers, who erected the city's first tall buildings, factory lofts, and other iron-framed structures. It chronicles the development of iron construction and the fortunes of the trade; analyzes the skills, tools, and machinery ironworkers used on the job; and describes their efforts to improve their lot in solidarity with other workers. Using project records, newspapers, and labor publications, this article reconstructs the history of a new building trade in a period of momentous change in the building industry.

In the late nineteenth century, New Yorkers witnessed the erection of skyscrapers, loft buildings, and other iron-framed structures that transformed the landscape of the city. Given the prominent role that architects, engineers, and manufacturers played in developing iron construction, the history of the industry is often portrayed as the triumph of design and engineering over craft. Yet it also created a new building trade that skillfully erected ironwork. The demand for iron construction elevated housesmiths, as these ironworkers were known at the time, into one of the most important trades in the building industry. Laboring in a loud, exciting, and dangerous trade, they became the iconic representatives of the big city construction worker.[1]

From the beginning of the city's iron age, architects, engineers, and manufacturers knew that building in iron would radically change how buildings were constructed. Building in iron produced taller, larger, and lighter structures but it also increased the speed of erection and thus lowered the cost of construction in comparison to traditional building techniques. Because every project was a custom job, iron producers depended upon workers with craft skills, mechanical ability, and training. The trade flourished with the expansion of the industry and drew upon the talents of working people of widely different backgrounds. Empowered by their starring role on large building operations, ironworkers staked their claim as a skilled trade by assembling ironwork at great speeds in what were often brutal working conditions.

Unlike many building trades which could trace their history back to a preindustrial past, iron construction was forged in the fires of an emerging industrial capitalism. Throughout the second half of the nineteenth century, iron producers and ironworkers lived in a state of nearly permanent conflict that often crippled the entire building industry. Seeking to maintain their control of the trade and maximize profits in a competitive market, iron producers sabotaged workers' efforts to form unions. Ironworkers found success by joining forces with more established trades to seek higher wages, lower hours, and better working conditions. Positioned at the vanguard of construction practice, facing tyrannical bosses, and working in one of the most physically demanding trades, ironworkers fought to secure their place in the building industry.

## The Beginning of Gotham's Iron Age

In the second half of the nineteenth century, New York City became the nation's leading center of iron construction. The city's rapid economic growth and demand for fireproof buildings, combined with its abundance of capital, technical expertise, and labor, all contributed to the emergence of the industry in the antebellum era. New York's central position in the national railway system, the expansion of domestic iron output, and the drop in price of key production materials such as anthracite coal were also important to the industry's growth. Producing iron in the city was expensive given its high labor costs, land values, and property taxes, but the industry thrived close to the source of demand. Like many industries that concentrated in the city, iron producers were primarily oriented toward supplying the large urban market.[2]

The first architectural ironworks in New York were founded in the late 1840s by Daniel D. Badger, James Bogardus, John B. Cornell, and other enterprising artisans who joined the ranks of the local manufacturing elite. Based on their success producing cast-iron fronts for stores, architectural ironwork developed in a branch of the local metals industry which included shipbuilding, boilermaking, and related industries.[3] In 1847, Cornell's $1,500 contract for erecting a cast-iron front for a store on Broad Street was the largest undertaking of the season, suggesting his early contracts were quite modest.[4] Cornell and most producers operated workshops below Canal Street, where they could be near both their customers and the New York and Harlem Railroad, which delivered pig iron, coal, and other supplies. By the early 1850s city directories listed a dozen "housesmiths" carrying on their trade, a name that was also used to describe some of the craftsmen in their employ. Traditionally, a housesmith was an artisan who fabricated ornamental ironwork such as railings, but these iron producers set their sights higher. While they manufactured iron railings, shutters, light vaults, and stairways, they focused their efforts on developing the more lucrative field of structural ironwork.[5]

New York's architectural iron producers aimed to supply all of the iron needed in a given building contract, but they viewed the manufacturing of cast iron as the centerpiece of their business. Used for making fronts, ornament, and columns, cast iron was a type of iron created by casting molten pig iron with a relatively large amount of carbon. Cast iron was hard and brittle but strong under compression, giving it excellent structural qualities for making columns. Many firms also manufactured wrought iron, a type of iron forged by working heated pig iron into shape after removing most of the carbon. Wrought iron was soft, malleable, and had good tensile strength, and thus was excellent for making girders, beams, and trusses.[6] When a contract required rolled wrought-iron beams, they were ordered from a local rolling mill such as the Trenton Iron Works, which manufactured some of the first rolled beams in the United States.[7]

Beginning in the 1850s, New York's master housesmiths oversaw the erection of an impressive array of structures, including the New York Crystal Palace (1853, Figure 1), the Harper & Brothers Building (1854), and the E. V. Haughwout Building (1857). By the late 1850s, the construction of dozens of "commercial palaces" was underway along Broadway south of 14th Street featuring cast-iron fronts, ornament, columns, and stairways, wrought-iron beams, and other iron components. Reaping the rewards of these big contracts, manufacturers reinvested their profits back into their shops, expanded their facilities, and began to plan for the future. By the end of the decade, the major architectural ironworks relocated along the waterfront north of 14th Street, where they could spread out over entire city blocks. Gotham's iron age had begun.

Most architectural iron producers saw themselves as manufacturers but they also operated as contractors in the building industry. Under the terms of their contracts with building owners, iron producers agreed to furnish all labor, materials, and equipment needed to assemble ironwork, requiring them to employ craftsmen in several trades. One of the most important trades on the payroll was the journeymen housesmith, the workers who erected iron on site and prepared the material in the shops for use. From the earliest days of the trade people were dazzled by the

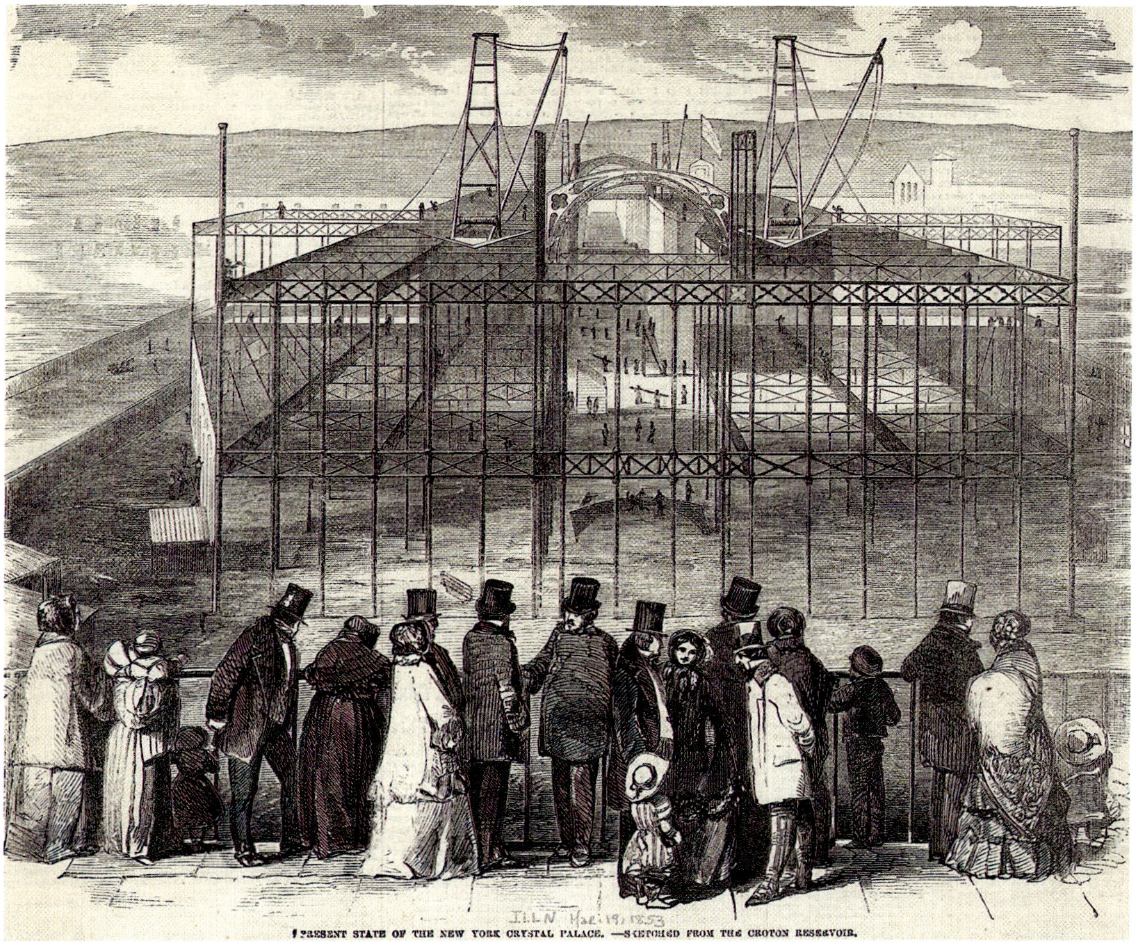

Figure 1. "Present state of the New York Crystal Palace, sketched from the Croton Reservoir," 1853. *Illustrated News*, May 19, 1853, New York Public Library.

sight of men putting together buildings while hovering over the void. In 1853, in one of the first descriptions of the trade, Horace Greeley praised the ironworkers erecting the Crystal Palace at 42nd Street. "Workmen perched," he wrote, "like autumnal pigeons on lofty boughs, clustered within and without the vast edifice."[8] Gawking at the spectacle, crowds gathered along the walls of the Croton Distributing Reservoir to get a better look at one of the city's newest occupations.

The men who erected the city's first cast-iron structures and formed the nucleus of a new building trade were trained specifically for the job, but many entered the industry with a background in a related metalworking trade (Figure 2). Due to the novelty of iron construction, the first architectural ironworks were not only places of production but also incubators of a body of knowledge that served as the foundation of the trade. While ironworkers were the only workers that erected ironwork on site, in the shop they worked alongside other metal workers, including blacksmiths, modelers, patternmakers, molders, and puddlers. Most shops employed carpenters, painters, and glaziers, in addition to machinists who repaired equipment. The yards of an iron manufacturer also resounded with the shouts of cartmen who loaded iron into horse-drawn wagons and transported materials to the job. Engaged in the design, production, and erection of iron, these workers labored at the cutting edge of industrial production.

By the late 1850s iron producers employed three broad classes of ironworkers. First, there were the skilled mechanics knowns as "outside" and "inside" ironworkers. The outside ironworkers worked on-site and comprised the setters who positioned members into place, the connectors who made connections in the field, and the riggers who prepared materials for hoisting. They were joined on-site by a special class of derrickmen who operated the equipment that lifted materials into place. Most outside workers started out as inside ironworkers, also known as finishers, who prepared ironwork before it was delivered to the site. Finishers chipped, filed, and sanded cast iron to remove imperfections from the casting process before fitting it together on the shop floor. They drilled and reamed bolt holes before fastening together the cast iron to guarantee a

Figure 2. Idealized view of Daniel D. Badger's Architectural Iron Works, showing the trades involved in producing and erecting architectural ironwork. Frontispiece, *Illustrations of Iron Architecture, Made by the Architectural Iron Works, New York* (New York: Baker & Godwin, 1865), Smithsonian Institution Archives.

good fit. Finishers also ensured that the iron was numbered and ready for erection by the outside crews. The third class of worker, known as helpers, assisted mechanics in the field and shop in the completion of their tasks (Figures 3 and 4).

The first ironworkers erected simple post-and-lintel frames using cast-iron columns which they connected to girders using different techniques. Many of the first buildings using cast-iron columns were erected by placing the columns on top of traditional timber girders, which caused the girder to shrink over time due to the weight of the load. Seeking to avoid this problem, dowelled cast-iron columns were employed that passed through a drilled timber beam, transferring the load to the column below.[9] Beginning in the 1850s, cast-iron columns were fastened to wrought-iron beams by placing the beam on a bracket cast into the column and bolting it together by hand (Figure 5). By the mid-1850s, riveted connections were introduced in the floor framing of some structures to connect wrought-iron girders with wrought-iron floor beams, thus eliminating timber framing altogether.[10] While the trade of ironworking remained based in the arts of metalworking, framing, and rigging, the rapid development of new building techniques meant that workers needed mechanical ability to keep pace with the state of the art.

Many of the trades' defining characteristics were apparent in the earliest days of iron construction. One of the main differences that separated ironworkers from other building trades was the weight, size, and bulkiness of the members they handled. A typical twelve-foot-tall cast-iron column with a twelve-inch diameter weighed nearly a ton and required careful coordination during erection.[11] Because iron members were lifted directly into position, the process of hoisting, setting, and fastening a column, girder, or beam into place was carried out as a single integrated operation. Ironworkers worked particularly closely with the derrickmen who operated the hoisting machinery that became essential to the on-site assembly process.

From the earliest days of the trade ironworkers were recognized as craftsmen due to their skills,

Figure 3. Detail from frontispiece view of the Architectural Iron Works, 13th and 14th Streets, East River, New York, in *Illustrations of Iron Architecture*, pl. 2, Prints and Photographs Division, Library of Congress, LC-DIG-pga-08213.

Figure 4. Loading cast-iron column into a spring wagon with a hand crank. Detail from "Excelsior Iron Works," ca. early 1860s. Prints and Photographs Division, Library of Congress, LC-DIG-pga-00087.

Figure 5. Front elevation, section, and rear elevation of cast-iron columns from a building by James Bogardus showing bolted connections, ca. late 1840s. "Architectural iron construction," *The Iron Age* 13 (April 30, 1874): 1.

mechanical ability, and training. Long before ironworkers went into the field, they apprenticed for five years in the shop. In their training ironworkers learned how to connect ironwork; to chip, file, and drill iron; to rig a block and tackle; to use a pulley, windlass, and derrick; to make a rope sling for hoisting; and to make a variety of knots they used in their work. They also learned to use the tools of the trade, including hammers, files, and wrenches; to operate drill presses, punches, and other types of metal-working machinery; and to read shop drawings. Most ironworkers specialized in particular tasks when they became journeymen, but their training gave them an understanding of every aspect of the trade. Ironworkers did not participate directly in the manufacturing of ironwork, but they learned about the production process. Like all crafts, the trade's maturation was cumulative as more experienced workers passed down a body of knowledge to the next generation.[12]

For many New Yorkers iron construction had a futuristic connotation, but the erection of iron buildings was a form of custom handcraft production. Working with a few basic tools, the setting crew erected, aligned, and fastened iron columns, girders, and beams into place. Riggers eyed members as they arrived on-site and determined how to place the hoisting sling. Derrickmen studied the layout of the site; built the necessary masts, guy wires, and booms; rigged the block and tackle; and operated the boom to swing iron into position. Mastering all of these tasks took special abilities, particularly since workers had to labor for ten hours a day, day after day, week after week, and month after month during the busy building season. Laboring outside in the stifling heat of late summer and early fall, ironworkers also worked in the wind, the rain, and the snow that came with the onset of winter before their season wrapped up for the year. Like most construction workers, ironworkers remained idle for several months while they awaited the beginning of the next building season.

New York's small but growing number of ironworkers belonged to a prosperous trade, but like most urban craft workers in the mid-nineteenth century, they found themselves in a precarious position. Due to the capital-intensive nature of iron production, few ironworkers became independent masters and the gulf between employers and their men was growing. As a result, most ironworkers became permanent wage workers and had to survive in a society in which they sold their labor as a commodity. Recognizing the tremendous power that employers held over their lives, ironworkers thus formed organizations to secure higher wages, lower hours, and better working conditions. Unlike more established trades that were trying to protect crafts with long traditions, ironworkers organized to protect a trade still in its infancy.

In 1850, a group of ironworkers organized the first journeyman's protective society at a meeting at the Fourteenth Ward Hotel at the corner of Grand and Elizabeth Streets in the emerging tenement district where many workers lived. Their main grievance was their inability to meet the rising cost of living in the city, particularly the cost of housing. According to press accounts, two hundred of the three hundred workers at the meeting voted to form a union and went on strike the following day, seeking an increase of 12.5 percent in wages from every employer. Iron producers initially resisted their demands but relented after several weeks, making the first strike a success. In the years that followed, ironworkers sought periodic wage increases from their employers but also began to complain of problems stemming from the breakdown of the artisan system as bosses failed to fulfill the terms of apprenticeships, blacklisted troublesome workers, and attempted to flood the trade with poorly trained workers.[13]

While the first ironworkers' protective society focused on improving their specific trade, they were also likely inspired by a groundswell of trade union activity in the city. Sparked by the first shocks of an emerging capitalist economy, collective action was especially prevalent among carpenters, bricklayers, and painters, but it also proved popular with other skilled trades, including printers, bookbinders, and tailors. In 1853, ironworkers answered the call of these larger trades to form a citywide federation of craftsmen that would unite all its unions, protective societies, and benefit associations into a single body. Before the potential of these efforts could be realized, however, the Panic of 1857 delivered a terrible blow to the craft economy. The depression was especially devastating for the building trades that depended on new construction, such as the ironworkers. Workers had only begun to reap the rewards of their labor activities when a collapse in demand for iron construction returned power to their employers.[14]

By the beginning of the Civil War, iron construction was still a small part of the city's building industry, but iron producers and ironworkers had established a place in the urban craft economy. Dominated by a few enterprising artisans who founded the first architectural ironworks, the business of iron construction flourished as part of the emergence of capital-intensive manufacturing. Like other kinds of manufacturing that found a home in the city, building in iron was a labor-intensive industry that relied on skilled hands to master a variety of techniques. As in many other craft industries, the erosion of the artisan system and the rising cost of living caused tensions between employers and wage workers. Proud of their skills and defensive of their trade, ironworkers felt confident in seeking a greater share of the fruits of their labor and rallied to the cause of the city's labor movement.

### The Post–Civil War Boom

Iron construction in New York City took a leap forward as rapid urban growth drove the expansion of the industry in the decade following the Civil War. In Lower Manhattan, prominent businesses commissioned the first tall office buildings, including the ten-story Western Union Telegraph Building, the New York Tribune Building, and the Evening Post Building—all completed in 1875 (Figure 6).[15] Retailers, merchants, and manufacturers continued to erect huge cast-iron department stores and factory lofts on Broadway between Chambers and 34th Streets. Expanding commerce translated into new iron-framed factories and warehouses along the waterfront. Iron producers competed vigorously for this work, and particularly for the contract for the huge train shed of Grand Central Depot, completed in 1871 at Park Avenue and 42nd Street. Won by Daniel D. Badger's Architectural Iron Works, the contract was reputedly worth more than a million dollars, an astounding sum for the time (Figure 7).[16]

The city's first tall buildings and train sheds represented large contracts for producers but they also showcased the expanding repertoire of the ironworkers' craft. The tall mansard roof of the

Figure 6. Western Union Telegraph Building, 1875. Prints and Photographs Division, Library of Congress, LC-DIG-stereo-1s06993.

Figure 7. "Grand Central Depot (1871), New York—Interior View," *Harper's Weekly* 16 (February 3, 1872): 105.

Western Union Telegraph Building, for example, was assembled more than two hundred feet above the street. It was framed with wrought-iron rafters and king-post trusses, creating an enormous column-free room for telegraph operators on the eighth floor. The building's thick load-bearing masonry walls were designed to work in tandem with oversized cast-iron columns, rolled wrought-iron girders, and floor beams. Ironworkers also pioneered the use of steam-powered machinery in the construction of these early tall buildings. According to one account, ironworkers on the Tribune Building applied steam power to the traditional mechanisms of pulley, windlass, and derrick, multiplying their power to raise ironwork with impressive speed.[17]

The construction of these buildings also changed the character of work in the trade. As projects grew in size, ironwork ballooned in weight, and the pace of work increased on-site. Many of the large structures of the era employed oversized columns to handle increased loads, which in turn required more muscular hoisting equipment and a larger number of setting crews. The spacious gallery hall of the nine-story Equitable Building, for example, used double-story columns sixteen inches in diameter and twice the weight of a typical cast-iron column. To keep track of these operations, iron manufactures relied on the foremen who represented their interests on-site. Foremen—often promoted from the ranks of journeymen ironworkers—drove the pace of work in the field, which became critical in commercial construction.[18]

With such large contracts in hand, Badger, Cornell, and other founders of the industry retired from business after forming partnerships with family members and transforming their firms into dynastic industrial enterprises. By the early 1870s, several of the first ironworks had grown into large plants that combined foundry work, forging, and rolling, enabling them to fulfill larger contracts and a larger total volume of work as well.[19] The five largest postwar firms were J.B. & W.W. Cornell, Badger's Architectural Iron Works, Jackson's Iron Works, the Excelsior Iron Works, and the Aetna Iron Works, each of which employed more than five hundred workers.[20] Smaller shops continued to work on a more modest scale, building the storefronts that gave the industry its start. By the early 1870s, twenty-five firms in the city specialized in some form of architectural ironwork.[21]

One of the main challenges iron manufacturers faced in the post–Civil War era was cobbling together a larger workforce to meet growing demand. Abandoning the use of formal agreements with apprentices, employers solicited workers from throughout the region and adjacent industries, quadrupling the number of workers in the trade in just a few years. By the 1870s, the trade included workers who had grown up in the first architectural ironworks, itinerant bridgemen seeking better wages in the city, and even sailors who drifted into the trade. Most ironworkers still completed their training in the shop before going out in the field—in 1870 W.W. Cornell's plant was described as an "Iron University"—but the terms of this training became informal.[22] While native-born American workers were still prominent in the trade, British, Irish, German, and Scandinavian immigrants began to enter the workforce in large numbers as employers looked to newcomers to address their labor shortage. Having secured their place in the building trades, the Irish in particular played a major role in the postwar labor movement.[23]

Just as they were starting to put the first touches on the skyline in Lower Manhattan, ironworkers began to organize once again to advance their interests. In 1864, they founded the Housesmiths' Mutual Protective Association, the first durable ironworkers' union in the city. Led by British-born ironworker George Linton, the organization grew from five hundred to fifteen hundred members to represent most ironworkers in the city by the early 1870s. Unlike previous efforts, this organization represented a more permanent style of trade unionism that worked fulltime to raise the status of the trade. Ironworkers continued to prioritize an increase in wages on account of the high cost of living in the city, as a union circular declared in 1867. "The nature of our trade compels us to live within a reasonable distance of our business," they asserted, "and through the rapacity of Metropolitan landlords, many of us are compelled to live in unhealthy locations, in crowded apartments, endangering the health of our families."[24] Like many building trade unions, the ironworkers held regular meetings to encourage political education, raised funds for death benefits for members, and organized picnics at commercial pleasure gardens.[25]

Despite the growing importance of their trade, ironworkers belonged to one of the smallest building trades in the city, which compelled them to stand shoulder-to-shoulder with their fellow trade unionists. In 1869, the union appointed Linton, Patrick Murphy, and John McCann to serve as delegates to the Workingmen's Union, a new citywide labor federation that was incorporated in 1866 to unify the efforts of urban craft workers in their fights against employers. Building trade leaders—from the ranks of bricklayers, carpenters, plasterers, and painters—were prominent in the organization and ensured that it would represent the interests of construction workers. Of all the issues that animated working people in the postwar years, the eight-hour movement garnered the most enthusiasm. By reducing the working day to eight hours, workers could reduce the strain of labor and also have more time for rest, leisure, and self-improvement. According to the leaders of the eight-hour movement, workers would thereby also gain more time to exercise their rights as citizens.[26]

Beginning in the late 1860s, ironworkers also began to participate in the national labor movement. In 1868, when the National Labor Union (NLU) held a congress in New York at Germania Hall on the Bowery, ironworkers participated in heated discussions on how to improve the political, economic, and social status of American workers. Founded in 1866, the NLU was the first nationwide federation of trade unions and brought together trade union leaders, labor reformers, and other representatives of the working classes. At the congress, they debated the

Figure 8. In 1871, prior to ironworker participation in the strike of 1872, workers conducted a procession in support of the eight-hour day. "New York City—Great Eight-Hour Labor Demonstration—The procession of workingmen as it appeared on passing the Cooper Institute," *Frank Leslie's Illustrated Newspaper* 33 (September 30, 1871): 33.

eight-hour day, women's suffrage, and the need for a labor party. Ironworkers' delegate Henry J. Keating supported the eight-hour movement, defended the legitimacy of strikes, and called for the formation of a labor party to advance workers' rights. However, Keating was opposed to elevating women's suffrage to the labor reform platform. After an eloquent speech by Elizabeth Cady Stanton, he arrogantly declared that women must "first learn to fight capital."[27]

The ironworkers' efforts to improve their lot in solidarity with other skilled male workers culminated in their participation in a strike for the eight-hour day in the spring of 1872 (Figure 8). Although the strike began in Manhattan, ironworkers walked off the job in forty shops throughout the metropolitan area, including some in Brooklyn and Jersey City. Smaller employers agreed to their demands, but Badger, Cornell, Jackson, and other large manufacturers refused to negotiate with the union. Manufacturers were further emboldened by the fact that ironworkers had limited their union membership to skilled mechanics, thus excluding the large number of helpers in their trade. Working outside the union, helpers were immediately hired to replace strikers, thus putting an end to the strike.[28] Yet ironworkers remained confident. In the summer of 1873, the union leader Linton was elected as vice president of the Workingmen's Union, giving the trade a prominent voice in the city's major labor organization.[29]

No sooner did ironworkers begin to plan their next strike, however, than the Panic of 1873 brought the building industry to a standstill. Although the trade had survived a panic before, the ensuing depression was more severe. As the number of contracts dwindled, iron producers regained the upper hand and the union dissolved. Virtually every employer reinstituted the ten-hour day and lowered wages, abolishing the gains of a decade of effort. Throughout the mid-1870s, the largest iron producers survived by building Manhattan's new elevated lines or other forms of infrastructure throughout the metropolitan area, but even with these contracts in hand they laid off half of their workforce (Figures 9 and 10). For the second time in fifteen years, many ironworkers found themselves unemployed, biding their time for better days. Many others, however, left the trade altogether.[30]

**Ironworkers Come of Age**

Surging demand for iron construction in New York at the end of the nineteenth century created a brief golden age for the industry. Beginning in the early 1880s, architects began to design structures that were twelve, fifteen, and even eighteen stories tall. The economic elite that built office buildings downtown also built major cultural institutions and luxury apartments uptown, all of which translated into more business for iron manufacturers. The construction of the Mills

Figure 9 *(left)*. "New York City—The Development of Rapid Transit—The Gilbert elevated railroad on New Church Street, in the rear of Trinity Churchyard," *Frank Leslie's Illustrated Newspaper* 46 (May 25, 1878): 200.

Figure 10 *(below)*. "New Jersey—The Great Iron and Tubular Pier at Long Branch—An illustration of the method by which the pillars are driven and drilled into the sand," *Frank Leslie's Illustrated Newspaper* 48 (May 31, 1879): 197.

Building, the New York Produce Exchange, the Dakota apartments, and other large buildings required miles of structural ironwork, generating enormous contracts and attracting more workers into the industry. By the mid-1890s, iron construction assumed enormous importance in the building industry, as most large buildings utilized the material in some way. Fifty years after the construction of the first cast-iron fronts, ironworkers finally had the leverage they needed to secure a lasting place in the industry.

The best examples of the ironworkers' craft were on display in Lower Manhattan, where several major structures were built using an innovative "cage frame" structure. In a cage frame building, exemplified by the Mills Building (1882), the outer masonry walls were designed to support themselves independently, whereas the interior iron frame carried the floors. Using this technique, buildings became likened to an "elaborate bird-cage" in which increasingly thin brick walls encased a robust iron frame.[31] An even more dramatic example of this technique was used in the New York Produce Exchange, an enormous commodity exchange erected on Bowling Green (Figure 11). J.B. & J.M. Cornell's contract for the Produce Exchange was worth $675,000 and kept more than sixty ironworkers busy for thirteen months.[32] Although their bid was higher than those submitted by out-of-town manufacturers, New York's iron producers like Cornell had an established reputation for their expertise in the

Figure 11. The New York Produce Exchange under construction, February 15, 1883. George B. Post Collection, New-York Historical Society.

field. As the Building Committee of the New York Produce Exchange explained to a despondent Syracuse iron manufacturer, "we do not know of any establishment or firm in the country having resources equal to theirs in their line."[33]

In the late 1880s, Cornell muscled ahead of its competitors and became the largest architectural ironworks in the nation, with over 1,200 workers. In 1887, John Milton Cornell finally assumed full control of the firm after the death of his father, John Black Cornell. Cornell employed a salaried staff of architects, engineers, draftsmen, foremen, and assistant foremen to supervise different branches of production, as well as a large workforce of craftsmen, including several hundred structural ironworkers. "Without a thorough inspection of this establishment," noted a visitor, "one can scarcely form an idea of the variety of work or the multitude of trades employed," including "housesmiths, blacksmiths, machinists, pattern-makers, molders, patent light glaziers, modelers, safe-makers, painters and carpenters."[34] By the early 1890s, Cornell was one of a dozen large architectural ironworks in a local industry that included over sixty shops throughout the metropolitan area.

Over the course of the 1880s the ranks of the ironworkers doubled once again, further diversifying the trade with new recruits. By this time the trade was largely composed of second-generation Irish, Scottish, and Canadian immigrants. According to one source, the trade also included "Germans, Englishmen, Frenchmen, Scandinavians, Italians and several other nationalities."[35] In the early 1890s eastern European Jewish workers began to enter the trade as finishers.[36] Skilled outside and inside workers constituted the majority of the workforce, but the trade also saw an expansion in the numbers of helpers, "whose chief requirements," one journalist observed, "are physical strength in handling the material finished by the mechanics and assisting the latter in placing them in the prescribed position."[37] The demand for helpers was so great that the building season attracted longshoremen who returned to the docks in the winter.[38]

Cast-ironwork continued to form the centerpiece of the iron producers' business, but they also began erecting riveted wrought-iron columns, girders, and trusses, which necessitated a more precise process of assembly. In the New York Produce Exchange, riveted girders, arches, and trusses were employed to suspend a skylight over the trading floor.[39] At Carnegie Hall, ironworkers riveted a large roof truss to create a column-free interior for the concert hall. Over the course of the decade, field riveting became routine on most large projects and iron producers began placing orders for specially designed compound columns from such firms as the Phoenix Iron Works in Phoenixville, Pennsylvania. In the eighteen-story New York World Building, completed in 1889,

Figure 12. New York World Building under construction, 1889. Milliken Brothers, *Allowable Working Loads for Phoenix Columns of Iron and Steel* (New York: Milliken Brothers, 1890), n.p., Hagley Museum and Library.

ironworkers created the tallest building in the world by riveting Phoenix columns to rolled wrought-iron girders (Figure 12). Riveted connections provided a more rigid—and therefore stronger—bond compared to bolting. As riveting grew in importance, the assembly of ironwork became an increasingly complex procedure.[40]

With the rise of riveting, the tasks of ironworkers became more specialized and their day-to-day work more labor-intensive. Up on the job site, setters had to inspect every rivet-hole, align members with drift pins, and temporarily bolt them into place. They were followed by hand-riveting teams, consisting of four men, "a heater, a right-hand riveter, a left-hand riveter, and a holder on," who made field connections (Figure 13).[41] While iron producers relied on other firms such as the Phoenix Iron Works to fabricate large riveted wrought-iron members, they assembled smaller members in their shops using rolled wrought-iron shapes. The process of fabricating riveted members was lengthy: shapes were marked off, punched with holes, straightened through the rolls, temporarily bolted, and the holes were reamed before the member was riveted together.[42]

The use of compound riveted members also made their work more dangerous. The largest cast-iron column used before the Civil War was twelve feet long and weighed a ton, while riveted wrought-iron members ballooned to fantastic

Figure 13. Riveting teams assembling roof truss, Carnegie Music Hall, 1889–1891. Louis de Coppet Berg, "Iron Construction in New York: Past and Future," *Architectural Record* 1 (April–June 1892): 460.

sizes and weights (Figures 14 and 15). The girders used in the Produce Exchange weighed twelve tons each.[43] The thirty-five foot tall wrought-iron Phoenix columns used in Edison's new Pearl Street Station, completed in 1891, were fifteen thousand pounds each.[44] J. Cleveland Cady's extension to the American Museum of Natural History, completed in 1890, used twenty-eight box girders that were six feet deep, sixty-two feet long, and weighed forty thousand pounds. After horse-pulled wagons collapsed while moving the girders from the Hudson River to the site on Central Park West, a tramway was built to deliver them to the job. Erecting ironwork had always been inherently dangerous, but ironworkers became prone to severe crushing injuries working with massive iron elements. Workers were lucky if they retired from the trade with a missing finger, a bad back, and a few other aches and pains.[45]

The hazards of the trade took their toll on workers. According to trade union leaders, many ironworkers struggled to keep "body and soul together," let alone buy property or properly raise a family according to the customs at the time. Their burials were often paid for by collections, a frequent event in a trade in which, as another union leader noted, "a misstep will throw a man into eternity."[46] People familiar with the trade believed a lifetime on the job also transformed the mentality of workers. "Facing danger daily develops in the ironworker," one writer later claimed, "a sort of desperate recklessness, that the workman in a less hazardous occupation does not understand."[47] While the outside workers faced the greatest dangers, shop conditions were little better. Bernard Weinstein, a Jewish labor leader,

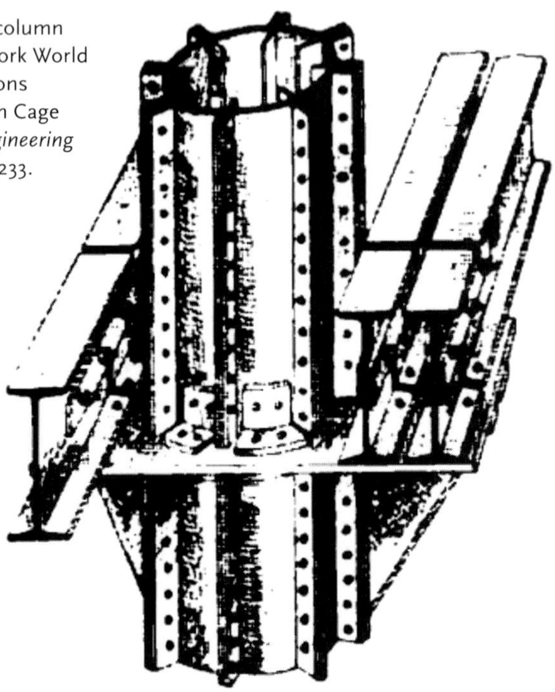

Figure 14. Detail of Phoenix column connections from the New York World Building, "Column Connections and Wall Supports in Modern Cage Construction Buildings," *Engineering Record* 38 (August 13, 1898): 233.

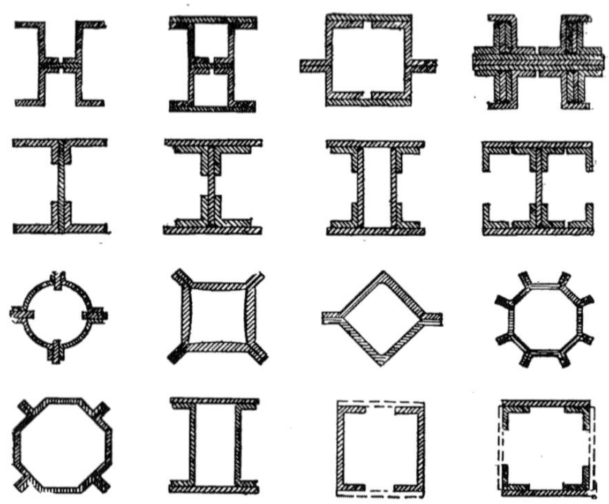

Figure 15. Typical compound column sections for a riveted wrought-iron or steel column, William H. Birkmire, *Skeleton Construction in Buildings* (New York: 1893), 22–23.

recalled the grueling working conditions faced by the inside helpers, who "worked from fifty to sixty hours a week." "Sweat pours over them all day, and the iron rust mixes with it and oozes into their skin," he wrote. "This often swells up their faces, sending them to the hospital."[48]

The rapid expansion of iron construction in the 1880s and the growing hazards of the trade set the stage for a far more acrimonious conflict between employers and workers (Figure 16). In the early 1880s, Cornell and other large producers established an employers' association, which acted as a cartel to ward off competitors and counter the growing power of organized labor.[49] At the same time, ironworkers regrouped to found the Housesmiths' Benevolent and Protective Union. Organized by the Knights of Labor in 1884, the Housesmiths' Union grew to over four thousand members and aimed to organize everyone in the trade, including inside workers, helpers, and even drivers who delivered ironwork to the site. Recalling the failure of their strike in the 1870s, ironworkers recognized the necessity of organizing every worker involved in the trade—including helpers. By embracing all workers, they were able to mount effective strikes that forced employers to raise wages, lower hours, and improve working conditions.[50]

Seeking to strengthen their position in the building trades fraternity, ironworkers in the early 1880s also elected a delegate to serve on the Building Trades Council, an organization founded by the bricklayers, carpenters, painters, plasterers, and other major building trades to plan collective actions in the building industry. Such "walking delegates," as they became known, recruited new members to the union, nominated shop stewards to impose union rules, and raised strike funds. Ironworkers also sent a delegate to the citywide trade council known as the Central Labor Union, which was founded in 1882. Organized as a trade, working in solidarity with other building trade unions, and affiliated with other workers in the city, ironworkers were finally prepared to go on the offensive.[51]

In 1885, ironworkers began with a strike against the most powerful employer, the J.M. Cornell Iron Works, in which one hundred and fifty workers walked off the job to protest the employment of nonunion workers. In 1887, the ironworkers launched eight successful strikes, in 1889 they launched thirteen, and in 1890 they launched over thirty-nine strikes involving five hundred workers. As a result of these strikes, the union organized virtually every worker in the trade and began to shift its attention toward reducing the length of the work day. Reeling from the threat of more strikes, employers signed the first collective agreement with the union in 1890, guaranteeing a nine-hour day without a reduction of wages, as well as a sliding wage scale for every branch of the trade. Iron producers also offered to recognize the union, take care of sick members, and cover their burial expenses if the union abolished the walking delegate and gave employers freedom to hire nonunion men, an offer the union refused.[52]

Figure 16. "New York City—Grand Demonstration of Workingmen, September 5th—The procession passing the reviewing stand at Union Square," *Frank Leslie's Illustrated Newspaper* 55 (September 16, 1882): 53.

Emboldened by their successes, ironworkers launched an enormous strike for the eight-hour day in the spring of 1891 involving four thousand workers—virtually the entire union membership. The principal firms involved in the strike were J.M. Cornell Iron Works and four other large producers. Given the large number of contracts they handled, the strike halted every major construction project in the city for six weeks—over eighty jobs in total.[53] The ironworkers increased their leverage throughout the strike by securing the pledges of the other building trades to strike in sympathy should any nonunion ironworker be employed on their jobs. The Central Labor Union also rallied to their cause and raised several thousand dollars for their strike fund. Workers found success once again in pressuring smaller employers to meet their demands; large firms refused to meet with strikers and put out advertisements soliciting workers to the city.[54]

Large iron producers—firms capitalized at values of several million dollars—were able to weather the strike, and, in the end, the ironworkers' union was unable to sustain it with their meager strike fund. "The whole contest," as one journalist put it, "was one of the stomach against the money-bag, buttressed by the political machinery of capital."[55] It thus came as a surprise when ironworkers found manufacturers tractable during their settlement talks. Having been taken aback by the militancy of the strike, iron producers agreed to hire back workers under their old terms and to weed out workers who did not belong to the union. Even more surprising was their suggestion that they would be willing to grant the eight-hour day, if it was not for the competition they faced from "less settled states."[56]

Despite the failure of the 1891 strike, ironworkers' fellow trade unionists and labor radicals came away impressed by the tenacity they exhibited in the contest. Most New Yorkers did not know much about the history of the trade, but veterans of the labor movement were aware that the latest strike was part of a long history of labor activity. As one radical working-class newspaper put it in the early 1890s, ironworkers were engaged in a "thirty years' struggle for eight hours."[57] So much time had passed since the founding of the trade that its early years were fading into legend. As the article noted, the records of the first ironworkers' union had been destroyed long ago and "the few old men in the present membership do not agree in matters of detail as to the workings of that first organization in their trade."[58]

Sensing they were on the verge of a breakthrough, New York's ironworkers regrouped a few years later and founded the United Housesmiths' and Bridgemen's Union in 1894 which grew to five thousand members. Led by Frank P. Leary and affiliated with the American Federation of Labor, the union aggressively focused on securing the eight-hour day as well as the kind of union recognition that most building trades enjoyed by this time. The very specter of this union forced the Iron League of New York—as the employers' association was then known—into important concessions. In the spring of 1895, for example, the Iron League granted the eight-hour day to ironworkers. However, the league refused to implement a uniform scale of wages or to recognize the union. Without such recognition, the union was powerless to create a closed shop in which employers agreed to exclusively hire union members.[59]

Several months later, in the fall of 1895, the United Housesmiths' and Bridgemen's Union launched the largest strike in the history of the trade with the goal of compelling the Iron League to recognize the union. Over the course of several months, ironworkers were assisted by sympathy strikes from other building trades until the strike involved fifteen thousand workers on more than one hundred projects throughout the city. Workers and walking delegates met daily at Clarendon Hall on East 13th Street and picketed major projects, while the police guarded job sites to prevent walking delegates from entering (Figure 17). Resenting the action of the union after the recent concessions, iron producers brought in poorly

Figure 17. "Police guarding Siegel, Cooper & Co.'s building against strikers," *New York Herald*, November 27, 1895, 6.

trained workers to replace strikers, several of whom died in accidents on the job shortly thereafter. Construction workers who had crossed picket lines walked off the job in turn, fleeing from such hazards. Having reached an impasse, a settlement was reached between the Iron League and the union that brought the strike to an end in December 1895. Although the union did not win the recognition it sought, the concessions it received represented another step toward winning a greater share of the fruits of their labor.[60]

As all these strikes demonstrated, iron manufacturers could not crush the ambitions of ironworkers to improve their lot, but workers were not powerful enough to force the hand of the largest employers. Unlike many building trades that were able to win most of their demands, ironworkers faced some of the largest, wealthiest, and most belligerent employers in the city—a group of manufacturers who were keen to maintain their competitive advantage at the center of a national industrial landscape. Despite the employers' hostile attitude toward the existence of the union, their post-strike negotiations underscored their dependence on the trade.

Two months after the settlement of the 1895 strike, New York ironworkers traveled to Pittsburgh to meet with union leaders from Chicago, Boston, Buffalo, Cleveland, Detroit, and nine other cities. On February 4, 1896, they formed the International Association of Bridge and Structural Iron Workers of America (IABSIW) with a charter from the American Federation of Labor. Although ironworkers were loath to give up their autonomy, they recognized that the challenges of the trade were national in scope. Successfully confronting bosses, they believed, required a single international union that combined the strength of local organizations. Being members of the largest local, New York's ironworkers maintained a decisive voice in the national union, but they shared the stage with their fellow unionists from other cities.[61]

### Conclusion

Over the course of half a century, New York's ironworkers emerged from obscurity to become one of the most important building trades in the city (Figure 18). Though the trade only accounted for 5 percent of the city's construction workforce in the mid-1890s, they had an outsized presence in the industry. Formed in the throes of the industrial revolution, many believed that this new trade injected a more raucous spirit into the world of construction. "The housesmith has knocked a large section of sentiment out of the building trades," noted one observer in 1895. "In watching operations on one of our mammoth buildings at the present day the idler does not smell the fragrant shavings nor see the clean white lumber being put up" or hear the "cheering cry" of the carpenter. Instead, they heard the "howls of the housesmiths" and the pounding of

Figure 18. "How New York Is Growing Skyward—The twenty-story building of the American Surety Company, at Pine Street and Broadway, now in course of erection," *Leslie's Weekly Illustrated* 80 (April 25, 1895): 263.

the riveting hammer while beholding the spectacle of beams "swung into place by powerful hoists." The author nevertheless praised the abilities of workers "who can rig a derrick like an old sailor, and in running along a three-inch beam 100 feet above the ground . . . take chances that would appall the best trapeze performer ever seen in the circus."[62]

By any definition the development of iron construction changed the landscape of the city, revolutionized building methods, and introduced a more industrial character to building sites. Yet in spite of the dramatic changes introduced by this new building technique, all ironwork still had to be erected by skilled workers who used a few basic tools. Empowered by their growing role in modern building operations, ironworkers fought to improve their trade from a position of strength. The architects and engineers who began in the early 1890s to publish the first comprehensive textbooks on iron construction in the United States implicitly recognized the trades' importance by what was left unsaid in their treaties. Filled with information on how to design structures using iron and steel, they contained little information about how to build them. As in any other trade, the art of assembling iron structures had to be learned on the job.[63]

By the mid-1890s, New York's ironworkers enjoyed decent wages, a collective craft identity, and a history of labor activity—all of which proved critical for the years ahead. In 1892, the city's building code was revised to allow an all-steel skeleton frame, and a few years later structural steel began to show up on-site.[64] The introduction of steel did not change the day-to-day work of the trade, but it transformed the industry in which they worked. A few local iron producers transitioned into rolling steel, but most manufacturers lacked the technical expertise and capital to compete in this market. Many general contractors who specialized in erecting steel-framed buildings, such as the George H. Fuller Company, used steel that they bought from Carnegie's mills in Pennsylvania. In the decades that followed, ironworkers thus came into conflict with a new breed of general contractors, corporate steel interests, and their subsidiaries, a conflict that produced a spate of ruthless union busting, labor racketeering, and terrorism that appalled the nation. While the first cast-iron fronts began to rust and the first architectural ironworks faded away, ironworkers entered a new and tumultuous era in the history of their trade.[65]


## AUTHOR BIOGRAPHY

**Alexander Wood** was the Helen and Robert Appel Fellow in History and Technology at the New-York Historical Society in 2021–22, and he is currently working on a book about the building of New York City between the 1880s and the 1930s. He received his PhD from Columbia University and his BArch from the Cooper Union.



## ACKNOWLEDGMENTS

The author is grateful to *Buildings & Landscapes* editors Lydia Mattice Brandt and Michael J. Chiarappa for their helpful comments and suggestions.


## NOTES

1. In his classic study of the American building industry, Carl W. Condit argued that after the Civil War, "the craft technique of building was progressively transformed into a scientific technology." Carl W. Condit, *American Building* (Chicago: University of Chicago Press, 1968), 114. Following Condit, many scholars have examined the history of iron construction as part of the history of technology and engineering. See, for example, the important works by Thomas Leslie, Donald Friedman, and Sara E. Wermiel cited in the following.

2. Sven Beckert, *The Monied Metropolis: New York City and the Consolidation of the American Bourgeoisie, 1850–1896* (New York: Cambridge University Press, 2001), 51. For the early history of the New York iron industry, see Margot Gayle and Carol Gayle, *Cast-Iron Architecture in America: The Significance of James Bogardus* (New York: W.W. Norton, 1998); and Alfred D. Chandler Jr., "Anthracite Coal and the Beginnings of the Industrial Revolution in the United States," *Business History Review* 46 (Summer 1972): 141–81.

3. Richard B. Stott, *Workers in the Metropolis: Class, Ethnicity, and Youth in Antebellum New York* (New York: Cornell University Press, 1990), 42–48.

4. "The Cornell Iron Works," *New-York Tribune*, February 19, 1870, 11.

5. For short biographies of Bogardus, Badger, and Cornell, see Turpin C. Bannister, "Bogardus Revisited: Part I: The Iron Fronts," *Journal of the Society of Architectural Historians* 15 (December 1956): 12–22; "Daniel D. Badger," *The American Architect and Building News* 16 (November 29, 1884): 254; and "John B. Cornell," *The Architectural Record* 1 (October–December 1891): 244–45.

6. Peter Termin, "The Composition of Iron and Steel Products, 1869–1909," *Journal of Economic History* 23 (December 1963): 447–48; Margot Gayle, David W. Look, and John G. Waite, *Metals in America's Historic Buildings* (Washington, D.C.: U.S. Department of the Interior, 1992), 42–50.

7. William J. Fryer, "A Review of the Development of Structural Iron," in *A History of Real Estate, Building and Architecture in New York* (New York: Record and Guide, 1898), 455–83; Patricia Evelyn Malon, "The Growth of Manufacturing in Manhattan, 1860–1900" (PhD diss., Columbia University, 1981), 112–45; Sara E. Wermeil, "Introduction of the Rolled I-Beam in the U.S.A. in the 1850s, Revisited," in James W. P. Campbell et al., eds., *Iron, Steel and Buildings: The Proceedings of the Seventh Conference of the Construction History Society* (Construction History Society, 2020), 93–104.

8. Horace Greely, ed., *Art and Industry as Represented in the Exhibition at the Crystal Palace* (New York: Redfield, 1853), 16.

9. Louis de Coppet Berg, "Iron Construction in New York: Past and Future," *The Architectural Record* 1 (April–June 1892): 452.

10. "Early Iron Building Construction," *Engineering News* 1 (September 10, 1903): 214–15.

11. William H. Birkmire, *Architectural Iron and Steel and Its Application in the Construction of Buildings* (New York: John Wiley & Sons, 1891), 182.

12. "Tyranny and Oppression," *Sunday Dispatch*, March 16, 1851, 2.

13. "Meeting of Journeymen Housesmiths," *New York Herald*, March 13, 1850, 1; "Labor Movements," *New-York Daily Tribune*, April 11, 1850, 1; "Tyranny and Oppression," *Sunday Dispatch*, 2.

14. John R. Commons et al., *History of Labour in the United States*, vol. 1 (New York: MacMillan Company, 1926), 608–9; Sean Wilentz, *Chants Democratic: New York City & the Rise of the American Working Class, 1788–1850* (New York: Oxford University Press, 1986), 363–87; *History of Architecture and the Building Trades of Greater New York*, vol. 1 (New York: Union History Company, 1899), 140, 143.

15. Sarah Bradford Landau and Carl W. Condit, *Rise of the New York Skyscraper, 1865–1913* (New Haven, Conn.: Yale University Press, 1996), 62–107.

16. "Mr. Daniel D. Badger . . . ," *The American Architect and Building News* 26 (November 29, 1884): 254; Ada Louise Huxtable, "Progressive Architecture in America: Grand Central Depot, 1869–1871," *Progressive Architecture* 37 (October 1956): 125–28.

17. "The Western Union Fire," *Architecture and Building* 13 (July 26, 1890): 45; John L. Parish, "A Retrospect of Manhattan Real Estate," *Real Estate Record and Builder's Guide* 101 (March 13, 1918): 19; Landau and Condit, *Rise of the New York Skyscraper*, 80.

18. Landau and Condit, *Rise of the New York Skyscraper*, 67.

19. William J. Fryer, "A Review of the Development of Structural Iron," 455–83.

20. "The Cornell Iron Works," *New-York Tribune*, February 19, 1870, 11.

21. "The Workingmen," *New York Herald*, May 28, 1872, 5.

22. "The Cornell Iron Works," *New-York Tribune*, 11.

23. John R. McKivigan and Thomas J. Robertson, "The Irish American Worker in Transition, 1877–1914: New York City as a Test Case," in Ronald H. Bayor and Timothy Meagher, eds., *The New York Irish* (Baltimore: John Hopkins University Press, 1997), 301–3.

24. "House-Smiths' Association," *The Irish Republic*, May 11, 1867, 3.

25. "The Housesmiths' Consolidated Protective Union," *New-York Tribune*, August 4, 1868, 5; "The Housesmiths," *New York World*, September 4, 1868, 6; "Labor Movements," *New-York Tribune*, May 1, 1869, 5.

26. "Labor Movements," *The World* (New York), November 12, 1869, 8.

27. "Text of the New York Congress, National Labor Union, 1868," John R. Commons et al., eds., *A Documentary History of American Industrial Society*, vol. 9 (Cleveland: Arthur H. Clark Company, 1910), 195–227; David Montgomery, *Beyond Equality: Labor and the Radical Republicans* (New York: Alfred A. Knopf, Inc., 1967), 176–96.

28. "The Housesmiths," *The People* (New York), June 7, 1891, 1; "The House-Smiths to Strike on Monday," *The Sun* (New York), May 28, 1872, 2; "The Workingmen," *New York Herald*, May 28, 1872, 5; "The

Housesmiths," *New York Times,* May 28, 1872, 8; Iver Bernstein, *The New York City Draft Riots* (New York: Oxford University Press, 1990), 247.

29. "The Working-Men's Union," *The World* (New York), January 4, 1873, 8.

30. In the late 1870s, Cornell built eight stations for the New York Elevated Railroad Company, which owned and operated two of the city's four elevated lines. *Account Book on Cost Estimates for Elevated Railway Structures, 3rd and 9th Ave. Lines, 1878–1880,* New-York Historical Society; "The Effect of the Panic on the Iron Works," *Scientific American* 29 (November 8, 1873): 292.

31. "Early Skeleton Construction," *The Engineering Record* 40 (August 12, 1899): 238.

32. Minutes and reports to Subcommittee on Buildings, December 1881–March 1883, SN306, New York Produce Exchange Records, 1860–1955, MS449, New-York Historical Society.

33. "Letter from Building Committee to Mr. A. E. Orr," October 1, 1882, Minutes of the Building Committee, Vol. 3, SN273, New York Produce Exchange Records, 1860–1955, MS449, New-York Historical Society.

34. "The Cornell Iron Works," *Building* 10 (February 2, 1889): 1–2.

35. "The Housesmiths," *The People,* 1.

36. Bernard Weinstein, *The Jewish Unions in America,* trans. Maurice Wolfthal (Cambridge: Open Book Publishers, 2018), 305. For original reference, see Bernard Weinstein, *Di idishe yunyons in Amerika: bleter geschikhte un Erinnerungen* (New York: United Hebrew Trades, 1929), 542–43.

37. "The Housesmiths," *The People,* 1.

38. Richard J. Butler and Joseph Driscoll, *Dock Walloper: The Story of "Big Dick" Butler* (New York: Putnam's, 1933), 99–100.

39. Minutes and reports to Subcommittee on Buildings, November 13, 1882, SN306, New York Produce Exchange Records, 1860–1955, MS449, New-York Historical Society.

40. James Bogardus, *Cast-Iron Buildings: Their Construction and Advantages* (New York: J.W. Harrison, 1856), 6–7; Donald Friedman, *Historical Building Construction,* 2nd ed. (New York: W.W. Norton, 2010), 98–100; Thomas Leslie, "Built Like Bridges: Iron, Steel, and Rivets in the Nineteenth-Century Skyscraper," *Journal of the Society of Architectural Historians* 69 (June 2010): 234–61; David A. Simmons, "The Continuous Clatter: Practical Field Riveting," *Industrial Archeology* 23 (1997): 4–20.

41. "Structural Iron Workers," *Eleventh Special Report of the Commissioner of Labor: Regulation and Restriction of Output* (Washington, D.C.: Government Printing Office, 1904), 311.

42. J. B. Johnson et al., *The Theory and Practice of Modern Framed Structures* (New York: John Wiley & Sons, 1893), 501–7.

43. Landau and Condit, *Rise of the New York Skyscraper,* 116.

44. "High Unbraced Wrought-Iron Columns," *Engineering News* 25 (May 30, 1891): 514–15.

45. "Monster Girders," *New York Times,* May 17, 1889, 8.

46. "Housesmiths, New York," *Tenth Annual Report of the Board of Mediation and Arbitration of the State of New York* (New York: Wynkoop Hallenbeck Crawford, 1897), 49.

47. Luke Grant, *The National Erectors' Association and the International Association of Bridge and Structural Ironworkers, U.S. Commission on Industrial Relations* (Washington, D.C., 1915), 8.

48. Bernard Weinstein, *The Jewish Unions in America,* 305.

49. "Society of Architectural Iron Manufacturers," *Building Age* 4 (1882): 172.

50. *Eighth Annual Report of the Bureau of the Statistics of Labor for the State of New York, for the Year 1890,* vol. 1 (Albany: James B. Lyon, 1891), 146.

51. "Fighting the Non-Union Men," *New York Times,* August 25, 1883, 8.

52. "Leaving Work from Sympathy," *New-York Tribune,* May 3, 1890, 1.

53. State of New York, *Twelfth Annual Report of the Bureau of Statistics of Labor of the State of New York for the Year 1894* (New York: 1895), 484.

54. "Workmen Will Fight for the Eight-Hour Day," *New York Herald,* May 1, 1891, 3; "Labor's Great Battle with Capital Has Begun," *New York Herald,* May 2, 1891, 3; "Powderly Averted the Strike," *New York Herald,* May 5, 1890, 7.

55. "The Agony Is Over," *The People,* June 14, 1891, 1.

56. "The Agony Is Over," *The People,* 1.

57. "The Housesmiths: A Thirty Years' Struggle for Eight Hours," *The People,* June 7, 1891, 1.

58. "The Housesmiths: A Thirty Years' Struggle," *The People,* 1.

59. "After Eight Hours a Day," *St. Louis Dispatch,* March 24, 1895, 2.

60. "Big Strike in Prospects," *New York Times,* November 11, 1895, 1; "Housesmiths, New York," *Tenth Annual Report of the Board of Mediation and Arbitration,* 43–68.

61. Sidney Fine, *"Without Blare of Trumpets": Walter Drew, the National Erectors' Association, and the Open Shop Movement, 1903–1957* (Ann Arbor: University of Michigan Press, 1995), 12.

62. "The Housesmith," *American Manufacturer* 57 (December 20, 1895): 883.

63. William H. Birckmire, *Architectural Iron and Steel* (New York: J. Wiley & Sons, 1891); Joseph Kendall Freitag, *Architectural Engineering* (New York: J. Wiley & Sons, 1895).

64. Landau and Condit, *Rise of the New York Skyscraper,* 182.

65. Sidney Fine, *"Without Blare of Trumpets,"* 47.

JAMES I. KELLEHER

# *Object Lesson:* The Half House Made Whole

## *Evidence from Southeastern Massachusetts*

ABSTRACT

End-chimney houses were a common form in early New England. This article examines the ways in which these houses were used, based on physical and documentary evidence from southeastern Massachusetts and adjacent regions. Especially in their double-pile variety, these houses accommodated several different types of interior organization, each suggesting a different relation of the occupants to early modern conceptions of space, privacy, and refinement. Work functions such as cooking could be placed "forward" in the house, continuing an essentially medieval conception of the hall as a multipurpose space, or could be removed to the rear of houses. Private spaces such as bedrooms or parlors were often situated beyond or above this hall. Occasionally, concepts of material refinement and privacy were spatially linked, but often they were split, with expensive showpieces like beds appearing in halls, with less refined but more private spaces beyond. The architecture determined the ways in which these houses were used only to a limited extent; the flexibility of the house form was likely a factor in its continuing popularity into the eighteenth century.

Both the tourist and the scholar of New England architecture will likely imagine the center-chimney hall-and-parlor house as the region's archetypal early form, and not without reason: the majority of extant houses built in Massachusetts prior to around 1730 follow this pattern. Yet the past few decades of scholarship on early colonial New England's architecture have justly asserted that these large houses—the result of survivorship bias—are not representative of early housing stock more broadly.[1] Many of those large houses started life as what are sometimes called "half houses"—end-chimney houses that, as the name suggests, are about half the size of the central-chimney double-pile houses into which they were often enlarged. But many of these half houses were never expanded. As Thomas Hubka notes, they were probably never thought of as "half" of anything.[2] This essay takes a deeper look into the end-chimney, double-pile house: the ways it was used, the ways it was adapted, and what it might tell us about how early colonists organized the spaces in which they lived. These buildings were larger than the single-cell houses occupied by many colonists, but distinct from central-chimney hall-and-parlor houses. Structural and documentary analysis reveals the innate flexibility of these buildings, which could be made suitable to multiple approaches to household organization, perhaps deriving from various British regional attitudes. This flexibility helps account for the early appearance, persistence, and variety of this form throughout the region.

This essay evolved from documentary and field research in southeastern Massachusetts, in which the end-chimney, double-pile house seems to have been especially popular into the eighteenth century. Four houses, three of which are extant and one of which is known through archaeological and documentary sources, form the core of the investigation. The earliest of these is John Howland's mid-seventeenth-century house, known only through archaeological and documentary sources, that illustrates a particular approach to interior space that remained popular, if not dominant, in southeastern New England for several decades. John Churchill's 1661 house illustrates a related trend in interior organization, while the Hoxie and Church houses, each dating to the first quarter of the eighteenth century or earlier, illustrate an alternate pattern of use within end-chimney houses. Related houses throughout southeastern New England, as well as probate inventories and other documents, help clarify the way in which these houses, and those like them, were used. This research expands on the work of numerous scholars, particularly Robert Blair St. George, Abbott Lowell Cummings, Richard Candee, Dell Upton, and Myron Stachiw.

The earliest house informing this investigation was occupied by John Howland, who came to Plymouth on the Mayflower as a servant to John Carver and his family (Figures 1 and 2).[3] In 1638, he purchased from John Jenney a tract of land on Rocky Nook, a peninsula to the north of Plymouth, where he built his house and lived with his wife, Elizabeth, and their children. This homesite, now in modern-day Kingston, Massachusetts, was excavated in the 1930s by the architect, restorer, and amateur archaeologist duo of Sydney and Charles Strickland (the latter of whom would go on to design the first houses for what is now the Plimoth Patuxet Museums).[4] The house foundations they uncovered have been re-excavated and confirmed by more recent archaeological excavations, and suggest a structure roughly 17 feet deep and 34 feet wide, excluding a projecting stone chimney and hearth on the western side, with a lean-to addition to the north (the lean-to has been omitted in the drawing).[5] The house likely had a direct entry into a heated hall, as suggested by a stone doorstep. Archaeological data provides no evidence of how many stories the house stood, nor of the interior layout aside from the hearth, but Howland's probate inventory suggests the arrangement.

The probate divides the house into a "fire

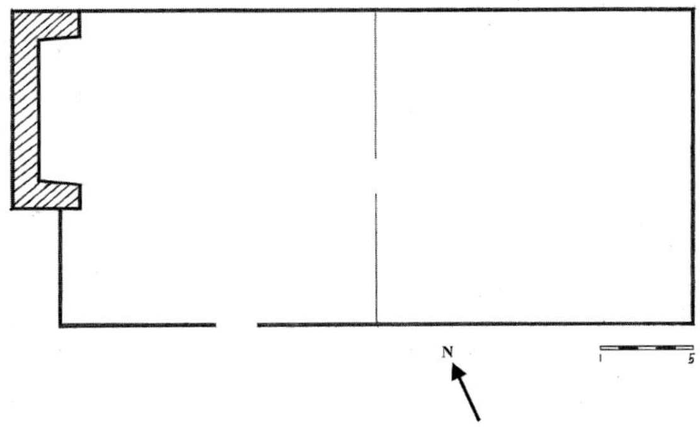


Figure 1. Conjectural plan of the John Howland house, mid-seventeenth century. Drawing by James I. Kelleher, based on archaeological work by Craig Chartier.

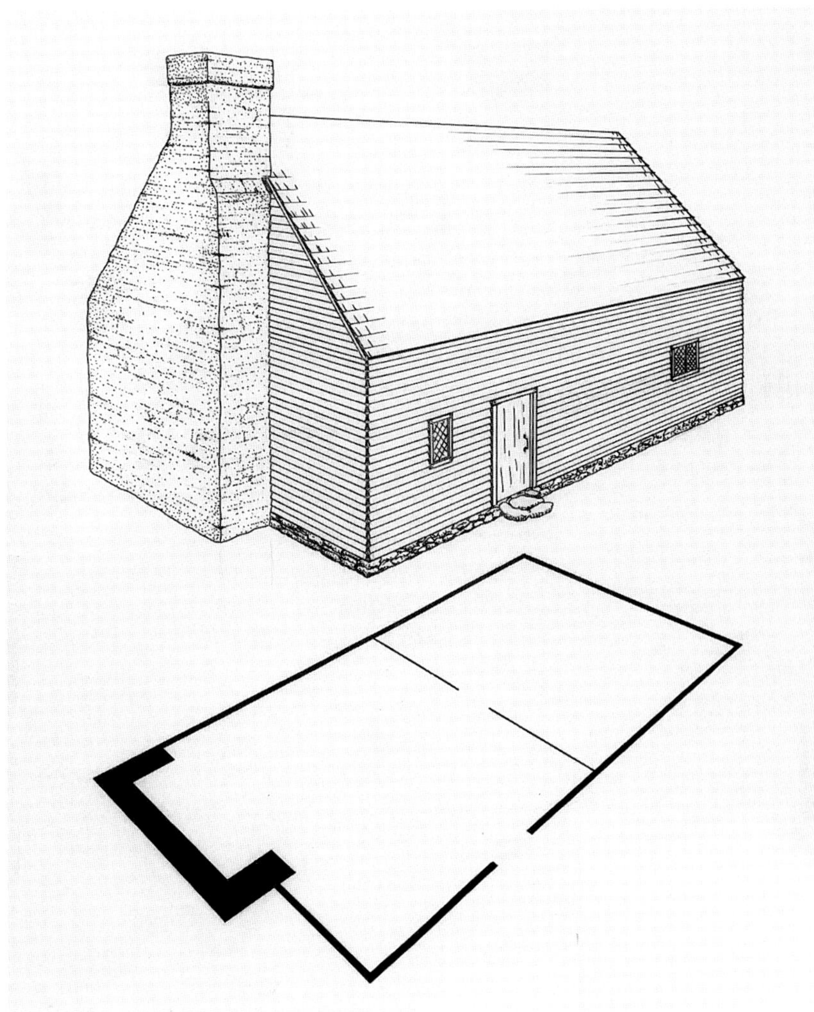

Figure 2. Conjectural reconstruction of John Howland house. Drawing by James I. Kelleher.

room" and an "inward room," functionally corresponding to a hall and parlor.[6] The arrangement differs, however, from a center-chimney house in that it is sequentially arranged—to arrive at the parlor, or inward room, a visitor must pass through the fire room, or hall. The fire room, into which the occupant or guest first entered, contained various tools, including a hatchel or comb for breaking coarse flax into the rudiments of linen, along with axes and adzes for cutting and hewing timber. Also included in this room was Howland's library of several books, with certain religious works explicitly mentioned—tools used for spiritual and mental refinement.

If the fire room contained tools used for refining natural resources (known as "improving" them) and cultivating crops, the inward room displayed the products of such effort.[7] Of the wealth stored within the house, more than half of it (over fifty out of more than eighty-nine pounds totaled in the inventory) was found in the inner room. Containing four chests and a cupboard, the room also housed Howland's collection of fine textiles. A visitor might see the room's wool bed (after passing the herd of sheep at pasture), linen tablecloths (after observing the hatchel in the kitchen), and a framed chair (after the axes and saws). Textiles, furniture, a good bed, and "reddy money"—the earthly fruits of labor and providence—were all seemingly crowded in the terminal room as occupants progressed through the land and house.[8] The room was refined both in the colloquial sense (well-appointed) and in a literal one: products therein had been worked, woven, carved, or otherwise processed into objects of use and ornament, and were not objects or tools in need of further processing.

Howland's house was therefore organized along an axis. At one end of this axis was a secluded space to which occupants could withdraw and sit among their refined material wealth. At the other was the fire room, both spatially and materially closer to the outside world of agriculture and its incomplete processes of cultivation and processing. The area above the first-floor rooms, referred to in the inventory as the chamber, was a less prominent multifunctional space accessed through a stair or ladder in an unknown location. Here too was material wealth, but of a more unprocessed kind. This was mostly a space for natural materials that had been harvested but not transformed into their final state (prepared food, fabric, etc.)—a storeroom for harvested goods and provisions such as meat, tallow and candles, and grains. However, the chamber also contained the second- and third-best beds. Possibly serving as a space for children or overnight guests, in general it seems separate from the house's principal sequence of rooms, in which a more private and refined space was situated beyond a less formal and more public room.

John Howland's floor plan probably did not stand alone among those employed by his neighbors. Several room-by-room probate inventories that date from the first third of the eighteenth century and earlier for the Plymouth Colony, and later, Plymouth County, as well as adjacent areas, mention houses with an inner room, an outer room, and a chamber (or linguistic variants of the same).[9] In most of these cases, documented material furnishings more or less correspond to those of a hall and parlor—a greater concentration of material wealth is found in the inner room than the outward room. While this end-chimney, hall-and-parlor orientation is not well represented in New England among surviving early houses, documented examples occurred from Plymouth to Piscataqua in the current Portsmouth, N.H., area.[10] The thermal concerns of an unheated parlor space far from the chimney may ultimately have hastened the form's gradual decline and disappearance from the material record. The closest surviving examples are likely the stone-ender houses of Rhode Island, some of which (particularly the Clemence-Irons house) probably bear a marked resemblance to Howland's house.

These houses exhibit what Robert Blair St. George has characterized as a "long-and-low" plan, possibly derived from Britain's highland regions and their dependence on pasturage.[11] These houses included a direct entry to a multifunctional work and gathering space centered around a hearth, with private spaces oriented beyond (if any existed), typically under a long, low roof. This contrasts with the central-chimney, lobby-entry floor plan, in which a hall/kitchen and a parlor were opposed on either side of a chimney. If this central-chimney plan was expanded backward with the additions of lean-tos or full rear cells, kitchen functions were typically pushed into these rear spaces. This latter organization, much more familiar in New England today, may have descended from Britain's mixed-agriculture lowlands such as East Anglia. Regardless of their origins, these two approaches to household organization are experientially distinct from each other. The circulation pattern of Howland's house and those like it is linear: inner spaces must be accessed through outward rooms. The central-chimney, lobby-entry plan, meanwhile, compelled occupants or guests to choose between entering the hall or parlor, a choice undoubtedly influenced by status and social convention.

The prevalence of the long-and-low house *form* in the seventeenth and early eighteenth centuries is difficult to determine. But the circulation pattern enabled by that form—that of public and private space arranged in a sequence or progression—may have persisted in other types of houses. Richard Candee has interpreted the several houses with "inner rooms" mentioned in probates as end-chimney houses with a lean-to, with a space in this lean-to serving as the inner room.[12] Candee was prudent not to ignore the linguistic connotations of "inner" or "inward," which does not imply a room opposite a hall in a center-chimney dwelling (as some have supposed), but rather a space entered after passing through some variety of antechamber.

John Churchill's 1661 house offers tantalizing material clues to this interpretation (Figures 3 and 4). Churchill (or Churchell, Churchwell) arrived in Plymouth from England sometime before his marriage to Hannah Pontus in 1643. In 1647, he bought a house and farm from Richard Higgens.[13] Higgens had already developed the land, which at the time of its sale featured a house, a garden, an orchard of more than thirty trees, and an indeterminate number of outbuildings. John and his family likely lived in this house until 1661, when he decided to build a new house. While Churchill's house was presumably an improvement over the previous structure on the site (which existed alongside the extant house for

Figure 3. Churchill house, 1661, with later modifications. Photograph by James I. Kelleher.

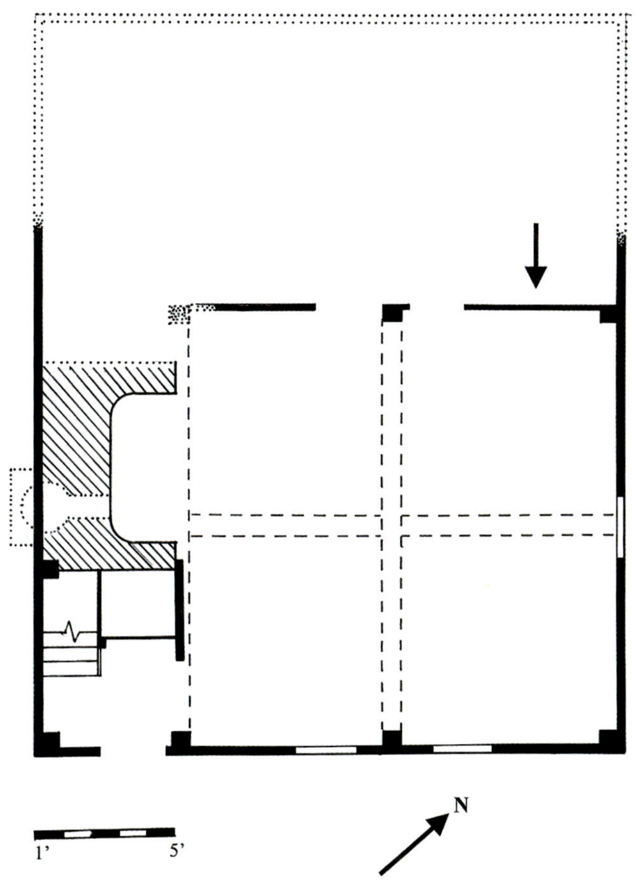


Figure 4. Conjectural, simplified original plan of the Churchill house, 1661. Arrow indicates location of crease-molded boards. Drawing by James I. Kelleher, based on fieldwork conducted by the author with the University of Delaware Center for Historic Architecture and Design.

an unknown number of years), the older house also had at least two ground-floor rooms, perhaps similar in plan to Howland's house. When John Churchill purchased Higgens's property, the latter party reserved the right "that it shall be lawful for the said Richard Higgens to take away the boards that line an inward room."[14] These were probably crease-molded boards similar to those seen in the Churchill house, and strongly suggest the partitioning of a more ornate interior space within Higgens's home.

As first built, the Churchill house was a story-and-a-half high, with an integral lean-to in the rear, evidenced by remaining original rear rafters in the roof framing (Figures 5 and 6). As a two-room-deep end-chimney house, it is the earliest local example of a type discussed through the remainder of this essay, a form that appears to have been popular in southeastern Massachusetts well into the eighteenth century.[15] The lean-to itself was probably divided into two rooms, accessed through the two doorways on each side of the hall's rear medial post. Interestingly, crease-molded paneling on the southeastern wall of the lean-to suggests that this space displayed a higher level of finish than the plastered hall in the front of the house, commensurate with our understanding of an "inner room" like that of Richard Higgens (Figures 7 and 8). It seems likely that the hall was undivided, while the lean-to was divided into perhaps a general storage space to the west and a smaller but more formal inner room to the east, lined, at least on one wall, with crease-molded boards.[16] The lean-to may or may not have been heated by a small fireplace when the house was built, but likely had one by 1767 at the latest, when the house was partitioned into two properties along the wall separating the lean-to from the hall.[17]

Explicit refinements were also made to the space above the Churchill house's principal room. Despite only boasting a second half-story in the front, the house included a cross gable that presumably allowed for one or more windows.[18] This inclusion potentially turned a modest garret space into a wholly functional second level, albeit one with marginally less headroom than a full story.[19] Likewise, a chamfered summer beam with simple but finely wrought stops supports the ceiling above, suggesting a level of finish comparable to the downstairs hall. Additionally, original floorboards in the attic story are beaded

Figure 5. Conjectural reconstruction of the Churchill house, 1661. Drawing by James I. Kelleher.

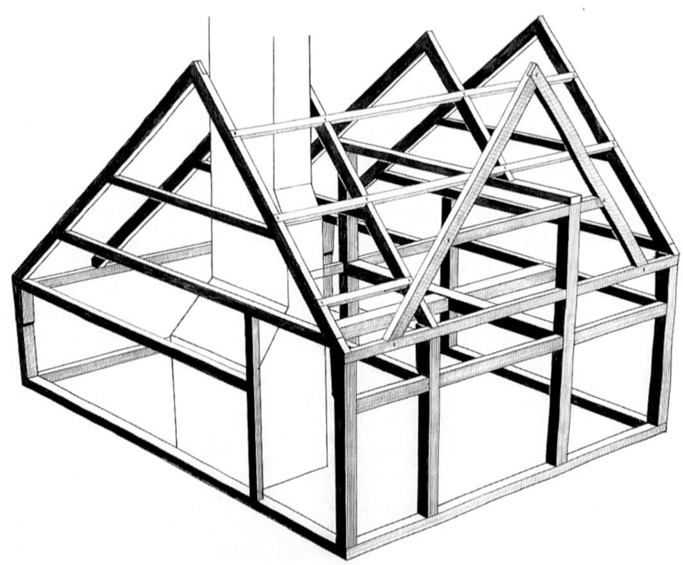

Figure 6. Conjectural frame of the Churchill house, 1661. Drawing by James I. Kelleher.

Figure 7. Crease-molded boards in the Churchill house. Photograph by James I. Kelleher.

at the edges, an unnecessary but decorative modification. House occupants, then, had the option to retreat from the main workspace, or semipublic room, both within the building's horizontal and vertical parameters, without being sequestered in an unfinished attic or strictly utilitarian lean-to.

Divisions of space were, of course, particularly consequential to the visitor's experience. An early court document relating specifically to the Churchill house (then in the possession of John's son, Joseph) helps illuminate the ways in which the space guided the behaviors of its occupants. Ephraim Tinkham of Plymouth understood a certain level of privacy when he came to the house on August 8, 1671, expecting to find Thomas Dotey (perhaps a mutual neighbor) to discuss some business. Per the Plymouth court:

> The said Sarjeant Tinkham, having occasion to speak with the said Thomas Dotey, went to the house of Joseph Churchill, expecting to meet with him there, and coming to the house, knocked att

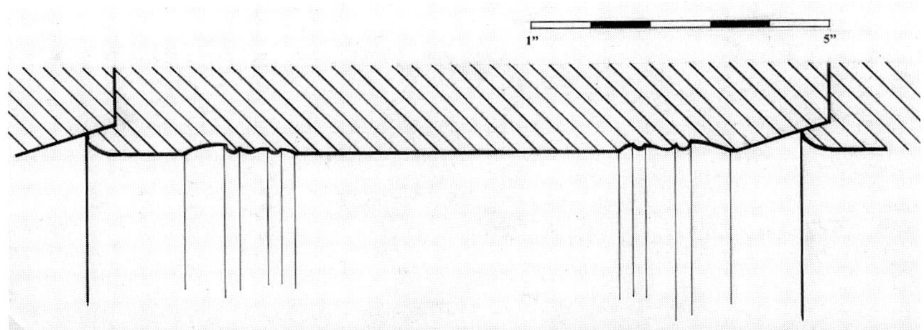


Figure 8. Crease-molding in lobby and lean-to of the Churchill house. This profile was taken from boards in the lobby; those in the rear are comparable in profile but are spaced more widely on wider boards. Drawing by James I. Kelleher.

> the dore; but noe body answared, and soe hee went in and stayed a while in the outward roome; and by some noise that he heard in the house, conceived that there was somebody within, although they answared not; but att length Mary Churchill [sister to Joseph Churchill] came forth.[20]

Mary, as she would confess to the court, was vigorously pursuing a developing romance with Thomas Dotey at the time of Tinkham's visit.[21] Knocking at the door, Tinkham received no answer, and freely entered into the "outward room" where he waited some minutes until Mary surfaced from her tryst.[22] We are left to wonder at the relative soundproof qualities of thin board and plaster partitions. Regardless, homeowner Joseph Churchill does not appear in the scene.

Tinkham's willingness to walk into Joseph Churchill's house looking for a third party, but not to move beyond an outward room, lends some color to the way in which visitors and residents alike understood these spaces. The outward room was a familiar space—a guest, at least a friend, obviously felt comfortable simply walking in. St. George has argued that it is this sort of interaction that more open, highland-derived houses facilitate, in which people "entered and left the houses of neighbors with little or no drama."[23] Probably because of this, Mary and Thomas stole away to an inward room (perhaps the molded-board-lined room in the lean-to) to canoodle. Here we can clearly see a motivation for lean-to (or any "inward" partitioned) spaces: a division of the home along a public-private axis. Undoubtedly, this motivation was especially pointed for occupants of smaller homes such as the Churchill house, where opportunities for private retreat were limited. The rear east room of the Churchill house was both comparatively private and refined, as attested by its position in the house plan (on an opposite corner from the entrance) and its surviving finish. Its specific function, however, is less clear. It may have served as a parlor, or as a private bedroom, or some ad-hoc combination of both as social desires dictated. If Churchill did in fact create a private, more elaborate space in the rear of his house, he would not have been the only person in early southern New England to do so. Henry Brown of Providence kept his best bed in the "leanto bed room" in 1702; as late as 1730 Samuel Barstow of Hanover, Massachusetts, similarly kept his "best bed in the leanto."[24]

Outwardly, the Churchill and Howland houses probably had little in common. But in each case, there was an arrangement of rooms along an axis stretching from the outside inward, with increasing levels of privacy. The line from public to private, and informal to formal, was sequential in nature. Both houses contained "inward" spaces only accessible after first passing through multipurpose workspaces (the hall of the Churchill house and the fire room at Howland's were both working kitchens as well as likely gathering spaces).[25] In Howland's house, this privacy was accompanied by elevated material refinement, and the surviving finish in the Churchill house suggests this may have been the case there as well. If probate room terms are consistent, these inner room/outer room arrangements were not uncommon into the early decades of the eighteenth century. Certainly, they gained purchase in neighboring Rhode Island, where houses such as the Clemence-Irons house, the Valentine Whitman house, and other stone-enders followed the same basic pattern as that of the Howland house in single- and double-pile variants.

Figure 9. Goodspeed house, Marstons Mills, Massachusetts, ca. 1700–30. Photograph by James I. Kelleher.

It is perhaps impossible to answer how many probate inventories reflected an outer room/inner room configuration such as that at Howland's house, or how many refer to those like Churchill's with a lean-to or rear room. Certainly, inventory takers occasionally used the word "lean-to" or its variants, but it is unclear if there were specific contexts in which one term and not the other (inner room) would be used. The early eighteenth-century Goodspeed house, in Marstons Mills on Cape Cod, demonstrates a possible source of linguistic ambiguity: the rear cell could structurally be termed an integral lean-to but could just as easily be called a back or inner room (Figure 9). From the inside of the house, there is no telltale element (a lower ceiling, for example) that would distinguish it as a "lean-to," with its connotations of being an appendage or subsidiary space.[26]

Despite their formal differences, the Churchill and Howland houses include "better" spaces that are basically additive in nature. These rooms, marked by certain refinements (the rear paneled room and the lit upper half-story on the Churchill house, the inward room on the Howland house), are appended to one side of (or above) a single, larger, multipurpose "hall" or "great room"—they are situated at the terminus of an architectural progression.

At the same time, end-chimney double-pile houses could accommodate a wholly different approach to interior organization. Rather than adding a private and more formal space onto or beyond a multipurpose room, builders also removed informal, unrefined, or messy practices from this room and pushed them into separate spaces farther from a house's entrance. In larger center-chimney houses, cooking functions were gradually being removed to the rear pile of the house by the latter half of the seventeenth century, as Cummings has discussed in depth.[27] The relegation of the kitchen to the rear of the house with the appearance of a third hearth has been regarded as emblematic of the same separation of work and leisure spaces that first resulted in the hall-and-parlor form.[28] The same impulse, adapted to the end-chimney two-room-deep form, may be found in southeastern Massachusetts and adjacent regions.

The removal of kitchen functions to a house's rear naturally required a rear hearth. In center-chimney houses, this rear hearth was usually part of the same chimney mass as the hall and parlor chimneys. Including a rear hearth was more of a technical challenge in the case of an end-chimney house, however, as the narrow chimney bay left little room for an additional fireplace. If end-chimney houses were enlarged into center-chimney houses, the width of the chimney bay was often enlarged partly for this reason.[29] Nevertheless, in southeastern Massachusetts and adjacent areas, builders found ways to incorporate rear hearths into end-chimney houses, accommodating an impulse to remove workspaces to the rear of the house while maintaining the end-chimney house form.

During the fieldwork that forms the basis of this essay, the author encountered a little-discussed subtype of end-chimney houses. This subtype has two hearths on the ground floor and, in the case of two-story houses, one on the second floor. Kitchen functions are apparently (though not universally) removed to the rear cell of the house, and the additional hearth is accommodated by a projection or jog against the chimney wall. These projections, on houses of varying sizes and forms, are often called Beverly jogs (Figure 10). In Sandwich, Massachusetts, the Hoxie house, while heavily restored in the mid-twentieth century, is relatively intact and a good example of this house type.

Unlike other houses in this study, the specific build date and occupants of this house are unknown, at least partially due to Barnstable County's incomplete records. Local tradition holds that it was built for one of the area's earliest ministers, John Smith, but this has yet to be verified. Finished, chamfered framing members with well-carved stops (especially the ceiling beams of the second story) suggest a first-period build date, likely in or before the first quarter of the eighteenth century.

Figure 10. Hoxie house, Sandwich, Massachusetts, 1680–1720, restored late 1950s. Leftmost extension is twentieth century. Photograph by James I. Kelleher.

The Hoxie house's rear hearth, projecting out the western side of the building under a pitched roof jog, is an oddity (Figure 11). Nevertheless, structural evidence suggests that this projection is original to the house's initial building. The rear plate of the lean-to is continuous from the northeast corner of the main block to the northwest corner of the projection. Additionally, if the house was initially built without the projection, there would by necessity be a corner post at the rear of the house, in line with the southwest corner post flanking the entrance. This is not the case, nor is there evidence to suggest that there ever was a post in that location.

George H. Sherwood, the Boston architect tasked with restoring the Hoxie house in the late 1950s, did not initially intend to reconstruct a rear hearth, as indicated in original plans for the house's restoration.[30] While working on the floor of the jog, Sherwood (or one of his contractors) found the footings for a hearth, and revised the plans accordingly. Unfortunately, neither photographs of this evidence nor the revised renovation floor plans could be found in the Sandwich town archives, and the author has not yet been

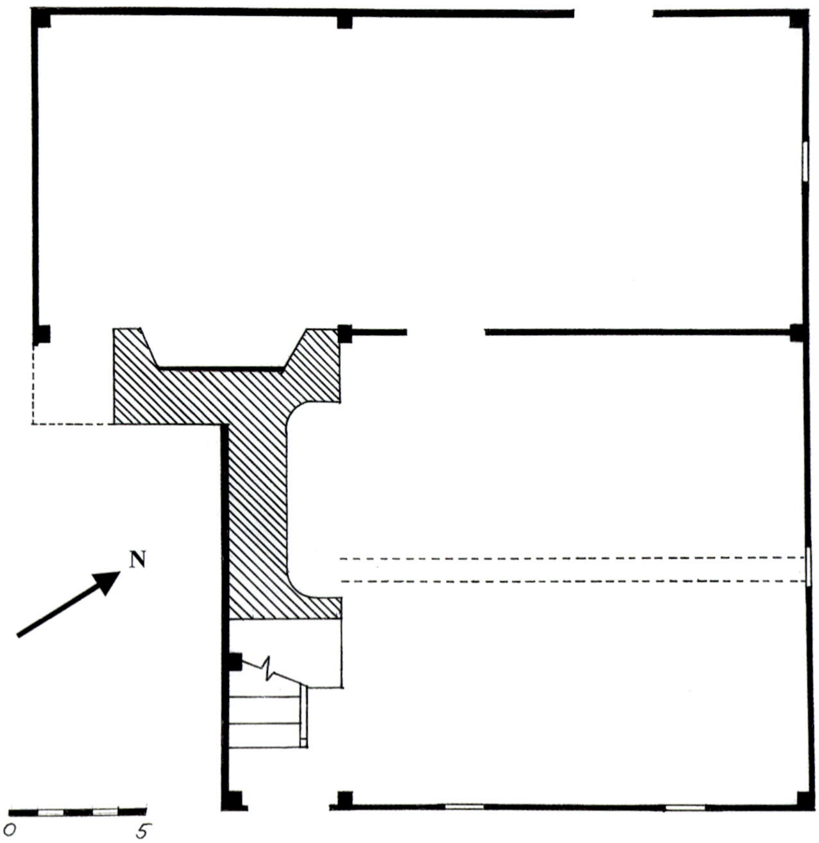


Figure 11. Simplified floor plan, Hoxie house. Drawing by James I. Kelleher.

Figure 12. Wall plate spanning chimney bay, Hoxie house. Photograph by James I. Kelleher.

permitted to pull up the flooring and check for the original chimney footings. Extant framing, however, suggests that the housewright built with a rear hearth in mind and designed the house frame accordingly.

In a typical end-chimney house, there are eight or more posts: three in the front wall, three in the wall separating the front room from the lean-to, and two in the rear wall at the corners, with possibly a third between. In the Hoxie house, the outer post in line with the corner post of the central room is missing. Instead, the second-story wall plate (supporting the garret floor) cantilevers out over the chimney bay, supporting the second-story western girt and supported by an up brace (Figures 12 and 13). This unusual framing was utilized to accommodate this hearth and chimney, suggesting that it was part of the house's first iteration even as the framing scheme was devised on the ground. Without the supposed chimney footings found by Sherwood, the framing alone would not be evidence enough for speculation about a third hearth in the Hoxie house, but together they form a compelling case.

It was only through acquaintance with the Hoxie house that the author was able to recognize the same structural scheme in a house on Plymouth's Summer Street, built in 1708 for Charles Church (Figure 14).[31] In this case, the hearth jog was eliminated when the adjoining house to the west was constructed, but framing evidence remains. The identification of an additional house with the same basic pattern suggests that the Hoxie house was more than an anomaly.

Charles Church likely moved to Plymouth, assumed control of the gristmill, and built his house after the settlement of his father's estate. Within three years, he constructed a barn on land formerly belonging to Nathaniel Jackson, a lot north of his house that he purchased in 1711.[32] In 1717, he bought out his mother's share of the mill, providing him with two-thirds ownership. By 1718, he had sold his shares in the mill, as well as his house and the barn and lands north of Summer Street.[33] It was probably around this time that he and his wife Mary moved to Freetown, Rhode Island, where Charles would drown nine years later at the age of forty-two.[34] At the time he sold them, Charles's land and mill shares were worth 160 pounds, indicating a level of prosperity commensurate with the size of his house, which, in its original form, was the largest of the four discussed in this article.

The Church house's plan probably mirrored that of the Hoxie house. Physical evidence suggests that the cantilevered second-floor wall plate and the absent post found in the Hoxie house were also employed at the Church house. Though a subsequent owner cut through the cantilevered plate to insert an attic stair, the spot where the plate projected into the plank siding is still visible. There is a robbed mortise for an up brace supporting the plate in the expected position on the south corner post of the main room.

The wall planking itself is cut at an angle roughly mirroring the rear roof pitch, declining toward the front of the house, in the position where a jog such as that at the Hoxie house would join the house. And in the western end of what would be the lean-to garret, where this theoretical projection seems to be occurring, short remnants of roof purlins extend beyond the westernmost rear rafter of the house. Nor are there any exterior planks in this space; it looks as if this small garret extended to the west and was cut short only by the construction of the adjoining house in the mid-eighteenth century. While the position of the rear posts in the lean-to cannot yet be determined, their positioning might offer further evidence for the existence of this jog. However, the evidence is convincing that the construction of the Church house approximately mirrors the Hoxie house in plan.

Unfortunately, there are no probate inventories associated with the Church house in its earliest configuration. The original use and furnishings of the house remain a mystery for now. Later in the eighteenth century, the chimney was vacated from the chimney bay and moved slightly north of the lean-to, reconfiguring the house into a hall-and-parlor plan turned sideways (with the best room remaining the best room, and the lean-to possibly turned into a hall/kitchen). The entrance at this point may have been moved to the east end of the house, but here the trail of modifications becomes hard to follow and is highly conjectural.

While the Hoxie and Church houses most likely shared a plan, they were constructed in markedly different ways. Their comparison suggests completely different craft traditions both responding to a particular impulse, namely, a desire to include a hearth in the rear of an end-chimney house. The builders of the Hoxie house framed its roof in an unusual way (see Figure 13). In New England, the traditional way to frame a ceiling is with a heavy summer beam that supports floor joists, as is seen in nearly all other houses discussed in this study. The Hoxie house's carpenters, it seems, could not effectively work out how to combine a summer beam/joist system with the necessary support that the lengthy lean-to rafters required. Instead, the house's builders dispensed with the summer beam and joists entirely, replacing them with five beams running from the front to the back of the house. These beams rest on the rear plate of the upper room and extend beyond, where two of them, along with the chimney and wall girts, are tenoned into rafters.

The Hoxie house's carpenters may have experimented with their framing, but they did not sacrifice the finish that their client presumably expected. These beams are planed and chamfered,

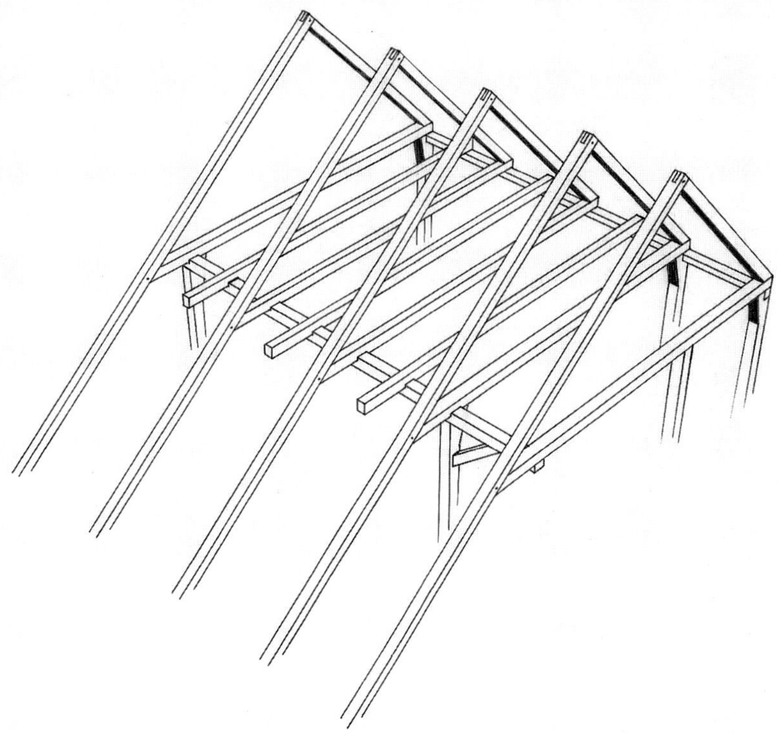

Figure 13. Hoxie house roof framing. Drawing by James I. Kelleher.

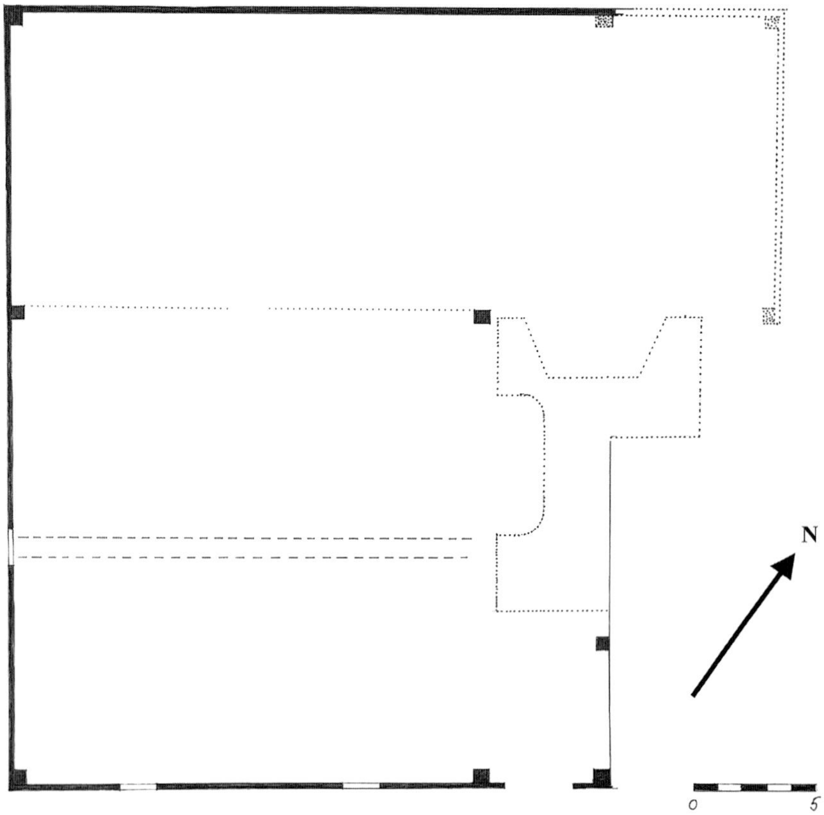


Figure 14. Conjectural, simplified floor plan of Church house. Drawing by James I. Kelleher.

with chiseled decorative stops more finely wrought than those on many early houses. The result is a ceiling and roof framing that, to the author's knowledge, is a unique survival in New England, which also lends a decorative flair to the chamber that is absent in the hall below.

The carpenter of the Church house was less radical (Figure 15). He retained the summer beam, and simply extended the joists beyond the rear plate. Two of these joists were tenoned into the middle two rear rafters. In a sense, the carpenter was conservative, employing tusk tenons that are generally assumed to be a seventeenth-century joinery technique, at least in this context.[35] But there was a technical rationale for this measure: under the pressure of the rafter, the summer beam end of the joist would be inclined to flip up, were it not securely tusk tenoned into the summer beam. There is a visible robbed mortise where one of the joists, now cut back, tenoned into the rafter, which was cut through in a later modification.

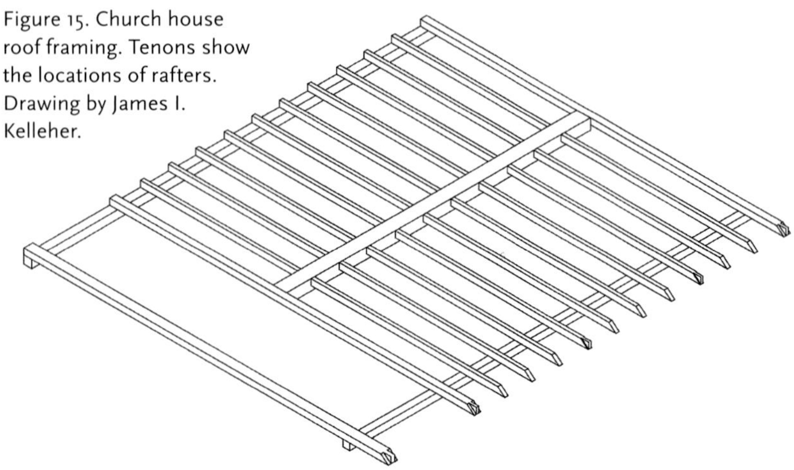

Figure 15. Church house roof framing. Tenons show the locations of rafters. Drawing by James I. Kelleher.

Documentary sources suggest there were earlier examples of arrangements like those in the Hoxie and Church houses. The 1675 inventory of Captain Nathaniel Thomas of Marshfield includes, on the ground floor, an inner room, outer room, "little room," and "outer room chimney lean-to."[36] This inventory might describe a four-room end-chimney plan. From the documentary record alone, it is impossible to say whether or not the Thomas's house had a projecting jog. Regardless, the "outer room chimney lean-to" included andirons, trammels, brass and iron pots and kettles—in short, all the makings of a rear kitchen, in what was likely an end-chimney house.

The same arrangement as the Hoxie and Church houses can be found in smaller houses as well, including two single-story examples in Plymouth and Wellfleet respectively. The small, gambrel roofed three-quarter Cape Cod style house at 119 Sandwich Street (Figure 16, now the Harlow House museum), has traditionally been ascribed to Sergeant William Harlow, who supposedly built it with timber recycled from the first fort on Plymouth's Burial Hill (constructed in 1621–22). Dendrochronological research suggests the timbers were instead felled in 1707–8.[37] In February 1709, Plymouth township granted John Harlow "Eighty foot of land square" at the southeast end of his father Samuel's lot, on the condition that he erect a house thereon within two years.[38] It seems likely that this is the house that remains today. Like his father, John Harlow was a cooper, and like most tradespeople in early Plymouth he probably farmed as well.[39] Harlow

Figure 16. Harlow house, Plymouth, Massachusetts, 1707–8. Photograph by J. Ritchie Garrison.

Figure 17. Rowell house, Wellfleet, Massachusetts, ca. 1720–40. Photograph by James I. Kelleher.

and his family would live in this house until they sold it to Robert Hosea in 1765.[40]

As built, this house was three bays wide with a jog accommodating a rear hearth. Today this projection is obscured by the subsequent addition of a full fourth bay.[41] While the present hearths were reconstructed by architect Joseph Everett Chandler in the 1920s, he claimed to have rebuilt them on original footings.[42] Like the Hoxie and Church houses, the lack of a post in the location of the rear hearth suggests the hearth's existence at the time of construction.

The expansion of the lean-to (or rear cell) beyond one side of the house occurred as late as the second quarter of the eighteenth century, as can still be seen in Wellfleet's Rowell house (Figure 17). This house probably looks similar to John Harlow's as it was first built. Until recently, a set kettle (a fixed kettle over a small hearth for cooking or perhaps laundry) existed alongside this house's rear hearth, probably identifying the space as a kitchen. Close examination of what Ernest Allan Connally called "house-and-a-half"-plan Cape Cod houses may reveal evidence of yet further examples, later expanded in the same vein as the Harlow house.[43]

This subtype may also be found farther afield in Rhode Island and Connecticut. In the early twentieth century, J. Frederick Kelly photographed and documented a house in North Guilford, Connecticut, similar in form to the Hoxie house, with an intact rear fireplace and oven housed in a jog (Figure 18).[44] This house, unfortunately demolished in 1921, is nearly the same in plan and construction as the Hoxie house, including the unusual roof framing discussed above. The primary difference is that the projection on the Norton house is capped with a hip roof, doubtless more complicated than the Hoxie house projection's pitched roof, and perhaps a later modification. Subsequent research has dated the Norton house to later in the eighteenth century, suggesting that this structural solution, while probably never common, at least had some longevity.[45] Likewise, the George Douglas house of North Kingstown, Rhode Island, dated to 1738, follows the same basic jogged plan, with an unusual protruding bake oven off the rear hearth specifying the back space as a kitchen.[46]

The original finishes of the front rooms of these various jogged houses differ. That of the Hoxie house appears to have been simply plastered, while the front room of the Church house has been significantly modified, obscuring any original treatments. The front room of the Rowell house has simple wainscoting and a paneled fireplace wall but is otherwise plastered. Regardless, the absence of work functions facilitated by the appearance of a rear hearth and kitchen constitutes its own sort of ornament. For example, given this arrangement at the Rowell house, the head of household or their guest need not be

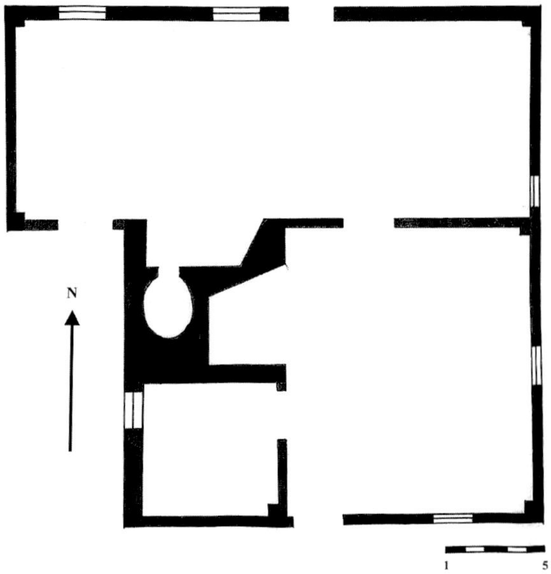


Figure 18. Simplified plan, Norton house, Guilford, Connecticut, mid-eighteenth century. Drawing by James I. Kelleher after J. Frederick Kelly.

confronted with a boiling vat of laundry in their front room, this being removed to the rear set kettle. Likewise, the messes of food preparation could be kept, relatively speaking, out of sight.[47]

There are undoubtedly more examples of this house type in various states of modification to be found throughout New England. And although the jogged plan represented by the Hoxie, Church, Rowell, and Douglas houses may be relatively rare, the same concept with a refined execution can be found in numerous "three-quarter" (or "house-and-a-half") cape houses of southeastern New England, wherein a roughly square plan contained a rear heated space/kitchen, and the front pile was divided into a hall and a small, often unheated, corner space.[48] Indeed, the Harlow house itself was converted to this arrangement (in which it remains) sometime after it was built. This execution of the concept was probably simpler for carpenters, obviating the need to construct two contiguous roofs of different sizes.

Even in those cases where the lean-to or rear cell had a hearth, the rear space's specific function is not always clear; one nineteenth-century writer notes of these houses that "the rear of the lower floor contained a small room at the northwest corner having a small fireplace, and was sometimes called the kitchen, but rarely occupied for that purpose."[49] In the Judge Freeman house of Wellfleet (ca. 1720–40), a later example of a jogged end-chimney house with two ground-floor hearths, kitchen utensils are listed in the great front room in 1764, rather than the rear heated space.[50] The long-standing identification of the hall as both kitchen and gathering space, with the parlor as a more private retreat, probably influenced the way these houses were used.

The purpose of discussing this subtype is not simply to expand the typology of New England house forms. It is instead to offer material evidence that the end-chimney double-pile house was specifically *preferred* by many colonists, to the point that different groups of carpenters executed unusual structural innovations in different ways to adapt it to changing cultural tastes. Cooking functions were (at least occasionally) removed to the rear of the house, just as they were in central-chimney houses, and builders engineered framing solutions allowing for an additional heated room on the ground floor while explicitly avoiding a center-chimney hall-and-parlor arrangement.

Thrift alone cannot explain the popularity of the end-chimney double-pile house, which did not necessarily represent a savings in cost of materials or workmanship. Two nearly contemporary houses illustrate diverging preferences in action. In 1714, Stephen Churchill (grandson of Joseph Churchill) built a single-cell, two-story house with the clear intention of expanding it laterally as his fortunes allowed, as evidenced by a framed chimney bay wide enough to accommodate back-to-back hearths. Five years later, he expanded his house to the southwest, resulting in a typical center-chimney, two-story, hall-and-parlor house with four heated rooms (Figure 19). Churchill essentially built his house in two installments. The 1714 structure was conceived not as a single-cell, two-story dwelling, but as the first half of a center-chimney house; the two building campaigns can reasonably be treated as an architectural whole.

A few miles north in Kingston, William Bradford constructed an end-chimney house with an integral lean-to just a year earlier (Figures 20 and 21).[51] Interestingly, Bradford's house is some eighty square feet larger in footprint than Churchill's center-chimney hall-and-parlor house. Churchill's house had the advantage of

Figure 19. Stephen Churchill house (commonly called Howland house), Plymouth, Massachusetts, 1714, with later additions. Photograph by James I. Kelleher.

Figure 20. Bradford house, Kingston, Massachusetts, 1713. Library of Congress, Prints & Photographs Division, HABS MASS,12-KING,1–1.

four heated rooms to Bradford's likely two (or possibly three), as well as two second-story chambers to Bradford's one (plus a small space over the lean-to). Nevertheless, the cost and amount of materials used was probably not substantially different; for his money, Bradford could almost certainly have built a house like Churchill's. There is no reasonable economic argument to be made for the construction and persistence of the end-chimney, integral-lean-to house. These houses are not necessarily smaller than center-chimney houses, and the framing involved is, if anything, *more* complex than center-chimney examples, particularly if a jog like those on the Hoxie and Church houses is considered. Bradford, for whatever reason, clearly preferred the arrangement offered to him by an end-chimney lean-to house, and probably had no immediate plans of expanding it. Stephen Churchill's house was explicitly *designed* to be enlarged—the nucleus of an expanded center-chimney house is encoded within the structure's initial framing. This was not the case with Bradford's house, which required partial demolition and reframing of the chimney bay to enlarge.[52]

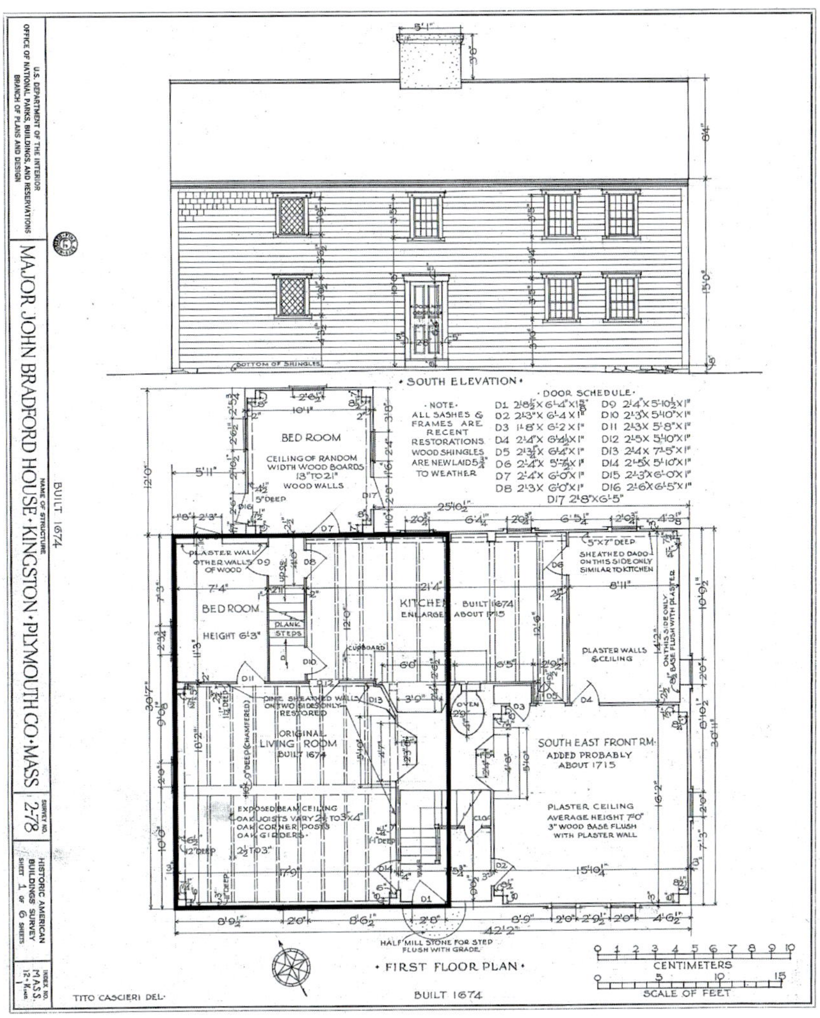


Figure 21. Bradford house plan, with probable original section highlighted in black. Library of Congress, Prints & Photographs Division, HABS MASS,12-KING,1- (sheet 1 of 6).

Of course, these end-chimney houses could be, and often were, expanded at some later date into center-chimney houses. The Samuel Stetson house in Hanover was not only doubled, but re-oriented from south-facing to north-facing.[53] Its fine Georgian façade facing the street belies its original status as a two-story, two-room-deep end-chimney house. This is a type of structural flexibility that provides the option to expand the house into an equally popular but organizationally distinct form, as taste and fortune allowed. These reorientations occurred at scales as large as the Stetson and Bradford houses and as compact as the Goodspeed house, which was also eventually enlarged into a center-chimney house.[54] The rising importance of formal symmetry as the eighteenth century progressed doubtless influenced many of these conversions.

The continuing preference for end-chimney double-pile houses in the Plymouth region may have been partly a result of their flexibility. Interior arrangements in these houses were highly variable. As mentioned above, Henry Brown of Providence and Samuel Barstow of Hanover kept their best beds in their lean-tos in 1702 and 1725 respectively, and John Churchill may have done the same decades earlier.[55] Others, such as John Maycomber of Taunton in 1725, still kept their best bed in the great room or hall, but kept lesser beds in the lean-to, offering differentiated sleeping spaces while still putting the proverbial best foot forward.[56] Similarly, Jonathan Morse of Bridgewater in the same year kept his second-best bed in the lean-to and third best in the chamber above.[57] By 1721, Johnathan Whipple's best bed was in the (upstairs) chamber of his Providence house, which nonetheless also contained feathers, salt, flaxseed, and cheese, recalling the multipurpose chamber of Howland's house. His "back roome" was apparently used strictly as storage, including cooking implements and other miscellaneous things. The lower room served as kitchen and hall with table and chairs.[58]

The three spaces of the end-chimney lean-to house could serve as bedrooms, parlors, halls, storage spaces, or kitchens (provided a hearth was available) almost indifferently. A common thread was the centrality of the lower front room, dictated by its position as the largest ground-floor space. In arrangements where the upstairs room was the best bedroom and the lean-to space was storage (such as Valentine Whitman's house in 1700–01), the hall served as a mediating space between the lowest-status service rooms in the rear and the highest-status chamber.[59] In the numerous cases where the same room served as both kitchen and best bedroom, the class distinctions of visitors were at least somewhat collapsed by their reception into a space simultaneously intimate and utilitarian. In these cases, the hall fulfilled much the same function that it had for centuries, combining a reception area with a cooking space. Perhaps it was this centrality that Churchill emphasized by including structurally unnecessary—but aesthetically arresting—crossed summer beams in his hall ceiling, a rare detail.

In this vein, St. George has written about "hybrid houses" that combine elements of highland and lowland housing forms into single dwellings, merging the direct entry (into the hall) of highland houses with the "up and back" expansion of lowland center-chimney dwellings. Hybridity in the organization of domestic spaces can be achieved through patterns of use as well as through distinct housing forms. John Churchill built a house that followed the structural program of a central-chimney house with an integral lean-to (and could easily have been expanded into one) but may have used it in a way like the highland-derived, long-and-low house of his peer John Howland: a sequential ordering of rooms, with private spaces of retreat located beyond a hall or kitchen.

The picture that emerges from the physical and documentary evidence is one of an almost unsatisfying ambiguity. There seems to be no hard and fast set of rules, no underlying grammar, that governed the use of the end-chimney, double-pile house. However, what could negatively be branded ambiguity could just as well be called flexibility, and it was likely this flexibility that sustained this house form and its variations for more than a century. In being a structure without a specific inherent logic, the form became amenable to an array of uses. It would be challenging and perhaps impossible to demonstrate that the end-chimney, double-pile house descended from houses like John Howland's. But it is clear that these houses could *accommodate* a similar way of organizing interior space along a single axis of both formality and privacy. In both the Howland and probably the Churchill houses, privacy and distance from the house's entrance was equated with material refinement. This orientation could come with a price: when Howland placed his best bed in his inner room, he may have distanced himself from vulgar kitchen functions, but he also sacrificed the fireplace's heat.

However, it also becomes clear that privacy and material refinement in these houses were not *necessarily* correlated. In the cases of rear kitchens like those of the Hoxie and possibly Church houses, the rear space's privacy relative to a front-facing hall was a matter of making work functions less visible, rather than placing an elite space beyond a more general one. Privacy and formality, in these cases, exist along crossed axes.

Perhaps colonists familiar with the long-and-low houses of Britain's highland regions preferred the sequential nature of the house, with its essentially linear circulation pattern. It would be haphazard to attribute these houses to some egalitarian impulse, but the fact is that minister and laborer alike, if invited into Howland's house, would have entered into a working kitchen. The same holds for Churchill's house, after passing through a small lobby. This was very much not the case with central-chimney hall-and-parlor houses, in which work functions could be bypassed entirely. The central-chimney house and the end-chimney double-pile house differed in kind, not in degree.

If nothing else, I hope that the term "half house" may be disposed of as an inadequate descriptor for buildings that, despite their relatively simple forms, simultaneously accommodated and enacted several approaches toward household arrangement. Stephen Churchill probably conceived of his 1714 structure as something like a "half house"; Bradford likely did not think similarly of his. As these houses changed hands or as their owners changed their minds, spaces could be used effectively in multiple ways to suit the occupants' tastes. Rear spaces were ambiguous, acting as bedroom, parlor, kitchen, or storage per the residents' wishes; so too with chambers. It is no surprise that such a flexible house form found purchase in southeastern Massachusetts' sandy soil, where disparate approaches to housing had coexisted since the time of initial settlement.

End-chimney double-pile houses were not necessarily the initial stage of center-chimney hall-and-parlor houses, nor were they motivated by thrift alone. They were distinct structures that were adaptable to varying conceptions of household organization that may ultimately have descended from English regional preferences. Their popularity suggests that New England attitudes toward domestic order remained heterogeneous well into the eighteenth century.

## AUTHOR BIOGRAPHY

**James I. Kelleher** is a PhD student in the American Civilization program at the University of Delaware.

## ACKNOWLEDGMENTS

I am grateful for the many people that have helped me put this manuscript together, including Ritchie Garrison, Lydia Mattice Brandt, Michael Chiarappa, Myron Stachiw, Catharine Dann Roeber, and Kathryn Blake, and my anonymous reviewers.

## NOTES

1. See Abbot Lowell Cummings, *The Framed Houses of Massachusetts Bay* (Cambridge, Mass.: Harvard University Press, 1979), 26; and Michael Steinitz, "Rethinking Geographical Approaches to the Common House: The Evidence from Eighteenth-Century Massachusetts," in *Perspectives in Vernacular Architecture III*, ed. Thomas Carter and Bernard L. Herman (1989): 16–26. Cummings points out that many center-chimney houses started life as smaller, side-chimney houses. Steinitz uses documentary evidence to convincingly argue that the majority of Massachusetts houses were likely single story into the late eighteenth century, probably reflecting a trend that continued back to the early colonial period.

2. Thomas Hubka, *Big House, Little House, Back House, Barn: The Connected Farm Buildings of New*

*England* (Hanover, N.H.: University Press of New England, 1984), 47–48.

3. Robert Charles Anderson, *The Great Migration Begins: Immigrants to New England 1620–1633,* 3 vols. (Boston: New England Historic Genealogical Society, 1995), 2: 1020–23.

4. James W. Baker, "'As Time Will Serve': The Evolution of Plimoth Plantation's Recreated Architecture," *Old Time New England* 74, no. 261 (Spring 1996): 51.

5. Craig S. Chartier, *Preliminary Report on Previous Archaeological Testing at the John and Elizabeth Howland Homesite* (New Bedford, Mass.: Plymouth Archaeological Rediscovery Project, 2015), https://www.plymoutharch.com/wp-content/uploads/2015/02/howland-final-report.pdf.

6. Inventory of John Howland, 1673, 3 (pt. 1): 51–54, Probate Records, Plymouth County, Massachusetts, 1633–1967, State Archives, Boston. Available online at Family Search, https://www.familysearch.org/search/collection/2018320. Family Search is the genealogical website of the Church of Jesus Christ of Latter-day Saints. You must create a free account to access the site. See also "The Inventory of the Goods of John Howland, deceased 1673," transcribed document available courtesy of the Pilgrim Hall Museum, https://pilgrimhall.org/pdf/John_Howland_Will_Inventory.pdf.

7. The link between cultivation, or "breaking," spiritual discipline, and physical space has been discussed by Robert Blair St. George, "Set Thine House in Order: The Domestication of Yeomanry in Seventeenth Century New England," in *New England Begins: The Seventeenth Century* (Boston: Museum of Fine Arts, 1982), 170–73. While he applies it to center-chimney house plans, where the acts of raw material processing and food preparation are gradually moved to the rear of the house, the same spatial progression could be applied to the sequence of rooms in Howland's house.

8. Archaeological evidence clearly points to the existence of a lean-to at the Howland site house; archaeologist Craig Chartier followed Strickland's example and interpreted this as the "inner room" referenced in the inventory in his report on the site. See Chartier, *Howland Homesite,* 21. This seems unlikely. First, this would result in a fire room nearly twice as long as it is wide—a proportion and scale that the author has not encountered in colonial architecture. Secondly, the roughly 7-by-22-foot lean-to is too small to feasibly contain the quantity of furnishings listed in the inventory, including four chests, a bedstead, and a cupboard. Because it was not mentioned in Howland's otherwise room-by-room inventory, the lean-to was probably an addition after Howland's death, and has been omitted from the figures here.

9. James Deetz and Patricia Scott Deetz, "Vernacular House Forms in Seventeenth Century Plymouth," The Plymouth Colony Archive Project, 1998. http://www.histarch.illinois.edu/plymouth/folkhouse.htm. For further discussion of room-by-room inventories of Plymouth colony/county, see James I. Kelleher, "Domestic Architecture of Plymouth Colony 1650–1720" (master's thesis, University of Delaware, 2020).

10. Richard M. Candee, "First-Period Architecture in Maine and New Hampshire: The Evidence of Probate Inventories," in *Early American Probate Inventories,* ed. Peter Benes (Boston: Boston University, 1987), 97–120. The Philip Call house of Ipswich is a likely example; see Margaret E. Welden, "Form B Form for 26 High Street, Ipswich, Massachusetts (IPS.117)" (Boston: Massachusetts Historical Commission, 1978); "26 High Street, the Philip Call House," Historic Ipswich, https://historicipswich.net/philip-call-house-26-high-st/. See also several of the Rhode Island stone-enders, particularly the Clemence-Irons house. Dorchester's Pierce house may have been similarly divided; see Cummings, *Framed Houses,* 101.

11. Robert Blair St. George, "A Retreat from the Wilderness: Pattern in the Domestic Environments of Southeastern New England 1630–1730" (PhD diss., University of Pennsylvania, 1982), chapter 3 passim. St. George's list of room-by-room probate inventories in southeastern New England prior to 1730 has been enormously helpful to the documentary portion of this investigation.

12. Richard M. Candee, "A Documentary History of Plymouth Colony Architecture," *Old Time New England* 59, no. 215 (1969): 59–71, 105–11; and 60, no. 218 (1969): 37–53, passim.

13. Nathaniel B. Shurtleff M.D. and David Pulsifer, eds., *Records of the Colony of New Plymouth in New England,* 12 vols. (Boston: William White, 1857), 12: 111–12.

14. Shurtleff and Pulsifer, *Records,* 12: 111–12.

15. For example, the late seventeenth-century Alden house (Duxbury), the late seventeenth- to early

eighteenth-century Sparrow house (Plymouth), the 1714 Bradford house prior to expansion (Kingston), the Church house (Plymouth, discussed here), Hanover's Samuel Stetson house prior to enlargement, and Sandwich's Wing House (erroneously "Old Fort").

16. I am choosing to interpret that both doors are original. It is possible that only one of them is original and one was added, but this does not especially affect the interpretation of the rear space, the evidence for which is only tangentially related to the doors.

17. Thomas Faunce, deed to Jonathan Churchill, 1767, deed book 53:203, Plymouth County Registry of Deeds, Plymouth, Mass.

18. For specific evidence of the cross gable as well as a more in-depth structural description of the Churchill house, see Kelleher, "Domestic Architecture," 47–51.

19. See, for example, the chamber in the oldest section of the Balch house, Beverly, for an almost identical arrangement of half-story with cross gable and finished summer beam.

20. Shurtleff and Pulsifer, *Records,* 5: 83. This quote occurred in court records during Mary Churchill's arraignment for fornication; she was later convicted and fined six pounds. Mary and Thomas were married thereafter.

21. Shurtleff and Pulsifer, *Records,* 5: 83.

22. Whether this was the porch or lobby (where the stairs are located) or the kitchen/hall (the largest front room) is unclear.

23. St. George, "Retreat," 122.

24. William G. Brennan et al., *Early Records of the Town of Providence,* 21 vols. (Providence, R.I.: Snow and Farnham, 1892–1915), 6: 221–25; Inventory of Samuel Barstow, 1730, 5: 814–15, Probate Records, Plymouth County, Massachusetts, 1633–1967, State Archives, Boston. Online at FamilySearch, https://www.familysearch.org/search/collection/2018320.

25. The Churchill house's hall is identified as a "kitchen" in a deed for part of the house in 1767. Thomas Faunce, deed to Jonathan Churchill, 1767, deed book 53:203, Plymouth County Registry of Deeds, Plymouth, Mass.

26. I would not ordinarily speculate on the historical connotations of words, but lean-to is so etymologically clear (i.e., leaning against) that the conclusion here seems natural. For information on the Goodspeed house, see Robert P. Frazee, "Goodspeed House Research Summary" (unpublished manuscript, September 1997). I am grateful to Mr. Frazee for sharing his helpful research and photographs with me.

27. Abbot Lowell Cummings, "Three Hearths: A Socioarchitectural Study of Seventeenth-Century Massachusetts Bay Probate Inventories," *Old Time New England* 75, no. 263 (1997): 13.

28. St. George, "Set Thine House," passim.

29. Cummings, *The Framed Houses of Massachusetts Bay,* 26. The 1714 Bradford house in Kingston was similarly enlarged in the 1750s; see Claire W. Dempsey and Betsy Friedberg, "John Bradford House," National Register of Historic Places Nomination Form (Washington, D.C.: U.S. Department of the Interior, National Park Service, 2006), Section 7.

30. George H. Sherwood, "Restoration of the Hoxie House for the Town of Sandwich, Massachusetts. June 15th 1959," typescript restoration plan, Hoxie House Folder, Sandwich Town Archives, Mass.

31. Personal communication with Dr. J. Ritchie Garrison, March 4, 2020.

32. Nathaniel Jackson, deed to Charles Church, January 3, 1712, Plymouth County Registry of Deeds, Mass.

33. Charles Church, deed to John Doane, June 16, 1718, Plymouth County Registry of Deeds, Mass.

34. *Boston News-Letter,* March 16, 1727.

35. Tusk tenons are tenons with a single, angled shoulder. More typically, joists are simply dropped into open pockets in the summer beam, and conceivably could be lifted back out.

36. Inventory of Nathaniel Thomas, 1675, 3:1:137, Probate Records, Plymouth County, Massachusetts, 1633–1967, State Archives, Boston. Online at Family Search, https://www.familysearch.org/search/collection/2018320.

37. Personal communication with Dr. J. Ritchie Garrison, June 25, 2019.

38. William T. Davis, ed., *Records of the Town of Plymouth,* 3 vols. (Plymouth, Mass.: Avery and Doten, 1889), 2: 22.

39. John Harlow, deed to Thomas Morton, February 1728/9, Plymouth County Registry of Deeds, Mass.

40. William T. Davis, *Ancient Landmarks of Plymouth* (Boston: Damrell and Upham, 1899), 322.

41. Michael Burrey, unpublished report on Harlow house, 2006, Plymouth Antiquarian Society, Mass.

42. Burrey, unpublished report on Harlow house.

43. Ernest Allen Connally, "The Cape Cod House: An Introductory Study," *Journal of the Society of Architectural Historians* 19, no. 2 (1960): 47–56.

44. J. Frederick Kelly, "The Norton House, Guilford, Conn.," *Old Time New England* 14, no. 3 (January 1924): 122–30.

45. James Cahill Sexton, "Craftsmen, Clients and Buildings: The Domestic Architecture of Guilford, Connecticut, 1689–1789" (PhD diss., Yale University, 1999), chapter 1.

46. It is interesting to note that protruding bake ovens apparently existed in old Cape Cod end-chimney houses, as well as on the Churchill house in some form, per Davis, *Landmarks,* 346. The oven at the Douglas house may be the only surviving example and warrants further study. See Amos Otis, *Genealogical Notes of Barnstable Families,* 2 vols. (Barnstable, Mass.: F.B. and F.P. Goss, 1888), 1: 490; and William T. Davis, *Plymouth Memories of an Octogenarian* (Plymouth, Mass.: Memorial Press, 1906), 484–85.

47. In the case of the Rowell, Norton, and Douglas houses, the identification of the rear heated spaces as kitchens is relatively clear given the attendant bake ovens and set kettles. In the Hoxie, Church, and Harlow houses, the original arrangement is less certain and is mostly implied by the former examples. The rear heated rooms could well have served as small parlors, in keeping with the sequential "inward room" arrangement discussed above.

48. These three-quarter cape houses are structurally distinct from the square-plan houses of the Narragansett Basin that Myron Stachiw has researched—the latter are descended from direct-entry highland houses by way of Rhode Island's stone-enders. See Myron O. Stachiw, "Domestic Architecture in the Narragansett Basin, 1636–1840," in *The Early Architecture and Landscapes of the Narragansett Basin: Volume I, Newport,* ed. Myron O. Stachiw et al. (Vernacular Architecture Forum, 2001). The relationships between these two house types, and to the jogged examples discussed in this essay, is an avenue for future research. Interestingly, some jogged houses (Norton and Douglas) clearly relate to the tradition of stone-ended houses, while others (Rowell and Hoxie) are fully framed, with a chimney bay.

49. Otis, *Genealogical Notes of Barnstable Families,* 2: 203.

50. Daniel Chase, "Form B, Form for 57 Hope Lane, Dennis, Massachusetts (DEN.60)," Massachusetts Historical Commission, Boston, 2019.

51. D. H. Miles and M. J. Worthington, "Bradford House, 50 Landing Road, Kingston, Plymouth County, Massachusetts," Oxford Tree-Ring Laboratory, https://www.dendrochronology.com/brd.html.

52. Dempsey, "John Bradford House," Section 7.

53. Sara B. Chase and Candace Jenkins, "Stetson House," National Register of Historic Places Nomination Form (Washington, D.C.: U.S. Department of the Interior, National Park Service, 2006), Section 7. The nomination does not clarify the sequencing and reorientation of the house aside from noting that it started as a smaller structure in the eastern half. See also Historic American Buildings Survey, Samuel Stetson House, Hanover Street, Hanover Center, Plymouth County, Mass., measured drawings (Hanover Center, Massachusetts, Plymouth County, 1933), https://www.loc.gov/item/ma0441/.

54. Frazee, "Goodspeed House," 31–32.

55. As beds were both intimate and expensive, their location serves as a shorthand for the relative level of material refinement in a room—the "best bed" tending to be in a better or best room.

56. Inventory of John Maycomber, 1725, 5: 186, Probate Records, Bristol County, Massachusetts, 1687–1916, index, 1687–1926. Available online at Family Search, Probate Registry, Taunton, Massachusetts, https://www.familysearch.org/search/catalog/277787?availability=Family%20History%20Library.

57. Inventory of Jonathan Morse, 1725, 5:185, Probate Records, Plymouth County, Massachusetts, 1633–1967, State Archives, Boston. Online at Family Search, https://www.familysearch.org/search/collection/2018320.

58. Brennan, *Early Records,* 16: 189–93.

59. The circulation into upstairs rooms is a thorny question, depending on the locations of staircases and front doors which are often modified or obscured.

CATHERINE W. BISHIR

# *Research Note:* Hiring Out

## *Enslaved Black Building Artisans in North Carolina*

ABSTRACT

Central to the construction of much of the architecture of the antebellum South were enslaved artisans in every building trade. A large proportion of these men were hired out as part of an economic system that operated in most slaveholding states, but their importance has seldom been addressed. Using North Carolina as an example, this article explores their work and their experiences.

> Henry, an enslaved carpenter aged about thirty, was hired out by a widow's executor and was working near Wilmington when he escaped. In an advertisement for Henry's return, the executor commented, "As he has never before ranaway [*sic*], and is supposed to have absconded without cause of complaint, it is thought that his object may have been his freedom."[1]

As I have studied the history of African American builders in North Carolina, I have realized more and more the importance of hiring enslaved artisans as well as laborers in the antebellum construction industry. Slave hiring was common in most slaveholding states, but its prevalence, operation, and significance in the building trades have seldom been addressed. I have discussed the topic as part of previous publications, which explored the experiences of enslaved as well as free Black builders and other artisans. This article brings together evidence from those publications and other sources to focus on the practice of artisan slave hiring in the construction industry.[2]

Historians have examined the larger topic of slave hiring in regional and state contexts. Studies such as Jonathan Martin's *Divided Mastery* and John J. Zaborney's *Slaves for Hire* address economic and political aspects of the practice, including its widespread use, its varied forms, the relationships between slaveholders and hirers, and the impact on the profitability of slavery.[3] Other studies have called attention to the roles of enslaved workers in the construction of selected landmarks, such as the White House, the United States Capitol, and the University of Virginia.[4] This article, by contrast, uses North Carolina as a case study both to depict the broad picture of hiring enslaved building artisans and to look closely at the day-to-day details of its operation and the varied experiences of the men involved. It thus provides a new perspective on a practice vital to the creation of much American architecture and to the lives of thousands of American artisans.

Within the wider economy, slave hiring facilitated the allocation of skilled labor as needed, including workers in most trade and service occupations, from shipbuilders and shoemakers to cooks and midwives. It played an especially vital—if unquantifiable—role in the sharply varying and site-specific labor needs of the construction industry. As far as I can tell, there is no way to estimate the number of enslaved building artisans, much less the number of those who were hired out. Few building projects are sufficiently documented to depict the roles of hired, enslaved artisans in their construction. But from cumulative anecdotal and circumstantial evidence, it is clear that the practice was widespread and long-lasting despite some Whites' efforts to quash it, and that much of the finest construction in North Carolina, as elsewhere in the South, depended on hiring enslaved artisans in essentially every building trade, including bricklayers, carpenters, plasterers, stoneworkers, and blacksmiths.

This article describes briefly the use of slave hiring in the North Carolina building industry, presents examples that provide the names and roles of the individuals involved, and considers the impact of the practice before and after Emancipation. Although most of the available documents were produced by White people—chiefly slaveholders—I have sought to illuminate where possible the experiences of the enslaved artisans themselves. I have looked especially for evidence of how they devised a degree of agency within the strictures of bondage—from their own words and actions and, more often, by reading between the lines of records left by White writers.

Regarding methodology, I have not discovered a strategy for finding evidence of the names and roles of hired enslaved artisans; rather, my findings are grounded in chance discoveries in research over the years, which turned up nuggets of information about slave hiring. Sources include letters, receipts, bills, and account books in private and public collections; wills, deeds, estate records, and inventories in public records; contemporary and later biographies and published and unpublished memoirs; and newspaper advertisements and accounts (newly available in recent years via Newspapers.com). Among the best sources are the rare cases in which records of hired enslaved builders' roles survive for specific private and public building projects, but these are few indeed; even where it exists in archives, such evidence is seldom noted in finding guides. Like much of the study of enslaved people's lives, the search for the human story of how slave hiring operated in construction is very much needle-in-a-haystack work, with luck as important as persistence to the process.

Crucial to the discovery of information about slave hiring in construction is simply noticing the evidence. During research in the 1980s for the book *Architects and Builders in North Carolina: A History of the Practice of Building* (1990), research assistant J. Marshall Bullock and I scoured the Southern Historical Collection at the University of North Carolina and the North Carolina State Archives and other collections for evidence of the people and practices involved in the state's building industry for our chapter covering the period from the American Revolution to the Civil War. In digging through the collections as well as studies by other historians, we were soon struck by the unexpected abundance of information about building artisans of color—more than we had imagined or could be included in the book. As a result, I published a separate article, "Black Builders in Antebellum North Carolina," in 1984, and included only some of that story in the book *Architects and Builders in North Carolina* in 1990. I uncovered additional information on Black building artisans in my studies of specific buildings and communities, such as the Hayes plantation house near Edenton, the Bellamy mansion in Wilmington, and the town of New Bern. Moreover, within the last several years, new digital resources have opened new expanses. Much of the data gathered about building artisans of color has been published on the North Carolina State University Libraries website as *North Carolina Architects and Builders: A Biographical Dictionary*.[5]

Recently, I agreed to give a paper on the importance of slave hiring in antebellum North Carolina, with a focus on the construction industry.[6] Taking a fresh look at my previous research, I began to realize just how prevalent slave hiring had been. For years I had concentrated on identifying artisans of color and their work and had noted that some of these men were enslaved artisans hired from their owners. But not until I sought to pull together the story of slave hiring did I recognize the scale of the practice in the state's antebellum architectural and social history. It was simply a matter of paying attention. One of the principal purposes of this article is to encourage readers to look closely at the records of antebellum building projects and other sources with an eye to evidence of hiring enslaved artisans and its architectural and social impact.

Although North Carolina's laws concerning enslaved and free people of color were more lenient than those in some other states, and regulations varied from one community to another, the financial arrangements for slave hiring were similar across the state and region. As historians Martin, Zaborney, and others have described, in some cases a slaveholder profited by hiring his or her enslaved workers to another employer, while in another, more controversial practice, they allowed or assigned enslaved workers to "self-hire" or "hire themselves"—to strike their own bargains with employers and turn over a given amount ("wages") to the slaveholder. Some hiring agreements were for short periods, while others covered an entire year, usually beginning about the first of January. Direct hiring, and especially self-hiring, changed the relationship between the enslaved person and the slaveholder into a more complex three-party dynamic that included the hirer.

Slave hiring had potential advantages and disadvantages to all three parties—employers, slaveholders, and enslaved workers. For the employer, hiring an enslaved worker enabled him or her to obtain services for a given task or period without the cost of purchasing a slave, which was substantial for a highly skilled worker. But there was also financial risk for the employer, especially in making year-long hiring contracts. White masonry contractors Dabney Cosby and his son, Dabney Jr., who owned enslaved artisans themselves, recognized this when they occasionally gambled on the utility of hiring additional workers. On November 28, 1850, the elder man wrote to his son, "You doubt the properity [*sic*] of hiring for another year because you have no prospects for imployment [*sic*]. Now I cannot but believe . . . sometime shortly some will be turning up that will alter the present state of business, there is to [*sic*] much public improvement going on not to make a stur [*sic*] in other ways and after the regular Hiring time not a hand can be let your wants be what they may—those you can get upon fair terms take."[7]

For slaveholders, hiring out slaves provided a significant source of income; some slaveholders, including widows and orphans, depended heavily on the earnings of their enslaved workers. Indeed, it is likely that in towns, at least, citizens who owned substantial numbers of enslaved people gained much of their income from hiring them out. Yet slaveholders also took the risk that the workers they hired out might be killed or injured or escape bondage, especially if the hirer was cruel or careless. As an eighteenth-century visitor from Europe commented after observing an auction of enslaved people in Wilmington, "a slave is capital, put out at a very high interest, but because of elopement and death very unstable."[8]

For an enslaved person, hiring out and especially self-hiring often offered the possibility of accomplishing their goal of freedom. The practice could bring greater latitude and agency as well as opportunities to make money independently, which until manumission laws were tightened in the 1830s, a good many enslaved workers used to obtain freedom for themselves or their family members. An enslaved artisan could gain experience in operating on his own and negotiating the White world. Hiring out, especially at a distance from home, also brought opportunities for escaping bondage, as witnessed by dozens of runaway notices cited below. But there were risks as well, especially the real fear that a hirer might mistreat, injure, or kill an enslaved person in whom he or she had no long-term interest. For the enslaved artisan who was hired out to work at a distance from home, the assignment could bring the trauma of separation from friends and family, including the loss of whatever degree of protection and care the workman had provided to his wife and children, siblings, and parents.

On balance, and despite complaints from White workers and new restrictions on the practice, slave hiring benefited employers and slaveholders sufficiently that it persisted until Emancipation, and enslaved people continued to use it to pursue their goal of freedom. An especially notable example was the enslaved brickmason Abraham Galloway (1837–70). Galloway was born in Smithville (now Southport) near Wilmington to a White ship pilot, John Wesley Galloway, of a long-established local family, and an enslaved woman,

Figure 1. Abraham Galloway, portrait. From William Still, *Underground Railroad* (Philadelphia: Porter & Coates, 1872).

Hester Hankins, who belonged to a White widow, Louisa Hankins. Moving to Wilmington as a youth owned by the widow's son, the young Galloway learned the brickmason's trade and was allowed—or required—to hire himself out at his trade and pay his owner "wages" of $180 per year. In 1857 Galloway, aged twenty, joined a friend in escaping by sea to the North, where he began a long career as a freedom fighter (Figure 1).[9]

Two seemingly unlikely sources convey the widespread use of slave hiring in general: the abundance of laws intended to regulate or forbid the practice and the repeated petitions and protests against slave hiring, and especially self-hiring. The many laws on the subject do not mean that the proscribed actions ceased. Rather, they indicate that slave hiring was prevalent enough to spur repeated laws and to evoke complaints that existing laws were not being enforced. As in many cases, laws and protests demonstrate the continuing existence of the practices they sought to end.

North Carolina laws concerning slave hiring also reveal lawmakers' evolving struggle to balance the economic advantages for slaveholders and employers against concerns over competition to White mechanics (a common term for skilled craftsmen, including builders) and the growing fear of "domestic insurrections" that might result from slaves operating without close supervision. A state law enacted in 1785 to regulate slave hiring in Wilmington, Fayetteville, Washington, and Edenton—leading towns all located in slaveholding areas in eastern North Carolina—actually acknowledged that it was "customary for many persons, as well in the country as in the several towns in this State, to permit their slaves to hire themselves out from day to day, by which great profits are acquired." Apparently accepting the practice but seeking to exert control over enslaved people and to assure that slaveholders who profited from their slaves' work in these towns would "contribute more than the ordinary taxes towards [the town's] support," the legislature enacted requirements for fees and badges for hired slaves and penalties for failure to adhere to the rule. In 1794, however, as Whites' fears of slave insurrections mounted (partly in response to the slave rebellion in Haiti), the legislature passed a law forbidding slaves in the state to hire their own time "under any pretense whatever." Leaders in Wilmington and New Bern, citing "the difficulty of obtaining White laborers," sought exemptions to the laws and passed their own regulations to permit the practice with certain conditions. Subsequent rebellions in South Carolina, Virginia, and elsewhere, coupled with growing complaints from White artisans, contributed to the passage of additional restrictions.[10]

Enslaved workers as well as enslavers often flouted the regulations for self-hiring, as indicated by Whites' repeated demands for better enforcement of existing rules. In 1803 Wilmington town commissioners ordered the local constable to arrest and jail any enslaved person "which shall hire himself out by the day without having obtained a Badge from the Town Clerk," indicating that many enslaved people did just that. Going further, in 1808 the "Incorporated Master Mechanics" of Wilmington pressed the general assembly to strengthen enforcement of laws forbidding owners of slaves from "hiring to them their own time" and slaves from hiring their own time from their owners; the White artisans claimed that the enslaved artisans worked for half what they did, and made it all but impossible for the White men to make a living.[11] Whites' concern over "domestic rebellions" continued to rise, as did complaints about enslaved workers' unfair competition with White artisans. But although local and state officials passed more restrictions on slave hiring and especially self-hiring, they were far from effective, and both practices prevailed in the building industry in much of North Carolina and the South.[12]

Perhaps influenced by antebellum White artisans' complaints about competition from craftsmen of color, some historians such as Carl Bridenbaugh in *The Colonial Craftsman* (1961) suggested that the presence of enslaved artisans resulted in inferior work. Other historians, including Ira Berlin and Herbert G. Gutman in their path-breaking 1983 article "Natives and Immigrants, Free Men and Slaves," indicated that during the late antebellum era, enslaved artisans were "stripped of their crafts," estimating their numbers in part from the number of slaves owned by free artisans.[13]

Greater understanding of the prevalence and the operation of slave hiring in construction challenges these notions. In fact, as examples discussed herein illustrate, many of the state's finest antebellum buildings were constructed and finished at least in part by enslaved artisans. Moreover, only a small proportion of these artisans belonged to other artisans; a large if unknown number were hired from non-artisan slaveholders. Indeed, the prevalence of slave hiring means that, contrary to earlier suggestions, the number of enslaved artisans has no relationship to the number of slaves owned by free artisans.

To be sure, some free building artisans—such as leading White builders John Berry of Hillsborough, Thomas Bragg of Warrenton, and Dabney Cosby of Virginia and Raleigh, along with the emancipated plasterer and bricklayer Donum Montford of New Bern—did own enslaved workers. Some of these, such as Montford's plasterer Isaac Rue, Cosby's plasterers Albert and Osborne, and Berry's carpenter Joe Nichols, were artisans in their owners' trades or complementary ones. Many other enslaved people owned by free artisans, however, were domestic servants or laborers. On the other hand, some major builders, such as contractors James F. Post of Wilmington and Jacob W. Holt of Warrenton, despite operating in communities dominated by slavery, did not own building artisans but hired them regularly, sometimes along with White workers.[14]

In any case, the artisans owned by other building artisans represented just a fraction of the population of enslaved construction artisans. As myriad examples demonstrate, most enslaved building artisans belonged to non-artisans—widows, single women, children, merchants, bankers, lawyers, or planters—who hired them out and often depended on their earnings. Slaveholding men sometimes willed their slaves to their widows and children to assure them an income. The practice was so woven into the social and economic fabric that it was employed by the most prominent White citizens. Stonecutter Allen Lane of Raleigh, for example, belonged to Susan and Emma White, unmarried daughters and heirs of North Carolina secretary of state William White. But Lane lived in the household of Governor Charles Manly with his wife Bertcha, a washerwoman for the Manly family, and their daughter Hannah, both of whom Manly owned. Lane hired out his time as a stonecutter and paid wages to the Misses White.[15]

Fuller understanding of slave hiring practices also challenges the supposition that enslaved artisans were "stripped of their crafts" in the late antebellum period. Again, figures are lacking, but it appears that the practice of slave hiring may have actually increased in the period. Several factors likely affected this pattern. Rising prices of enslaved people, spurred by demand for slaves in the burgeoning Deep South, meant that fewer free people could afford to purchase slaves and therefore turned to hiring them as needed. During the same era, large construction projects and the "contract mode" of building became more common: rather than clients hiring individual workmen themselves, a builder or other contractor took on a large building project and then assembled a workforce as needed; the flexibility of slave hiring facilitated this process.

Finally, newly stringent laws passed by the North Carolina legislature in 1831 and in subsequent years drastically reduced the possibilities for private manumissions, punitively raising the costs and requirements involved, and thus shrinking the number of owners who could emancipate the artisans they enslaved.[16] As a result, there were likely slaveholders who in former times might have freed certain slaves, including those kin to them and those who had saved money to facilitate the process, but who could no

Figure 2. Henry Taylor, portrait. Courtesy of New Hanover County Public Library.

longer do so. They could, however, allow their enslaved artisans to work and live with some degree of autonomy, including hiring their own time. Booker T. Washington provided a rare account of such a situation of carpenter Henry Taylor (1823–91), based on the account of his associate Robert Taylor, Henry's son: Henry Taylor was "the son of a white man who was at the same time his master. Although he was nominally a slave, he was early given liberty to do about as he pleased." Born near Fayetteville, Henry was a son of an enslaved woman and her owner, Angus Taylor. Angus allowed Henry to move to Wilmington, where he went into business as a house carpenter with his father's support. It is not known whether Henry Taylor "hired himself" and paid "wages" to his father–owner or operated essentially as a free man. How many other slaveholders followed such a course remains unknown and unknowable (Figure 2).[17]

Two well-documented great houses, Hayes plantation house near Edenton and the Bellamy mansion in Wilmington, demonstrate the role of enslaved artisans in buildings of the highest quality and highlight various aspects of slave hiring in construction, including the human details that often appear between the lines. One modest but well-recorded example, the work of the enslaved carpenter Harry in Chapel Hill, illustrates from the slaveholders' perspective the personal interactions among slaveholders, enslaved workers, and community members in a single small town.

We begin with the seemingly simple story of Harry, one of many enslaved artisans who built or helped build their owners' structures as needed and also earned money for their enslavers by being hired out. Harry (fl. 1840s) belonged to Judge William H. Battle, a native of Edgecombe County, who was married to Lucy Martin Plummer of Warrenton. Both were well-educated members of prominent slaveholding families and had inherited slaves from their fathers. The Battles moved to the village of Chapel Hill for their sons to study at the University of North Carolina, where William Battle became a professor of law. There they employed a White carpenter, a Mr. Jenkins, to enlarge a small house with Harry's assistance, and Harry subsequently built and repaired outbuildings for them. William Battle traveled frequently and Lucy managed the household, including the hiring out of slaves, which William encouraged. Lucy and William's correspondence offers an unusually detailed (and possibly too rosy) picture of slave hiring from the point of view of the enslavers. We come close at times to hearing Harry's voice as he participated in decisions about his schedule and the details of arrangements when he was hired by local employers to work on buildings important to the community.[18]

In March 1845, university president David L.

Swain hired Harry to build a fence around the university's Steward's Hall. In September, Lucy reported to her husband, "Harry is now nearly out of a job as there is no timber to be had—he went out to the Merritts' [a sawmill] this morning to see about it. He says Mr. Green speaks of hiring him next week." This was surely William Mercer Green, a university professor and chaplain instrumental in the construction of the Episcopal church, the Chapel of the Cross (built 1844–48), who likely hoped to hire Harry for that project. In October, Lucy wrote that Mr. Jenkins (the carpenter who had renovated their own house) had called upon her "to hire Harry to help him build Mrs. Scott's House—I told him he could have him . . . he does not seem to like to give $15 pr month unless I bord [*sic*] him which I don't like to do as I am going on the last side [of meat]." "Board" meant to provide the workman with his food; hiring agreements varied as to whether the hirer or the owner or the enslaved person would supply his food. Harry then entered into the discussion: "Harry says he has always received $15 and the person who hires him boards him—he wishes to know what you say." A week later, Lucy reported, "Harry has gone to work for Mr. Jenkins. I sent him [Jenkins] word that he must board him or pay me more than $15 a month so he concluded to do so."[19]

In 1848, Lucy Battle wrote, "I came near setting Harry to making an arbor for vines . . . as he said it would take only three dollars." A few weeks later, she reported, "Harry says he can do it, as soon as I get the timber—he is now working on the Presbyterian Church but says he can stop long enough to do my job. I expect that church will be finished now before ours [the Episcopal church]." The Chapel Hill Presbyterian Church, a stuccoed brick building designed by New York architect Alexander Jackson Davis, was built by Raleigh contractor Dabney Cosby, who specialized in stuccoed or "rough cast" brick construction and for which he typically employed his enslaved plasterers, Albert and Osborne (Figure 3). However, Cosby did not own skilled carpenters and whether Harry was employed by Cosby as a carpentry subcontractor or the congregation is not clear. By 1850, Harry was evidently employed

Figure 3. Chapel Hill Presbyterian Church, Chapel Hill, N.C., 1845–48. Alexander Jackson Davis, architect; Dabney Cosby, builder; Harry, carpenter. Photograph ca. 1910. Courtesy of Wilson Library, UNC-Chapel Hill.

by local White carpenter Kendall B. Waitt: Lucy wrote to her husband on April 13, "I went to Sis. Catherine's last night—she sends her love and says that her porch is just as it was—except that Harry came and told her that Mr. Waitt intended to send him there to finish it very shortly." How long Harry continued his work in Chapel Hill is uncertain, but during his tenure there he had helped build a good portion of its most substantial buildings.[20]

A much grander project was Hayes plantation house near Edenton, begun in 1814, where enslaved and free artisans, including sawyers, carpenters, bricklayers, and plasterers devoted hundreds of hours to building and finishing a large and elegant residence for planter James C. Johnston (Figure 4). In his accounts and correspondence Johnston recorded the story of the artisans he hired from other slaveholders. He was typical of his era in serving essentially as his own contractor, directly acquiring building materials and hiring workmen. He hired English-born carpenter-architect William Nichols to plan the house and superintend construction, but a large proportion of the artisans who worked on the house were enslaved men whom Johnston hired from their owners.[21]

Although James Johnston owned many slaves, few if any of them had specialized construction skills. This was the case for many slaveholders whose primarily agricultural or industrial workforces did not include the artisans necessary for an ambitious and fashionable construction project. Such slaveholders might assign their own workers as laborers on their building projects but usually hired any necessary specialists from other slaveholders who had invested in or inherited expert artisans and who profited from their work chiefly by hiring them out. Thus, when researchers seek the names of artisans who might have constructed a given slaveholder's buildings, their names may or may not appear among the men enslaved by the owner of the building under construction.

The records kept by James Johnston during construction of the Hayes house provide details of the hiring system along with the names of several hired workmen. An early step came in 1814

Figure 4. Hayes plantation house, Edenton, N.C., vicinity, 1814–17. William Nichols, architect and house carpenter; Joe Welcome, brickmason and plasterer. Photograph from southwest, C. O. Greene, 1940. Historic American Buildings Survey.

when Johnston hired two pairs of sawyers, Moses and Stepney and Gilbert and Randall, from their owner, W. W. Wilkins of Virginia, to undertake the sawing of timber for the large frame house. Two more enslaved sawyers, Wilson and Anthony, saw the job as an attractive opportunity and informed their owner, merchant David Clark, that they were "desirous to go" to Hayes with the other men. Clark acceded to their request, and the six men went to Edenton and worked for months for Johnston, making money for their owners and themselves.[22]

Among the other enslaved artisans Johnston hired to work at Hayes were carpenters such as Cato and Elijah, who made doors, and Dave and Jim, who installed floors. Especially notable was Joe Welcome (ca. 1774–1859), a plasterer, bricklayer, and stonemason who belonged to the great planter Josiah Collins. Among his 140 slaves counted in the United States Census of 1810, Collins owned a small if unknown number of men who possessed construction skills and worked frequently on local projects. Years earlier, Collins had recorded Joe Welcome's work in building the Edenton Academy in 1800–1801 and restoring the town's colonial St. Paul's Church in 1806–7. At Hayes from 1815 to 1817, Joe Welcome earned for Collins a dollar a day, leading a team of enslaved men who made mortar, laid bricks, and made and applied plaster. Johnston also noted extra payments to Joe Welcome and others, probably for work beyond their assigned "tasks."[23]

A glimpse of the dynamics among the hirer, slaveholder, and enslaved workers appears in Johnston's correspondence with W. W. Wilkins concerning the hiring of the latter's enslaved sawyers, Moses, Stepney, Gilbert, and Randall. Reading between the lines of the White men's letters suggests the agency the sawyers exerted on their own behalf. Johnston had settled on a pay rate with Wilkins, but when the workmen accomplished more than expected, Johnston wrote to Wilkins, "They inform me that give them a task and that all they saw over that they have—you will please to say what is their task, and whether I may pay them for all they cut over." Clarifying his own authority, Wilkins responded, "I make it a rule to give my sawyers all they get over their task but I settle with them myself for it and I do not wish any gentleman to pay them. I am glad to hear that they please you, they have done pretty well, and I will thank you to pay each sawer [*sic*] two dollars . . . and charge me with the same." On subsequent occasions when the sawyers exceeded their tasks, they repeated their requests to Johnston. In one missive, Wilkins authorized Johnston to pay them five dollars each "as an encouragement for further well doing and charge me for the amount $20." By the time Hayes was completed, a long roster of enslaved men had employed their skills and labor to fulfill the vision initiated by Johnston and architect Nichols, and some of them had earned substantial sums for their owners and for themselves.[24]

As at Hayes, many enslaved artisans were hired to construct the grand Bellamy house in Wilmington in 1859–60, but physician John D. Bellamy took a different approach to his project: he used the contract mode of building, which was becoming more common at that time (Figure 5). As more builders took on the job of contractor responsible for an entire building project—rather than providing the work of a single trade—they tended to hire more enslaved building artisans to provide the range of skills and number of workers needed.[25]

Rather than hiring artisans directly from their owners as did James Johnston, Dr. Bellamy contracted with a White architect-builder, James Post, who provided the design and hired and superintended the workmen. James Post, a native of New Jersey and leading Wilmington builder, did not own enslaved workers but hired many such men, either directly from their owners or through arrangements with self-hired laborers and artisans.[26]

During construction of the Bellamy mansion, Post also employed as assistant architect young Rufus Bunnell of Connecticut, who recorded his impressions of life in the slaveholding South. The carpentry subcontractor was a free man of color, Elvin Artis, but most of the other artisans as well as the laborers were enslaved. Architect Bunnell wrote that he "found it strange ever to keep in mind, that almost to a man these mechanics (however seemingly intelligent) *were nothing but*

Figure 5. Bellamy mansion, Wilmington, N.C., 1859–60. James F. Post, architect and contractor; Rufus Bunnell, assistant architect; William B. Gould and Price family, plasterers; Elvin Artis, Howe family, and Henry Taylor, attributed carpenters. Photograph, David Strevel, 2020. Courtesy of Preservation North Carolina.

*slaves* and capable as they might be, all the earnings that came from their work, was regularly paid over to their masters or mistresses." Bunnell also described the Saturday paydays in James Post's office, where he "had to calculate with Mr. P. the quantities of work done on the buildings during the week, setting prices to it and writing orders for the money for all the white mechanics and for their masters to draw their money for the labor of their slave mechanics. In the latter part of Saturday afternoons, they all white and black, flocked into the outer office room for their pay working on the various buildings, or 'jobs,' that Mr. P. had under his charge."[27]

Some of the free and enslaved workmen of color who built the house were well remembered by John Bellamy Jr., who was a child in 1860. As an old man, he stated in a 1934 article on "Interesting Houses" in the *Wilmington Star-News*, "it is a fact that the labor in the construction of the building was done chiefly by Negroes; in fact, nearly all the principal ante-bellum carpenters, masons, plasterers and interior finishers were Negroes." He recalled by name the "Howes, Artises, and Prices," among others, whom he probably remembered because these families continued in Wilmington after the Civil War.[28] The Prices were decorative plasterers George W. Price Sr. and Jr. According to the formerly enslaved John Jackson, who grew up in Wilmington, "The man that plastered the City Hall was named George Price, he plastered it inside."[29] George W. Price Jr., who followed in his father's trade, reportedly belonged to one William Benticott. The Prices were the best known of the plasterers John Bellamy Jr. cited as working at the Bellamy mansion: "Even the delicate and ornamental cornice work of plaster of Paris in the rooms was done by Negro mechanics" (Figure 6).[30]

Another of the enslaved decorative plasterers at the Bellamy mansion was William Benjamin Gould. The son of Englishman Alexander Gould and an enslaved Wilmingtonian, Elizabeth Moore, William Gould belonged to the Nixon family, who evidently hired him to architect and contractor James F. Post or allowed him to hire his own time. Besides mastering his trade, Gould also learned to read and write. One day in 1859, the twenty-two-year-old plasterer inscribed his initials "WBG" in flowing script on the back of a piece of ornamental plaster before attaching it. His surreptitious and perhaps defiant assertion of his identity and accomplishment remained hidden for well over a century.[31]

Enslaved artisans acquired their skills in various ways. Many learned their crafts informally from relatives, including their parents, or from other local or distant craftsmen. For an enslaved youth, such an apprenticeship could open the way to a future as an artisan whose position in the community stood well above that of unskilled laborers. Some enslavers selected promising youths for such opportunities, and even paid established artisans to train their slaves for profitable work. Planter Benjamin Smith advertised in a Wilmington newspaper in 1788 that he had for hire three carpenters, a shoemaker, and a bricklayer who had "served their apprenticeship in Charleston."[32] Raleigh banker William Polk offered for hire six carpenters, who in 1814 were nearing the completion of four years of apprenticeship. The enslaved youth Stewart Ellison of Washington, N.C., was assigned by his owner, Abner Neal, to learn the carpenter's trade through an apprenticeship to free master carpenter Mars Newton, and thereafter hired out Ellison for various jobs, including sending him to work on projects in Raleigh in the 1850s (Figure 7). Whether Neal hired Ellison directly to employers in Raleigh or had Ellison find his own employer and pay Neal "wages" is unknown. While in Raleigh, Ellison was exposed to a wider world than he had known in Washington. He returned to Washington within a few years, but when the Civil War began, he headed back to Raleigh to begin a new life.[33]

Apprenticeships for slaves were regarded as sufficiently important to warrant legal action if the terms were not met. In 1810, a mulatto boy named George was bound by his owner, merchant Stephen Forbes, for a term of four years to learn the house carpenter's trade from leading White House carpenter John Oliver; Forbes likely intended to hire George out or to sell him. But in 1815, Forbes sued Oliver, claiming that he had failed to meet the bargain and demanding damages of £250, indicative of the value placed on such training. Some free artisans offered their services to slaveholders seeking training for their

Figure 6. Bellamy mansion, Wilmington, N.C., interior detail showing decorative plasterwork. Photograph, Bill K. Blaine, 2020. Courtesy of Preservation North Carolina.

Figure 7. Stewart Ellison, portrait. Courtesy of Elizabeth Anne Ray Williamson and Preservation North Carolina.

enslaved youths. Raleigh carpenter John J. Briggs sought three or four "Negro" apprentices to the carpenter's trade: "Any gentlemen who may think proper to put their boys under my care" could be assured that the "greatest attention will be paid both to their usage and learning."[34] For some enslaved craftsmen, their apprenticeships became part of their identity. When plasterer Ulysses, aged about twenty-eight, ran away in 1818, his Hyde County owner noted that he had "served his time" with New Bern master artisan Donum Montford.[35]

Slaveholders came into ownership of artisans by various means. A good many inherited them from parents or spouses: slaveholders' wills sometimes included provisions to assure that their enslaved artisans would provide support to their heirs. Some individuals acquired skilled slaves with the specific purpose of hiring them out for profit, such as New Bern attorney John Donnell, who as we shall see purchased expert carpenters Ben and Simon and bought them the tools to practice their trades to supplement his income.[36]

The business of slave hiring often involved direct hiring of the enslaved workman from the owner. In a verbal or written agreement, the hirer promised to pay the slaveholder a certain sum to employ the enslaved person for a given task or period. In Warrenton, a typical agreement recorded the arrangements concerning the "negro man Hilliard," one of the many free and enslaved workers hired by White contractor Jacob W. Holt. Holt promised on January 1, 1858, "On or before January 1, 1859, we promise to pay M. K. Williams [a widow] $150 for hire of negro man Hilliard for the year 1858 and we bind ourselves to furnish said negro with the usual summer & winter clothing Hat shoes Blanket & witness our hands and seals 1st of January 1858." In another instance, Holt's arrangement for hired slaves such as Hilliard appears in an agreement to allow a planter-client to provide food as part of the client's payment: "Board of 1 white man from today [August 2] to 22 Decemr . . . $36.00; Board one negro same time . . . $18.00." Few of the slaves hired by Holt have been identified; one of these, according to local tradition, was Corbin Boyd, a skilled brickmason, who belonged to the Boyd family but worked regularly for Holt and earned a reputation for the excellence of his chimneys in houses built by Holt's shop.[37]

In some cases, slave hiring arrangements designated that the enslaved worker would keep a portion of the money he earned. The enslaved carpenter Ben, who was among New Bern's most highly regarded artisans, operated under a variety of arrangements. He was owned by White carpenter John Oliver, who hired him in 1817 to another White carpenter, Uriah Sandy, for $120 for the upcoming year, with Sandy to provide Ben with his board, a winter suit of clothes and two sets of summer clothes, a pair of shoes, and one blanket, as well to pay the necessary tax. Ben was likely one of the three outstanding house carpenters Oliver offered for sale in 1821 and again in 1823 as being equal to any such artisans in the state. In 1823 White merchant John Donnell purchased Ben for $615 from Oliver's agents. Donnell, who acquired Ben and other slaves as an investment and source of income, bought him a set of tools, and soon hired him to White master carpenter Martin Stevenson for $18 a month. This time Ben worked under a different arrangement. "Of this I allow him to pay Ben $1.50 per week," wrote Donnell, adding, "Ben to board and clothe himself—my object being to reserve $12 per month for myself."[38] Similarly, when New Bern free carpenter of color Rigdon Green—himself formerly enslaved—hired several artisans from the White widow Mary McKinley on January 1, 1840, they agreed that Green would pay McKinley $198 per workman for the coming year, of which each man was to have $48 for himself. Mrs. McKinley had provided in her will for her slaves to be freed at her death. She died before the agreement was to end, and when Rigdon Green settled with her estate, the executors gave the newly freed men their payments.[39]

In many other cases, enslaved artisans "hired themselves," the controversial practice in which slaveholders allowed or required their artisans to find work on their own and earn money from which they paid their owners a certain amount as "wages." Shade Green, a plasterer enslaved by merchant John Donnell, worked on his own and paid Donnell "wages" of $8 per month out of the $22 per month he earned. The two men settled up at intervals, sometimes with a bit of negotiation. In 1829 Donnell noted that Shade's payment for the previous year fell short of the expected amount. Donnell recorded, "I have told him I would strike out of my account the forward balance against him about $209 if he would make up the balance of $10.95 for last year and keep up the wages from the first of this year. I therefore open on next side a new account for him."[40]

How the parties kept track of their arrangements varied considerably. Aleck, a mason, carpenter, and blacksmith aged about eighty, had evidently hired his time from his owner, James Downey of Warren County, on a regular basis before he ran away in 1855. The artisan carried with him a carpet bag and, Downey surmised, "a memorandum book, in which I authorized him to keep and collect his accounts for work done in masonry." There is no record of how many building artisans engaged in self-hiring, but the anecdotal evidence coupled with the frequency of objections to the practice and laws against it indicate that self-hired artisans took a major role in the building industry and in the wider economy.[41]

Self-hiring was prevalent in the port town of Wilmington, North Carolina, the largest city in the state in the late antebellum period, where approximately 50 percent of the population was enslaved in 1850. Although some enslavers hired their workers directly to employers, many of the city's slaveholders found it to their advantage to permit their enslaved workers the flexibility to earn money for their owners and for themselves. Enslavers had to pay certain fees and provide a badge for each enslaved person authorized to hire his or her own time. Indicative of the remarkable autonomy of some enslaved artisans in the city is George W. Price Sr., an enslaved plasterer who in 1854 submitted a bid to repair plasterwork in the local customs house, a remarkable action for an enslaved person who legally had no right to enter into a contract.[42] Price was continuing a practice that led a writer for the Providence, Rhode Island, *Journal* to comment, "There is probably no place in the world where slaves are treated with more lenity and indulgence than in Wilmington."[43]

According to the formerly enslaved John Jackson, who grew up in Wilmington, many enslaved people "lived out" with their families and "hired theyselves where they pleased. They colle'ted they pay, an' the onliest thing the owner took was enough to support they fam'lies." Of Wilmington's imposing city hall, Jackson said, "I remember all the bricklayers, they was all colored" (Figure 8). In addition to citing George Price as a plasterer, he commented, "The men that plastered the City Hall outside and put those colum's up in the front, their names was Robert Finey and William Finey, they both was colored. . . . they was slaves, mos' all the fine work 'round Wilmin' ton was done by slaves. They called 'em artisans." Jackson commented, "None of 'em could read, but give 'em any plan an' they could follow it to the las' line."[44]

Not surprisingly, Wilmington was also the scene of White mechanics' strong objections to competition from enslaved artisans, especially those who hired their own time and even took contracts on their own and hired other slaves. Earlier in the nineteenth century, as noted above, the city's White mechanics had organized to persuade the state legislature to enforce laws against both slaveholders and slaves from participating in slaves' self-hiring, but the practice prevailed nonetheless.[45] Local protests over slave hiring took a violent turn in 1857. Late one summer night in Wilmington, about fifteen White mechanics "endeavored to tear down . . . the framework of a building" and left a note threatening similar attacks on "all buildings to be erected by Negro contractors or carpenters." Rumor had it that they represented an association of 250 or more White mechanics. Their grievance was not with free artisans of color but with the enslaved men whose low pay rates and low living costs enabled them or their owners to underbid White artisans. They asserted that enslaved workers "were cared for by their master's [*sic*], were at trifling expense for living, and were thereby enabled to underbid them in contracts." The practice, they said, "cheapened labor to such a degree that they the White mechanics could not live, and would be compelled to abandon their occupations or leave the place." At a public meeting held to address the "outrage" of

Figure 8. City Hall—Thalian Hall, Wilmington, N.C., 1855–58. John M. Trimble, architect; James F. Post, supervising architect; Wood brothers, builders; Price family, Robert Finey, and William Finey, plasterers. Photograph, Tim Buchman, 1988. Courtesy of Preservation North Carolina.

the attack on the building, a representative of the "gentlemen" of the city expressed his class's perspective: condemning the violence, he suggested that if the White mechanics found that "the present business did not justify them in remaining here, they were at liberty to leave the place and seek a living elsewhere."[46] As we have seen in the case of the Bellamy mansion, slave hiring continued to be central to Wilmington's building industry until Emancipation.

The ability to hire their own time or to keep a portion of wages earned for their owners allowed some enslaved building artisans to achieve important personal goals. Brickmason and plasterer Donum Montford of New Bern worked as an enslaved man for the first half of his life, paying wages to his prominent White owner but living with relative autonomy. He must have saved sufficient funds to participate in a transaction in which the leading free Black citizen John Carruthers Stanly purchased him in 1804 and promptly manumitted him. Montford became an important local builder who himself owned an enslaved workforce, trained free and enslaved apprentices, and manumitted two enslaved youths in 1827, including his son, who in turn became free building artisans.[47]

Within a few years, restrictions placed on private manumissions had become radically more onerous and made such actions as Montford's all but impossible. Working around the existing situation, in the late antebellum period, the enslaved carpenter and coffin-maker Dick Tucker found another way to take advantage of being hired out to benefit his family. Tucker belonged to New Bern merchant John Flanner, who hired him out for various projects. In 1858 the estate of Moses Griffin paid Flanner for eleven days work of "Dick Tucker and boy on house on Middle Street @ 17/6 [per day]." Flanner may have permitted Tucker to keep a portion of the wages, and Tucker also "hired his own time" and paid wages to Flanner. Tucker and his wife, Emeline, had as many as fifteen children, some of whom were sold away by her owner, White shoemaker Raymond Castix, who by law owned her children born while he owned her. The determined carpenter Tucker gradually saved enough money to persuade Flanner to purchase Emeline and their youngest child, so that the couple and their future children could stay together. Tucker then provided for his wife and children by hiring his own time. Tucker also took a fatherly role with his children enslaved by other owners: in 1858, a newspaper notice stated that Dick and Emeline's son Edward, aged about eighteen, had run away after being sold to another New Bernian. The notice related, "His father, Dick Tucker, belonging to Mr. John Flanner, lives in New Bern, and raised him, his former owner is Mr. Raymond Castix."[48]

Many other records left by Whites suggest ways in which enslaved artisans maintained a degree of agency within the framework of bondage. An enslaved artisan who hired his own time within a region where competent artisans were scarce could use his mobility and the demand for his work to assert his autonomy among his clientele. Enslaved plasterer Dave or Davy Dickinson or Dickerson, who had been employed at Hayes, kept his planter clients waiting for his services. In 1837, Clement Blount of Chowan County near Edenton and his cousin Ebenezer Pettigrew, who had a large plantation across the Albemarle Sound, were trying to track down Dickerson to do some promised work. Blount wrote to Pettigrew in June 1837 that he had "the promise of Dave Dickerson to go on the 15th July if nothing turns up to prevent him," but two months later Dickerson had not appeared. Blount was waiting to see if Dickerson had finished "Mr. [James] Johnston's work," but when he went to Johnston's residence "to see if he was done," Blount found that Dickerson "had not done one stroke of work there yet and has gone to Washington County to Plaster a House for Mr. Harrison at Lees Mills, which is treating you and myself very ill."[49]

Another enslaved carpenter, Jack Dewey, who had worked on some of New Bern's best houses, was sent in the 1830s by his owner, banker Charles Dewey, to build a house in Hillsborough for lawyer and planter Paul Cameron and another in Raleigh for Paul's father, the banker, attorney, and planter Duncan Cameron—some of the wealthiest men in the state. Jack Dewey ("Dewey's Jack") earned $100 per six-month term for his owner, a welcome sum at a time when New Bern's economy was slumping. Well regarded by both his enslaver and his employers, Dewey was given a copy of the plans and moved freely between towns, often working with little supervision and negotiating his schedule with his employers. A hint of Jack Dewey's approach occurs in an 1834 letter from Paul Cameron to his father, Duncan Cameron, concerning Jack's work on Paul's house, Burnside, in Hillsborough. Paul wrote to his father, "I went . . . to see how Jack and his company had employed themselves. They had not gone on as well as I had expected in laying down the floors—but said that they had waited until all the flooring plank had been carried up so that a selection might be made of the best for the floors of the lower rooms." Dewey's reported conversation with his employer evokes the seldom recorded negotiations that involved the enslaved worker as well as the owner and the employer, as here the artisan apparently employed his trade expertise to define his schedule without a direct confrontation.[50]

Demonstrating the pervasiveness and complexities of hiring enslaved building artisans are the scores of newspaper advertisements offering to hire out such men, a source made newly accessible via websites such as Newspapers.com. Many advertisements were general, such as a notice in the Halifax *North Carolina Free Press* in February 1825, offering for hire "an excellent Negro Carpenter, with a good set of tools."[51] In the *Raleigh Register* of August 17, 1827, banker William Polk of Raleigh sought to hire out by the month a bricklayer and a plasterer whose qualifications, were "not surpassed by any in the State."[52] Only occasionally did advertisers give the workmen's names. Brandon, a carpenter "qualified to do all kinds of Carpenters work," was to be hired to the highest bidder at noon on January 3, 1837, in Milton, North Carolina.[53] The *Hillsboro Recorder* of December 5, 1821, announced that Stephen, a carpenter, was to be hired out for the coming year on December 28, 1821, at the market house in Hillsborough by the executor of John Whitted's estate.[54] This was a common situation, for enslaved workers were often hired out during the settlement of estates. Several carpenters numbered among the forty or fifty "likely Negroes, all working hands," offered for hire in the *North Carolina Star* of December 15, 1836, by the executor of J. R. Eaton's estate in Granville County.[55] The dates of many such advertisements reflect the customary hiring date of about the first of January for the forthcoming year.

Some enslaved artisans took advantage of the ambiguities of slave hiring, such as carpenter Deman and bricklayer Limerick, who evidently represented themselves as self-hiring. Their owner published a notice in the *Wilmington Gazette* of February 3, 1807, to assert his authority over them. He offered the two workmen for hire by the month, quarter, or yearly and asserted, "As those Negroes have not permission to hire themselves, by jobbing or otherwise, any person wanting to employ them, will make application to the subscriber, T. Fitzgerald."[56]

Antebellum newspapers were also filled with notices seeking the return of runaway slaves who had been hired away from home. According to an advertisement in the Fayetteville *Weekly Observer* of March 28, 1838, Dick, a bricklayer and plasterer aged about twenty-six, had "worked in most of the Counties in the Eastern part of the state" before escaping from his Bladen County owner.[57] Carpenter Cornelius Williams had been hired out by his owner, J. G. Stanly of New Bern, to W. B. Flanner of Wilmington in 1854, and escaped from R. Wood of Jones County in 1855. According to Stanly's advertisement in the Wilmington *Daily Herald* of September 20, 1855, Williams had probably returned to Wilmington, where he was "well known"; he was believed to be planning to "escape by some vessel or the railroad, to the State of New York."[58] As both Williams and Stanly knew, the rail-connected port city had become a magnet for freedom seekers who sought safety among friends or kin while seeking a means of escaping to the North.

Although some enslaved artisans practiced their trades close to home—especially in towns such as Wilmington and New Bern where there was sufficient demand for their skills—others traveled good distances to earn money for their owners. Such mobility among hired artisans was a frequent if seldom documented practice in rural areas. An unusual record of such activity appears in the daily journal of planter Nicholas Massenburg of Franklin County, who made succinct notations of births, deaths, church attendance, weather, crops, and activities of his enslaved workers. In 1838 he noted each day's work on the expansion of his plantation house, Woodleaf, including that of stonemasons Wash and Willis, who belonged to a Warren County planter (Figure 9). The two men went to Franklin County to build a chimney for Massenburg, a job they began at noon on August 13, 1838, and completed in October. Massenburg also hired Albert, a plasterer, from Abraham Spencer, a leading brick and plaster contractor of Oxford. The chief carpenter for the project was William Jones, a White carpenter who employed both enslaved and free workers. Massenburg assigned some of his own enslaved workers to assist the artisans and accomplish other tasks, including Cary, who regularly drove the wagon to pick up supplies at the railroad depot. Such a scene was typical of building sites of all sizes in much of antebellum North Carolina, with hired enslaved artisans working alongside White artisans and other free and enslaved men of color.[59]

Large construction projects provided slaveholders with special opportunities to profit from their enslaved artisans' work. During the 1820s remodeling of the state house in Raleigh, architect William Nichols issued many payments to slaveholders for the hire of their workmen. In July 1821 "the hire of Peter the Carpenter" brought $19.45 for slaveholder John Marshall; and during June and July enslaved Raleigh carpenters Jacob and Mumford, together with two enslaved laborers, made $118 for their owner, state treasurer John Haywood. In some cases, slaveholders sent their artisans long distances to work on large projects: in the 1850s, the enslaved carpenter Stewart Ellison, who as we have seen was trained through an apprenticeship with free carpenter of color Mars Newton, traveled from Washington, N.C., to Raleigh to make money for his owner by working along with many other free and enslaved men on the North Carolina Hospital for the Insane designed by New York architect Alexander Jackson Davis (Figure 10).[60]

Figure 9. Woodleaf (Massenburg) Plantation, Louisburg, N.C., vicinity, 1838 (addition including stone chimney). William Jones, carpenter; Abraham Spencer, plastering contractor; Albert, plasterer; Wash and Willis, stonemasons. Photograph, David Anderson, 2019. Courtesy of Preservation North Carolina.

Figure 10. North Carolina Hospital for the Insane, Raleigh, N.C., 1850–52. Alexander Jackson Davis, architect; Eleazar Colbourn, Conrad family, Dabney Cosby, and David and S. L. McKnight, contractors; Stewart Ellison, carpenter. Postcard courtesy of Wilson Library, UNC-Chapel Hill.

A major employer of enslaved artisans appeared with the antebellum construction of railroads. Railroad companies advertised to employ not only enslaved laborers but also artisans including carpenters. In 1849, the *Raleigh Register* promoted investment in the state-sponsored east-west railroad by citing the benefits to trade and agriculture and touted an immediate boon to slaveholders: "There are thousands of slaves in North Carolina whose labor . . . is utterly unprofitable to their owners," but slaveholders who contracted their enslaved workers to help build the railroad would find that "this is greatly the most profitable employment that ever slave labor engaged in as a general business."[61]

Slaves hired to work for the railroads brought profits to their owners, but they also used their new situations to escape from bondage, embodying the earlier comment that "a slave is capital, put out at a very high interest, but because of elopement and death very unstable." An especially determined runaway was the carpenter Harry, who escaped in 1849 while he was hired to the "Railroad Company" by his Edgecombe County owner, Guilford Horn, probably to repair and build structures for the line between Wilmington and Weldon that traversed the locality. Harry was evidently a skilled and valuable artisan, for Horn advertised in various newspapers for his return for over a year, offering a substantial reward of $125. Like many freedom seekers, Harry had planned his escape carefully and made use of a series of connections. He was last heard of in Wilmington at the terminus of the railroad and was believed to have departed by ship, as did so many freedom seekers despite increasingly severe penalties against ship captains permitting such departures (see sidebar below).[62]

Scholars have only begun to explore the multiple impacts of slave hiring in the construction industry. One question is how the practice affected the physical character of buildings. When we realize that many buildings attributed to White craftsmen were crafted at least in part by enslaved artisans hired from local or distant owners, we must wonder anew whose hands actually shaped

### Harry, Carpenter and Freedom Seeker

According to Guilford Horn's notice placed on October 5, 1849, the enslaved carpenter Harry was about forty years of age, a "stout built" man about five feet five inches tall, with a yellow complexion, a scar on his left leg, missing upper front teeth, a loud voice, and a "very dark spot on his jaw, supposed to be a mark." Experiencing many changes in his lifetime, Harry had once been "the property of Mrs. Copage, of Edgecombe county; afterwards he fell into the hands of Asiel Farmer, from whom he was purchased by Mr. Barnes, of said county, from whom I purchased him about six years ago." Using his network of relationships, Harry had laid plans for his escape: "It is supposed that he has obtained, or will endeavor to obtain free papers from a free colored man living in Nash County, by the name of Moses Hagens, and assume his name, in order to make his way to a free state." "Well known along the railroad line," Harry had been heard from on September 11, 1849, on the New Bern Road not far from Wilmington, "enquiring the way to the Sound." Horn added a typical notation: "All Captains of Vessels are cautioned against taking away the above negro under penalty of the law." In June 1850, Horn updated the posting: Harry had been seen in New Bern calling himself Henry Barns or Burns, or possibly Copage or Farmer. He had a wife, the free mulatto woman Sally Bozeman, who had recently moved to Wilmington in New Hanover County, where Harry was supposed to be "lurking." Accompanying Horn's advertisement was a legal notice issued by the New Hanover County justices in response to Horn's complaint to them. It stated that Harry was "lurking about" New Hanover County and "committing acts of felony or other misdeeds." This notice took the extreme step of outlawing Harry, commanding him to surrender and return to his master, and authorizing any member of the public to capture or, if necessary, kill Harry without penalty. Such a threat sometimes led runaway slaves to surrender their freedom. That announcement ran as late as November 1850. Evidently Harry continued to elude the authorities, and Guilford Horn continued his advertisement well into 1851. Harry's fate remains unknown.[70]

the patterns of stonework, brickwork, woodwork, or ornamental plaster that appear from one building and one locale to another. Seldom do we find the kind of evidence that planter James Johnston recorded about the carpenters who made the doors at Hayes or the decorative plastering that William B. Gould produced at the Bellamy mansion. In New Bern, much of the town's notable and similarly executed federal-period woodwork is cited to White House carpenters including John Oliver, Martin Stevenson, and Asa King. What we do not know is how much of the fine work associated with these White artisans was actually executed by the highly regarded enslaved house carpenter Ben, who was owned for a time by Oliver and hired out to Stevenson, or Jack Dewey, who was associated with Asa King, or other enslaved artisans whose names are unknown. With an awareness of the frequency and importance of slave hiring in construction, however, researchers may look more closely at documentation and buildings in hopes of tying specific works to specific artisans.

Another important topic is the effect of antebellum slave hiring on builders and buildings after Emancipation. It is striking to observe how quickly freed people entered into postwar economic and political life despite many Whites' insistence that they were not competent to do so. Although no figures indicate how many of North Carolina's post–Civil War Black leaders had been enslaved and how many had been free before the war, it is clear that a substantial proportion of them had been enslaved, and many had been hired out or self-hired while in bondage. Various aspects of that experience—the craft training obtained through apprenticeships in slavery, the prestige associated with the status of skilled artisan, along with their experiences of working with some degree of independence and even negotiating terms of employment—undergirded their effective transitions into their lives as independent artisans, family men, and political figures.

Taking on roles they had envisioned before Emancipation, the Black political leadership, during and after the war, included a substantial number of formerly enslaved and hired-out artisans, including those involved in building. Conspicuous among the early political leaders was Abraham Galloway, the bricklayer who hired his own time in Wilmington before escaping to the North by sea and becoming a Union spy. He returned to North Carolina during the war and spent time in New Bern, which had been liberated by Union forces in 1862, and became a daring and effective advocate of equal rights. Shortly after the war, he and other New Bernians initiated and took leading roles at the North Carolina Freedmen's Convention in Raleigh from September 29 through October 3, 1865, a benchmark event that brought together Black leaders from across the state, including many formerly enslaved artisans, to express their vision for their future in freedom and make lasting connections to pursue that vision. After returning to Wilmington, Galloway continued as a radical political leader and served in the North Carolina senate. At his death at age thirty-three in 1870, his funeral was attended by some six thousand people.[63]

Another, longer-lived, political leader was carpenter Stewart Ellison, who had mastered his trade in bondage in Washington, N.C., was hired out to work in Raleigh in the 1850s, and returned to the capital during the war. By 1867 he had "commenced business at his trade, taking large contracts and erecting many elegant residences in and around Raleigh, and in other sections of the State," and in 1874 he was described as "probably the most extensive colored contractor in the state."[64] Entering immediately into politics, he joined Galloway and others in leadership at the Freedmen's Convention of 1865, serving as a vice-president. He became one of the first three men of color elected to Raleigh's board of commissioners, and he served as a member of the North Carolina general assembly. He continued as a prominent builder for many years. In 1896 the Raleigh *Gazette* reported, "We are pleased to note that St. Paul A.M.E. Church of this city is rapidly nearing completion. Hon. Stewart Ellison, who is general manager, is due much praise for the rapid dispatch with which he is having the work done. This church, when completed, will be one of the finest in the State. It will be a credit to the denomination, to the city, and to the race."[65]

Wilmington plasterers George W. Price Sr. and

Jr. likewise dove into public life. On April 27, 1865, when Black Wilmingtonians held an Abraham Lincoln memorial procession honoring the slain president, George W. Price (probably Sr.) served as "Marshal on Horseback" leading a half-mile long throng of mourners through the streets, an event vital in spurring local Black political life in the city. Meanwhile, George W. Price Jr., who had escaped from Wilmington by sea in 1862, soon joined Abraham Galloway in the political leadership in liberated New Bern. With Galloway, he led in organizing and participated in the 1865 Freedmen's Convention in Raleigh, and then returned to Wilmington. There he joined in political leadership, winning elections to the city's board of aldermen and to the North Carolina house of representatives in 1869–70 and the state senate in 1870–72. He was a popular public speaker on many topics, including the role of Black citizens. He also continued the trade he had mastered in slavery. The *Wilmington Star* of July 26, 1871, commented favorably on Mr. R. P. Barry's house with its ceiling "ornamented with plaster of paris cornice work," which was "the handiwork of George W. Price, the colored Senator from this county." Well into the 1890s, Price advertised as a contractor, builder, and plasterer, and a manufacturer of "Ornamental Decorations for Cornicing and Ceilings, Centre Pieces and Stucco Work."[66]

After Emancipation, New Bern house carpenter Dick Tucker—who had earned and saved money in bondage to enable his owner to purchase his wife Emeline and their youngest child—became known as Richard Tucker and emerged as one of the wealthiest Black men in town. He legally wed Emeline in December 1865. The couple brought together friends and some of their fifteen children for a ceremony that celebrated their thirty years together with "tears of grateful joy" and the singing of hymns, including the old freedom anthem, "Sound the Loud Timbrel o'er Egypt's dark sea/ Jehovah has triumphed, his people are free," which now took on new meaning.[67]

In a common diversification of carpentry skills, Tucker ran an undertaking and funeral business as well as other enterprises, and by 1870 owned real estate valued at $1,000. He joined other New Bern artisans in political life, serving in 1866 in the second Freedmen's Convention in Raleigh and in the 1868 constitutional convention (which enfranchised Black men, among other accomplishments). He also held office as a justice of the peace, state legislator (1870, 1872) and state senator (1874). In 1878 Tucker was described by a local White minister as "a prominent colored man who has been a member of N. Carolina Senate from Craven Co.—about 60 or 65 years old; bright and enterprising Negro; with two daughters teaching school."[68]

Like Richard and Emeline Tucker, whose daughters became schoolteachers, many formerly enslaved building artisans joined the upwardly aiming Black people who worked to educate their children to succeed in a new world. They organized to promote good schools for local Black children, and they devoted themselves to educating their own children. Wilmington house carpenter Henry Taylor, who had operated essentially as a free man in slavery, prospered after the war as a builder and grocer, and with his wife, Emily, saw to the education of their four children at local schools and prestigious colleges. His son, Robert, studied at local schools and also learned practical building skills by working with Henry. Setting his sights high, in 1888, with his father's encouragement, Robert Taylor entered the Massachusetts Institute of Technology (MIT). He became MIT's first Black graduate in any field, probably the nation's first professionally trained Black architect, and an architect and teacher at Tuskegee.[69]

Many more stories remain to be uncovered, but judging from the example of North Carolina, it is clear that the hiring out of enslaved bricklayers, carpenters, plasterers, and stonemasons played a central role in the construction of antebellum architecture, and their work, often unacknowledged, encompassed many of the finest buildings in the state. Their experiences also undergirded their subsequent roles as builders in the post–Civil War era as well as leaders in postwar political life.

It is well known that men of color, including enslaved workers, constituted a substantial though uncountable proportion of the artisans involved in antebellum construction in the South. Less widely understood is that a large proportion of these enslaved building craftsmen, perhaps the majority, were hired out. Along with earning wages for their enslavers, many of them earned and saved money for themselves and their families, learned how to operate with a degree of autonomy, established networks of allies, and searched for and sometimes found ways to attain their goal of freedom.

Far from being an anomaly found in a few notable examples, and despite laws meant to limit the practice, the hiring out of enslaved building artisans was so vital to antebellum construction that our understanding of the Southern architectural landscape must take into account these artisans' diverse experiences and accomplishments. Tracing their long-hidden stories and making them known is our challenge.


## AUTHOR BIOGRAPHY

**Catherine W. Bishir**, a member of the Vernacular Architecture Forum since its founding, is architectural historian emerita with Preservation North Carolina. Among her publications are articles on Black artisans going back to the 1980s and the book *Crafting Lives: African-American Artisans in New Bern, North Carolina, 1770–1900* (2013). She is also the author of *North Carolina Architecture* (1990) and author or coauthor of other publications on North Carolina architecture and building practice.



## ACKNOWLEDGMENTS

The author wishes to thank her friends J. Marshall Bullock, Louis P. Nelson, Lydia Mattice Brandt, and Julianne Patterson for their invaluable help on this article.


## NOTES

1. *Wilmington Daily Herald,* October 4, 1859.

2. The author's previous publications, from which this article is largely derived, were produced over several decades. Notes in this essay primarily cite those sources, which contain more extensive documentation. From the twentieth century are "Jacob W. Holt, An American Builder," *Winterthur Portfolio* 16, no. 1 (Spring 1981), republished in *Common Places: Readings in American Vernacular Architecture,* ed. Dell Upton and John Michael Vlach (Athens: University of Georgia Press, 1985), 447–81; "Black Builders in Antebellum North Carolina," *North Carolina Historical Review* 61, no. 4 (October 1984): 423–61; and "'Severe Survitude to House Building': The Construction of Hayes Plantation House," *North Carolina Historical Review* 4 (October 1991): 373–403. These three articles have been republished in Catherine W. Bishir, *Southern Built: American Architecture, Regional Practice* (Charlottesville: University of Virginia Press, 2006), and page citations herein are to that publication. Some of the research represented in these articles is also included in *Architects and Builders in North Carolina: A History of the Practice of Building,* with Charlotte V. Brown, Carl R. Lounsbury, and Ernest H. Wood III (Chapel Hill: University of North Carolina Press, 1990). More recent works include *The Bellamy Mansion, Wilmington, North Carolina: An Antebellum Architectural Treasure and Its People* (Raleigh: Preservation North Carolina, 2004); "Urban Slavery at Work: The Bellamy Mansion, Wilmington, North Carolina," *Buildings & Landscapes: The Journal of the Vernacular Architecture Forum* 17, no. 2 (Autumn 2010): 13–32; *Crafting Lives: African American Artisans in New Bern, North Carolina, 1770–1900* (Chapel Hill: University of North Carolina Press, 2013); "Searching for Donum Montford: Methods and Mysteries in Researching an African American Artisan," *Buildings & Landscapes* 21, no. 1 (Autumn 2014): 126–50.

3. Jonathan D. Martin, *Divided Mastery: Slave Hiring in the American South* (Cambridge, Mass.: Harvard University Press, 2004); John J. Zaborney, *Slaves for Hire: Renting Enslaved Laborers in Antebellum Virginia* (Baton Rouge: Louisiana State University Press, 2012).

4. See for example Jesse Holland, *Black Men Built the Capitol: Recovering African-American History in and Around Washington, D.C.* (Guilford, Conn.: Globe Pequot, 2007); Louis P. Nelson, "Slavery and Construction," in Maurie D. McInnis and Louis P. Nelson, eds., *Educated in Tyranny: Slavery at Thomas Jefferson's University* (Charlottesville: University of Virginia Press, 2019); and Renee K. Harrison, *Black Hands, White House: Slave Labor and the Making of America* (Minneapolis: Fortress Press, 2021). See also White House Historical Society, "Building the White

House," at https://www.whitehousehistory.org/building-the-white-house. This subject was addressed by the White House Historical Society in response to First Lady Michelle Obama's 2016 observation, "I wake up every morning in a house that was built by slaves," a statement that surprised many people and generated attention to the topic of slave hiring.

5. Especially useful local studies include Lynda Vestal Herzog, "The Early Architecture of New Bern, North Carolina, 1750–1850" (PhD diss., University of California, Los Angeles, 1977); Elizabeth Reid Murray, *Wake: Capital County* (Raleigh, N.C.: privately printed, 1983); and William M. Reaves and Beverly Tetterton, eds., *Strength through Struggle: The Chronological and Historical Record of the African-American Community in Wilmington, North Carolina* (Wilmington: New Hanover County Libraries, 1998); see also North Carolina State University Libraries, *North Carolina Architects and Builders: A Biographical Dictionary,* https://ncarchitects.lib.ncsu.edu/. Thanks to these historians for their generous assistance and contributions.

6. Catherine W. Bishir, "The Importance of Slave Hiring in Antebellum North Carolina," Society for Historians of the Early American Republic, annual meeting, 2021.

7. Bishir, "Black Builders," 81; and Bishir et al., *Architects and Builders in North Carolina,* 158; quote, Dabney Cosby to Dabney Cosby Jr., November 28, 1850, Dabney Cosby Papers, Southern Historical Collection, University of North Carolina, Chapel Hill [hereafter SHC].

8. Bishir, "Black Builders," 84; quote from Johann David Schoepf, *Travels in the Confederation (1783–1784),* 2 vols., trans. and ed. Alfred J. Morrison (New York: Burt Franklin, [1911], 1968), 2: 148.

9. David S. Cecelski, *The Fire of Freedom: Abraham Galloway and the Slaves' Civil War* (Chapel Hill: University of North Carolina Press, 2012). According to Cecelski, Abraham Galloway later indicated that his father acknowledged his paternity and "protected me as far as he was able," Cecelski, *Fire of Freedom,* 4. Cecelski writes that Galloway's difficulty in earning the full amount his enslaver required, coupled with the fear of being sold, spurred his escape by sea to Philadelphia.

10. Guion Griffis Johnson, *Ante-Bellum North Carolina: A Social History* (Chapel Hill: University of North Carolina Press, 1937), 531–32; *Revised Statutes of North Carolina,* 1837, 1, Ch. 111, sec. 21; and *Session Laws,* 1827, Ch. 92. Typically, the punishment for flouting such laws involved fines for free offenders and whippings for enslaved ones.

11. *Wilmington Gazette,* February 10, 1803; November 15, 1808.

12. See the *New Bern Weekly Journal,* November 29, 1854, for a summary of complaints about self-hiring of slaves and a demand to prohibit slaves from learning skilled trades.

13. Carl Bridenbaugh, *The Colonial Craftsman* (Chicago: University of Chicago Press, 1961), 31, 120, 138, 140; Ira Berlin and Herbert G. Gutman, "Natives and Immigrants, Free Men and Slaves: Urban Workingmen in the Antebellum American South," *American Historical Review* 88 (December 1983): 1192.

14. See entries for these individuals in *North Carolina Architects and Builders,* https://ncarchitects.lib.ncsu.edu/. See also Bishir et al., *Architects and Builders in North Carolina,* 157–59, 185–86.

15. Bishir, "Black Builders in Antebellum North Carolina," 83–84.

16. Several newly restrictive laws came in 1831, partly in response to the 1829 publication of David Walker's *An Appeal to the Colored Citizens of the World* (Boston: 1830) and other abolitionist tracts and to growing White fears of slave rebellion. These fears were intensified by Nat Turner's rebellion in Virginia, which occurred shortly after the North Carolina legislature passed the new laws of 1831. See Bishir, *Crafting Lives,* 102–3.

17. Bishir, *Bellamy Mansion,* 27; *North Carolina Architects and Builders,* s.v. "Henry Taylor," by Catherine W. Bishir, Beverly Tetterton, and Ellen Weiss (2010), https://ncarchitects.lib.ncsu.edu/people/P000488; quote from Booker T. Washington, *The Story of the Negro Volume II: The Rise of the Race from Slavery* (London: T. Fisher Unwin, 1901), 81.

18. Bishir, "Black Builders," 86–87; *North Carolina Architects and Builders,* s.v. "Harry," by J. Marshall Bullock (2009), https://ncarchitects.lib.ncsu.edu/people/P000331; quotes from Battle Family Papers, SHC.

19. Bishir, "Black Builders," 86–87; *North Carolina Architects and Builders,* s.v. "Harry," https://ncarchitects.lib.ncsu.edu/people/P000331; quotes from Battle Family Papers, SHC.

20. Bishir, "Black Builders," 86–87; *North Carolina Architects and Builders,* s.v. "Harry," https://ncarchitects

.lib.ncsu.edu/people/P000331; quotes from Battle Family Papers, SHC.

21. Bishir, "'Severe Survitude to House Building,'" 126–56; see also materials from the Hayes Collection, SHC.

22. Bishir, "'Severe Survitude to House Building,'" 135–37.

23. Bishir, "Black Builders," 76; *North Carolina Architects and Builders,* s.v. "Joe Welcome," by Catherine W. Bishir (2009), https://ncarchitects.lib.ncsu.edu/people/P000186. For Josiah Collins's account of the daily work of Joe Welcome and other enslaved workmen at the Edenton Academy, see Bishir, "Black Builders," 98–100. For James Johnston's records of Welcome's payments for work at Hayes see Bishir, "'Severe Survitude to House Building,'" 139–40.

24. Bishir, "'Severe Survitude to House Building,'" 135–36.

25. On the "contract mode" of building and the rise of contractors in building in the antebellum period see Bishir et al., *Architects and Builders in North Carolina,* 145–61.

26. Bishir, *Bellamy Mansion,* 28. An important source used therein is Rufus W. Bunnell, "The Life of Rufus William Bunnell" (ca. 1900), Bunnell Family Papers, Sterling Library, Yale University, New Haven, Conn., photocopy in possession of the Bellamy Mansion, Wilmington. On James F. Post, see *North Carolina Architects and Builders,* s.v. "James F. Post," by Janet K. Seapker (2009), https://ncarchitects.lib.ncsu.edu/people/P000212. As noted by Seapker, Post's records include the names of several enslaved workmen whom he hired.

27. Bishir, *Bellamy Mansion,* 20.

28. *Wilmington Star-News,* July 16, 1934.

29. Bishir, "Black Builders," 97.

30. Bishir, "Black Builders"; *North Carolina Architects and Builders,* s.v. "Price Family," by Catherine W. Bishir (2010), https://ncarchitects.lib.ncsu.edu/people/P000475; *Wilmington Star-News,* July 16, 1934.

31. Bishir, *Bellamy Mansion,* 27–28; William B. Gould IV, "William B. Gould," in Reaves and Tetterton, *Strength through Struggle,* 471–72; William B. Gould IV, *Diary of a Contraband: The Civil War Passage of a Black Sailor* (Stanford, Calif.: Stanford University Press, 2002); *North Carolina Architects and Builders,* s.v. "William B. Gould I," by Catherine W. Bishir (2015), https://ncarchitects.lib.ncsu.edu/people/P000320.

32. Bishir, "Black Builders," 72.

33. Bishir, "Black Builders," 84–85; Elizabeth Reid Murray, "Stewart Ellison," in William S. Powell, ed., *Dictionary of North Carolina Biography,* 6 vols. (Chapel Hill: University of North Carolina Press, 1986) 2: 152–53; *North Carolina Architects and Builders,* s.v. "Stewart Ellison," by Catherine W. Bishir and Elizabeth Reid Murray (2009), https://ncarchitects.lib.ncsu.edu/people/P000337. Because of his postwar political prominence and Murray's research, Ellison is one of the few formerly enslaved building artisans in the state whose biography has been well known for many years.

34. Bishir, *Crafting Lives,* 76; quote from *North Carolina Star,* December 6, 1810.

35. Bishir, *Crafting Lives,* 53; quote from *Ulysses, Norfolk and Portsmouth (Va.) Herald,* February 2, 1818.

36. Bishir, *Crafting Lives,* 53–60.

37. Bishir, "Black Builders," 81–82; *North Carolina Architects and Builders,* s.v. "Jacob W. Holt," by Catherine W. Bishir (2009), https://ncarchitects.lib.ncsu.edu/people/P000039; *North Carolina Architects and Builders,* s.v. "Corbin Boyd," by Catherine W. Bishir (2009), https://ncarchitects.lib.ncsu.edu/people/P000151. The fact that the substantial number of slaves listed under Holt's name in the United States censuses is not confirmed in either tax records or in the valuation of personal property in the 1860 census calls into question whether listings of slaves under a given person's name in the census always indicate ownership. In Holt's case, it appears not to.

38. Bishir, "Black Builders," 82–83; Bishir, *Crafting Lives,* 58–59. The source of Donnell's dealings is the John R. Donnell Account Book, Bryan Family Papers, SHC.

39. Bishir, *Crafting Lives,* 115–16.

40. John R. Donnell Account Book, Bryan Family Papers, SHC.

41. Bishir, *Crafting Lives,* 60; *Raleigh Register,* June 27, 1855.

42. Bishir, "Price Family."

43. Bishir, "Black Builders," 94.

44. Bishir, "Black Builders," 97.

45. *Wilmington Gazette,* February 10, 1803, and November 15, 1808.

46. Bishir, "Black Builders," 96–97.

47. Bishir, *Crafting Lives,* 71, 76.

48. Bishir, *Crafting Lives,* 117–18, 288–89; *New Bern Daily Progress,* December 14, 1858 (final quotation).

49. *North Carolina Architects and Builders,* s.v. "Dave Dickinson (Dickerson)," by Catherine W. Bishir (2009), https://ncarchitects.lib.ncsu.edu/people/P000189. As noted therein, "Dave Dickinson was evidently enslaved for most of his life but operated almost as a free man. An intriguing entry in the United States census of 1840 listed in Edenton one David Dickinson who, according to the check marks on the census form, was head of a household that included no free people, White or of color, but four slaves—the total number of people cited for the household. Three members of the household were occupied in manufacturing or a trade. It is possible (though it would be unusual) that the census taker might list a slave household in this way, perhaps thus identifying the household of a well-known person living essentially as a free man. (There are also a few other heads of households listed in Edenton in the same census in which no free persons are included, and the total number of household members is the same as the number of enslaved people. Whether these listings were errors or actually represented separate households of enslaved persons is unknown.)"

50. Bishir, "Black Builders," 116–17; quotes from Paul Cameron to Duncan Cameron, November, 1834, Camerone Family Papers, SHC.

51. *Halifax North-Carolina Free Press,* February 18, 1825.

52. *Raleigh Register,* August 17, 1827.

53. *Milton Spectator,* January 3, 1837.

54. *Hillsboro Recorder,* December 5, 1821.

55. *North Carolina Star,* December 15, 1836.

56. *Wilmington Gazette,* February 3, 1807.

57. *Weekly Observer* (Fayetteville), March 28, 1838.

58. *Daily Herald* (Wilmington), September 20, 1855.

59. Bishir, "Black Builders," 69. Illustrating the luck involved in finding such evidence, I was shown the privately owned Massenburg journal during fieldwork in Franklin County, N.C., in the mid-1970s.

60. Bishir, "Black Builders," 79. By contrast, among the many workers employed in the 1833–40 construction of the state capitol, all of the artisans were free men, and nearly all were White, whereas a large number of the laborers and quarrymen were enslaved men hired from their owners. Reasons for the absence of enslaved artisans in the project will be explored in the author's current study of the capitol builders.

61. *Raleigh Register,* March 14, 1849. The east-west railroad was soon named the North Carolina Rail Road. As its proponents predicted, it made commercial agriculture and manufacturing more profitable.

62. *Wilmington Journal,* October 26, 1849; *Weekly Standard* (Raleigh), June 19, 1850, and July 10, 1850; *Wilmington Journal,* November 1, 1850; *Semi-Weekly Standard* (Raleigh), February 22 and April 9, 1851.

63. Cecelski, *The Fire of Freedom,* 217.

64. Elizabeth Reid Murray, "Stewart Ellison," in Powell, *Dictionary of North Carolina Biography,* 2: 152–53; *North Carolina Architects and Builders,* s.v. "Stewart Ellison," by Catherine W. Bishir and Elizabeth Reid Murray (2009), https://ncarchitects.lib.ncsu.edu/people/P000337. Quote from Charles N. Hunter, "Stewart Ellison," *Daily Examiner,* February 19, 1874, clipping in Charles N. Hunter Scrapbook, Charles N. Hunter Collection, Rare Book, Manuscript, and Special Collections Library, Duke University, Durham, N.C.

65. *Gazette* (Raleigh), December 5, 1896.

66. Bishir, "Price Family"; Reaves and Tetterton, "Strength through Struggle," 449–50; *Wilmington Star,* July 26, 1871; *Wilmington Dispatch,* June 13 and August 20, 1895.

67. Bishir, *Crafting Lives,* 234–35; quote from Horace James, "A Freedman's Wedding," 1866, in *Household Reading Selections from the Congregationalist, 1849–1866* (Boston: Galen James and Co., 1867).

68. Bishir, *Crafting Lives,* 288–89; quote from Elizabeth Vass Wilkerson, ed., *The Diary of Rev. L. C. Vass, D.D., Chaplain, Stonewall Brigade* (n. p., privately published, 2008).

69. Bishir, "Henry Taylor." On Robert Taylor, see Ellen Weiss, *Robert R. Taylor and Tuskegee: An African American Architect Designs for Booker T. Washington* (Montgomery, Ala.: New South Books, 2012).

70. *Wilmington Journal,* October 26, 1849; *Weekly Standard* (Raleigh), June 19, 1850, and July 10, 1850; *Wilmington Journal,* November 1, 1850; *Semi-Weekly Standard* (Raleigh), February 22 and April 9, 1851.

ROBERT W. CRAIG

# *Research Note:* Fire Insurance Records and the Architectural Historian

ABSTRACT
One of the largest bodies of descriptive information about the American built environment lies hidden in fire insurance records, especially those from the late eighteenth through the early twentieth centuries. Insurance companies faced a universal need to describe the properties they insured for reasons related to the proper management of their businesses, recording these "risks" in written volumes called policy registers and daily reports and in graphic documents known as insurance surveys. Local insurance agents also kept their own policy registers and sometimes copies of the surveys they produced for the insurance companies. As this case study of research from New Jersey indicates, architectural historians who actively search for surviving collections of fire insurance records will find tremendous reward for their efforts, especially in the discovery of vernacular buildings and landscapes.

For architectural historians in the United States, the vast scope of recordkeeping produced by and for the nation's fire insurance companies and their agents holds great potential to inform, and sometimes to transform, vernacular architecture studies.[1] Any type of building that one may wish to research was probably insured, and surviving records may document it. Fire insurance companies faced a universal need to describe the buildings they insured, to ascertain their real estate values, to confirm that they were neither underinsured nor overinsured, and to ensure that damage claims could be paid out in the proper amounts. Even from the early years of the American fire insurance industry in the eighteenth century, companies produced and collected descriptive records of their insured "risks." The very ubiquity of fire insurance coverage almost rivals that of land title records. If architectural historians can discover the many collections of century-old and older fire insurance records that likely still exist, and make them yield their riches, researchers will discover a broad trove of information bearing directly on features of the built environment.

Some of the information these records provide is otherwise virtually undiscoverable. For example, New York City socialite Kate Shippen Roosevelt, whose late husband, Hilborn Roosevelt, was a first cousin of President Theodore Roosevelt, had a house designed and built for summertime entertaining in a secluded area of western Monmouth County, New Jersey, about 1907. Many memories must have been made there, and Roosevelt wrote about her experiences as the house was constructed. But the house burned in the 1960s, no photographs are known to survive, its precise location is obscure, and only a site plan sketch produced by an insurance agent survives as a graphic representation (Figure 1).

Architectural historians have yet to tap much of this material. When asked what they know of the records of insurance companies or agencies, architectural historians almost universally respond that they are familiar with maps produced

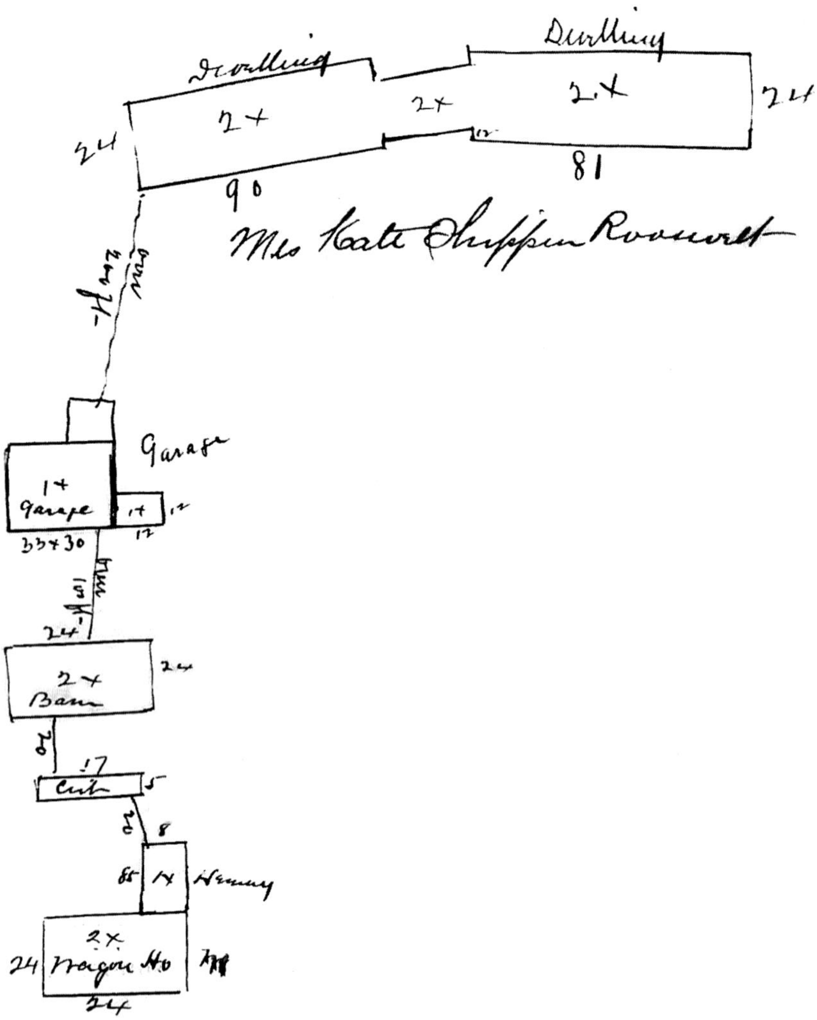


Figure 1. Sketch site plan of the Kate Shippen Roosevelt farm in western Monmouth County, New Jersey, ca. 1907. Roosevelt, a New York City socialite, used this house for summertime entertaining. The house no longer stands and this sketch is its only known graphic representation. Allen & Stults Company fire insurance surveys, vol. 1, p. 24. Courtesy of the Allen & Stults Company.

by the Sanborn Fire Insurance Company. Sanborns, of course, have long been the most popular type of insurance-related mapping, but the Sanborn Company and its competitors were suppliers *to* the insurance industry, not, strictly speaking, part of it. Others might respond, "I guess you mean old insurance policies?" Not really. Of course, the written policy issued to the insurance customer was the industry's most basic and fundamental document, but the policy itself never provided much architectural information since the property owner did not need a paper from the insurance company to describe his own house. Policies did state how much insurance was placed on a building, and in the case of a property with multiple buildings, like a farm, they enumerated each building and stated the amount of coverage placed on it. This, even by itself, can be useful information in the absence of superior records, but companies and agents kept more detailed ones.

A major attraction of studying insurance records is that almost any kind of building one can imagine was insured. Companies accepted a wide variety of risks: residential, agricultural, commercial, industrial, civic, educational, and religious. The same companies also began selling casualty insurance in the nineteenth century for disasters that did not involve a fire. Insurance companies provided coverage for furnishings and for industrial equipment inside factories. Specialized firms arose to exploit niche markets, including insuring farmers' livestock and the plate glass of commercial windows. Identified collections of surviving insurance records, although still relatively few in number, make clear that buildings of all kinds and values were being insured.

This article introduces the reader to the most common and widespread types of fire insurance records that contain architectural information. Though they are not traditionally considered "architectural," they nonetheless matter-of-factly and routinely convey physical and spatial information about buildings from the perspective of a profession that, while very attuned to building design and construction practices, was nonetheless a dispassionate outside observer. The insurance industry worked steadily to improve practices to make fires less frequent and less damaging when they did occur. It needed to know much about the cost of building construction to ensure that in the event of the loss of a $2,000 house, for example, they would not be pressured into paying $4,000 for replacement. The industry's records of the buildings it insured allowed it to settle claims fairly.

For descriptive architectural content, the key fire insurance records are chiefly of three types: the policy register, the insurance survey, and a record that became popular later called the daily report. These types of records hold the architectural information that the companies and their agents collected. I have illustrated each of them below from examples that depict New Jersey buildings, the state where I have made most of my insurance-related finds, but the record types they represent were in widespread use and not unique to any state.

### The Policy Register

A policy register is a record book in which each of a company's (or an agent's) insurance policies are abstracted. Such a register is almost always organized by policy number in ascending numerical order. Both companies and agents kept policy registers. An agent would keep a register for each company for which he was writing coverage. Periodically, each company would send a field representative to visit each agency to consult their agents' corresponding policy register, to copy out information to update their own registers, and to collect the company's premiums, minus the agents' commissions. This explains why registers kept by the companies themselves were derivative of those produced by the agents, and may be less informative than the agents' registers, since the companies may have been selective in the information they copied. Registers also became the agent's (or, when necessary, the company's) essential instrument for customer relations, since one could easily find the proper entry by policy number if the customer could provide that information, or, if not, then by the customer's name through the volume's own index. Policy registers also enumerated the amount of insurance placed on each building.

Insurance "blotters," which were kept by the Insurance Company of North America (INA) between 1794 to at least 1805, and which take the form of manuscript booklets describing insured properties, are a primitive form of policy register. For example, Philemon Dickinson, who insured his Philadelphia property with INA, took out policy number 1495 for his New Jersey farm, "called the Hermitage, near the east bank of the Delaware, about one mile and a quarter from the City of Trenton." The blotter described the property as containing "a Two-Story Stone Dwelling House, a framed Dwelling House adjoining the foregoing with a Piazza in front and rear, a Stone Kitchen, a framed Kitchen, and a Piazza connecting the framed Dwelling House and the framed Kitchen." He insured the buildings for $3,000 and the furniture in the stone dwelling for $800. These were one-year policies that he renewed several times.[2] Later registers almost always take the form of a folio-sized bound volume. Such registers are almost entirely text-based and have very little to no graphic content. Their descriptive value depends on the length of their entries.

Policy registers vary widely. The most meager entries would not support a detailed investigation of an individual building. Some contain little more than the number of stories of a building, its type—for example, a dwelling—and whether its walls were of stone, frame, or brick. The entries in most registers, however, contain at least some further description of a building's footprint and three-dimensional massing. Still more useful registers include descriptive information that may be hard to find elsewhere, including the sizes of additions, porches, and outbuildings. Some policy registers go beyond even this to describe the number of rooms inside, along with their sizes and uses. This information provides clues to the interior floor plans.

A policy register produced by Haddonfield, New Jersey, insurance agent J. Lewis Rowand survives, covering the years 1854–81. The following entry from 1880 illustrates the "moderate" level of detail common to this record type:

524 Re-Survey for Isaac Browning Taken April
29, 1880, for Ten Years . . . as follows
To wit: on his 1 1/2-story Brick Tenant house
4x28 ft. $600.
on his Leanto frame shed back 14 x 4
Premium note at 5 per ct $30.
cash on % of Premium note $6.00
Incidental expenses 2.75
Total Cash $8.75
Situate in the City of Gloucester, County of
Camden New Jersey, on the Eastwardly side
of Burlington
Policy street, 28 feet North of Somerset Street, aged
No. 30389 about 25 years and in good condition
and repair—used as a dwelling house
only and occupied by a careful tenant—
Adjoins two other brick buildings of
the same description—the one on the
North, the other on the South of the one
described—in front is a 60 feet wide
street and in the rear an open lot—No
Manufactories or special uses and no
other insurance on the premises.[3]

While the description of this small row house is meager, the entry takes pains to characterize its condition, describe its surroundings, and identify that it was occupied by a tenant. The frequency with which such entries identify tenant-occupied buildings, for example, might enable a researcher to map the material culture of tenancy across a community and contrast it with the material culture of owner-occupancy. Combined with city directories, one could add occupational dimensions to such a study.[4]

Policy registers are useful in other ways as well. They sometimes report the age of a building, from which its construction date could be deduced (though this information often needs to be treated with caution). Rowand's policy register, for example, often states that a building was either "new" or that it had been constructed within the past building season. They routinely report the name of the policyholder, often explicitly indicate the ownership of the property, and, if leased, the names of tenants (sometimes the tenant was the policyholder). Over time, they may include the names of a succession of owners or tenants, which may be very helpful in checking the accuracy of land title evidence and provide a fuller history of occupancy than might otherwise be obtained, either from decennial census records or even annual city directories. Hidden family connections sometimes emerge. Register entries also sometimes report the construction of additional new buildings or the removal of older ones from coverage. Such removals from a policy may be the result of destruction, or because the owner no longer needed to pay for insurance on a building no longer in use. These entries may be the best source of information for ephemeral buildings, or perhaps identify ephemeral uses of buildings.

### The Insurance Survey

To fully understand what they were insuring and to make certain that their agents were applying good underwriting judgment, many companies required their agents to provide a document known as an insurance survey. These surveys began as careful written descriptions of the insured properties. Among the best are those of the Philadelphia Contributionship, the United States' oldest fire insurance company, founded in 1752.[5] The Contributionship's early surveys are particularly descriptive because they were produced by members of the Carpenters' Company of the City and County of Philadelphia, master builders whose business included measuring construction work to ensure that builders were properly paid.

By the early nineteenth century, surveys for many companies came to commonly include a top-down, site plan view of the property. William R. Tharp, for example, chronicled the evolution of the Short Pump Tavern, near Richmond, Virginia, and reproduced two early nineteenth-century fire insurance surveys that provided plan views of the tavern itself and other nearby buildings.[6] They show the footprint of each section of the buildings, the size of each footprint, the buildings' uses, and often the materials of their walls and roofs.

Even after insurance mapping of the Sanborn type became available, surveys were still produced in rural areas that lacked Sanborn coverage, as well as for properties where significant recent changes rendered existing Sanborn coverage out of date. Importantly, surveys came to characteristically show the distances in feet between one building and another. This was vital to insurance companies, who understood that if fires occurred, they would more likely be contained to a single building if that building was at a sufficient remove from others. Especially in towns or cities, surveys often showed the locations of buildings on adjoining properties, sometimes up to one hundred feet away. Survey by survey, one can sometimes piece together entire small villages or neighborhoods that did not have Sanborn coverage.

The Historical Society of Pennsylvania holds a large collection containing tens of thousands of surveys of both the Franklin Fire Insurance Company of Philadelphia and the Pennsylvania Fire Insurance Company, collectively called the Franklin Fire Collection. The surveys were issued during the period from about 1830 to the early 1880s. Although the great majority of these records describe Philadelphia buildings, perhaps as many as two thousand describe New Jersey buildings, chiefly in the cities of Camden, Burlington, and Trenton, and elsewhere in their respective counties. In nearly every case, these surveys provide a much higher level of architectural description than the policy registers do—the most detailed written description of any insurance record that this author has seen—with information about interior features and finishes. The survey of the Reeve-Shepherd house in Greenwich, Cumberland County, New Jersey, in 1838 describes it in part as follows:

> The 5 front windows have marble heads and sills—the front door is finished with a wooden frontispiece and has a threshold 2 steps and a platform of marble. The windows are finished with shutters six pairs paneled and 4 pair are venetian. . . . The lower floor [consists of] 2 rooms, [an] entry and staircase. The front room or parlour is 15 by 17 feet fire place with a wooden mantel and jambs faced up with variegated marble—hearth of the same material.[7]

Nearly all include graphic representations of the building's footprint and plan, either drawn to scale or with interior dimensions provided. Some provide a plan of each floor of the building. An 1853 plan of the First Presbyterian Church of Trenton, New Jersey, prepared for the Franklin Fire Insurance Company, in-

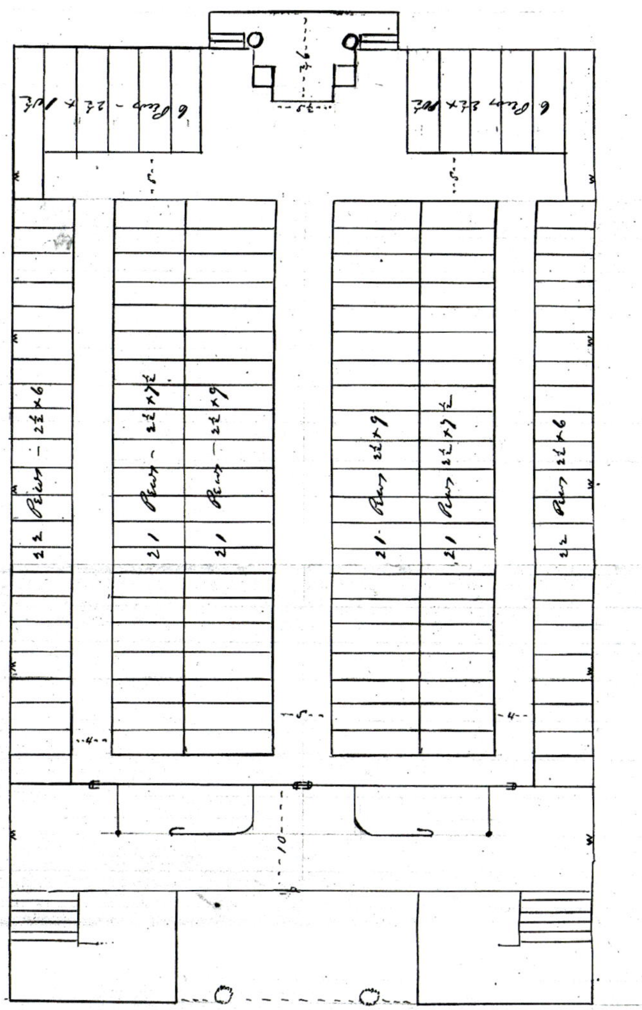

Figure 2. Franklin Fire Insurance Company survey no. 19407, plan of sanctuary, First Presbyterian Church of Trenton, New Jersey, 1853. Henry Austin, architect. Collections of the Historical Society of Pennsylvania.

Figure 3. First Presbyterian Church of Trenton, 2021. Photograph by Robert W. Craig.

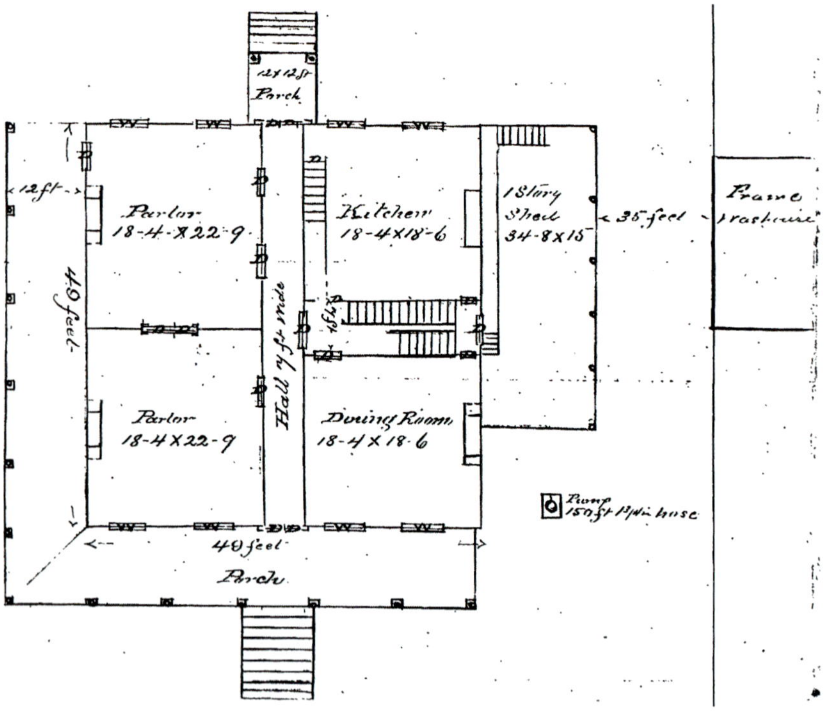


Figure 4. INA survey of the Atsion mansion, 1870. The first-floor plan depicted here was the only interior representation of the house the restoration design team had available to inform its work, and thus was crucial to the outcome. INA Records, Chubb Archives, Philadelphia.

Figure 5. Atsion mansion, Burlington County, New Jersey. Built in 1826 as an ironmaster's house, the building is shown here following a restoration completed in 2014. Photograph by the New Jersey Department of Environmental Protection. Used with permission.

cluded plan drawings of both the basement story and of the sanctuary above (Figure 2).[8] Listed in the National Register of Historic Places for its Greek revival design, it was the work of Henry Austin, a prominent New Haven, Connecticut, architect who completed it in 1840 (Figure 3). Its survey includes a written description of the church's architectural features. The plans depict it substantially as completed little more than a decade earlier, before later alterations were made. The sanctuary is shown with its chancel, the shape and placement of its pulpit, and the original plan of its pews.

Such records of alteration can be crucial to restoration efforts. The Atsion mansion, built in 1826 in Burlington County, New Jersey, was an ironmaster's house. A later owner insured it with INA in 1870, and the house was surveyed (Figure 4). The survey includes a plan of the mansion's first floor, showing an unusual interior arrangement that separated public and private circulation and provided large first-floor rooms resulting in a narrow central hallway. The survey also documents the presence of a washhouse (long since disappeared) near the mansion, and a well with a water pump supplied with 150 feet of one-and-a-quarter-inch hose. The state of New Jersey, the mansion's owner, finished restoring the building in 2014 (Figure 5). The survey provided crucial information that helped distinguish original walls and finishes from post-1870 alterations.[9] The mansion had been previously remodeled on the inside with additional room partitions that produced a confusing puzzle to the architectural team who planned the restoration, who did not have access to any other surviving historical drawings of the house. The insurance survey's first-floor plan, with its interior room measurements, allowed the identification of the walls that were still in their original locations.

Such plans also convey a fair amount of information about the structures of adjoining properties, such that a researcher who is studying one property might benefit from finding a site plan for any of its abutters. A survey of the Garwood house in Salem City, New Jersey, shows how a survey can provide useful information beyond its borders (Figure 6). The building stands today as a surviving nineteenth-century hotel in the center of the city's downtown. Beginning in the middle of the eighteenth century as a fancy patterned-brickwork house on Market Street near Broadway (its origin only rediscovered about two decades ago), the building was enlarged into a four-story hotel in the 1850s.[10] A circa 1888 photograph of the Garwood House shows a building very consistent with the survey conducted in 1880 (Figure 7). Hotels were multiuse properties that provided food and lodging, livery service, public meeting rooms, and sometimes offices for select local businesses. Garwood provided the amenity of a reading room for its guests, conveniently located in front of the barroom, in the portion of the building that had been the mid-eighteenth-century house. The survey implies that the interior partitions in that part of the building had been removed in the transformation of it into a hotel. A long, transverse hallway linked all the major spaces of the first story. How these ancillary uses were arranged is seldom made clear in other records. But this survey also suggests how spaces *outside* of the buildings were used.

Some companies apparently did not require surveys, but surviving records suggest that more companies than those known from identified collections surely did. One example is a surviving policy of the Mercer County Mutual Fire Insurance Company of New Jersey, dated July 10, 1848, stated on the printed policy form, "agreeably to a Survey on file in this Office," meaning that the company, like Franklin, used, collected, and filed its own insurance surveys (its collection of surveys has not been found).[11] Sometimes, one company would note in its policy register the existence of a survey held by another company. Surveys were, however, the responsibility of the agents to produce, and where large numbers of these surveys exist, one sees the same agents' handwriting repeatedly. Some surveys are signed, others not. Insurance companies retained their surveys, while many agencies also evidently kept copies (or draft copies).

To the great advantage of architectural historians, nineteenth-century fire insurance records were extremely redundant. This is especially noteworthy when a researcher is focused on a specific building. Descriptions or surveys no longer available may have been copied in a different, surviving collection. Companies and agencies kept similar information, and over time the

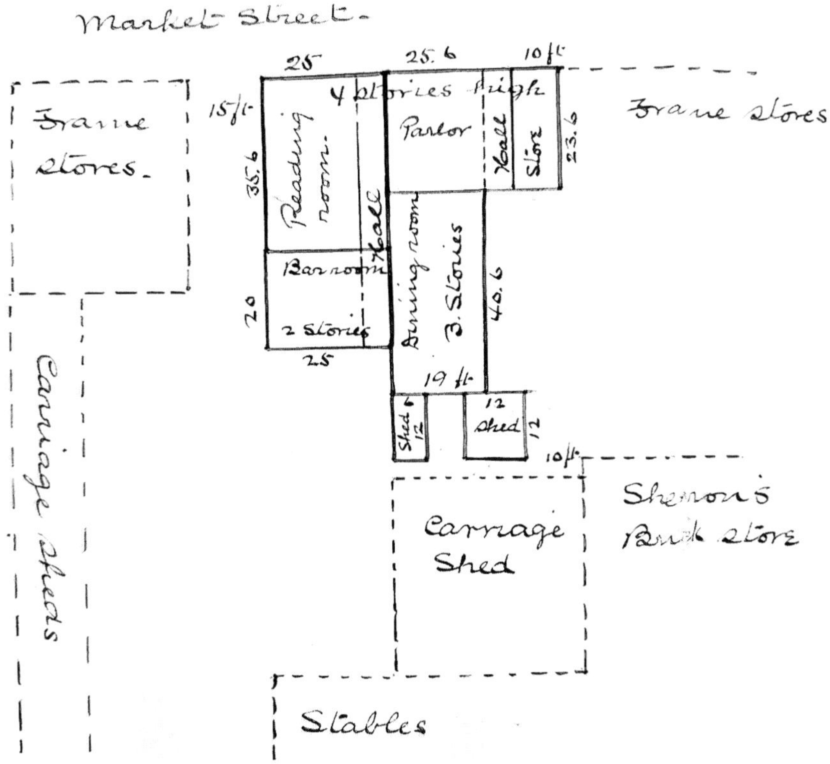


Figure 6. Insurance survey of the Garwood house, Salem City, New Jersey, in 1880. Salem County Mutual Insurance Company Collection, Salem County Historical Society.

Figure 7. The Garwood house in downtown Salem City, New Jersey, from a photograph taken ca. 1888. Collections of the Salem County Historical Society.

same building was likely the subject of multiple insurance records. As long as the same owner continued to insure a property through the same agency, the time horizon of a policy register entry would lengthen. The longer such an entry continued, the more information it would accrue, including minor changes to buildings thought to be not so extensive as to require a new survey. If insurance continued to be placed with the same company, a survey previously prepared could continue to serve. Agents handling insurance renewals would refer to their policy register to update their entry. Changes in ownership or tenancy would also be recorded. Few policy register entries, however, covered more than a decade or two—most covered just a few years. Over several decades, therefore, a property was likely to be the subject of several entries in policy registers, as different owners chose different agencies or different insurance companies. In such situations, more than one survey was likely made, suggesting that a property's evolution over decades might be revealed.

### The Daily Report

About 1885, some of the major national insurance companies developed similar printed forms for use by their agents. Called daily reports, these point-of-sale forms served the same purposes as the insurance survey but could be completed more quickly and cheaply.[12] They can provide similar information to the researcher as do surveys, including evidence of long-demolished buildings.

Agents completed daily reports on the day a policy was purchased, then mailed the documents to the company on the day on which the insurance took effect (the postmark on the form would serve as evidence of the date of activation). The forms consisted of two sides of a single sheet of paper and apparently were intended to supplant the survey for all but industrial properties and the largest nonindustrial ones. Daily reports did not replace the policy register, however, which continued to be maintained throughout the nineteenth century and beyond. Companies also created their own versions of daily reports to serve special purposes. The Continental Insurance Company, for example, created a Farm Daily Report.

The front side of a daily report form provided space for the policy number, and to identify the property, its location and its owner or tenant (Figure 8). The space was further divided to categorize the information about improvements to the property, though descriptive text was mostly kept to a minimum. A series of directed questions triggered a series of short or one-word answers. Space is provided on the reverse side for a floor plan or site plan sketch, within a box usually containing a quadrille of lightly printed broken lines to aid in keeping the sketch in scale (Figure 9). In many of the versions of this form that companies supplied their agents, the letters N, E, S, and W mark the cardinal points of the compass to encourage surveys to be properly oriented.

In the case of farmsteads, the site plan sketches usually identified each building by its use, provided the size of its footprint, and provided the spacings between buildings. For example, in Figure 9, which shows the reverse side of a daily report prepared about 1895, the central focus is not the dwelling that faces the Hightstown and Perrineville Turnpike, but rather the gristmill that stands behind it to the northeast. This document is the only known representation of this building, built about 1773 in the village of Etra, near Hightstown, and of the sawmill attached to it. The daily report states that the mill was still in operation and that it remained a profitable business, which is somewhat unusual for local gristmills in central New Jersey in this period. When the mill was destroyed about 1900, it was not rebuilt.

### Factory Surveys

As the insurance industry grew and matured in the fourth quarter of the nineteenth century, it became too expensive to continue to produce individual surveys for all but the largest and most complex properties. Sanborn maps and their competitors had begun to appear by the 1870s, and competition between firms led to continuing downward pressure on the rates charged for insurance premiums. Such surveys accordingly found their highest expression in the insuring of industrial properties, which had much higher valuations and dollar premiums. These surveys continue to provide invaluable information to

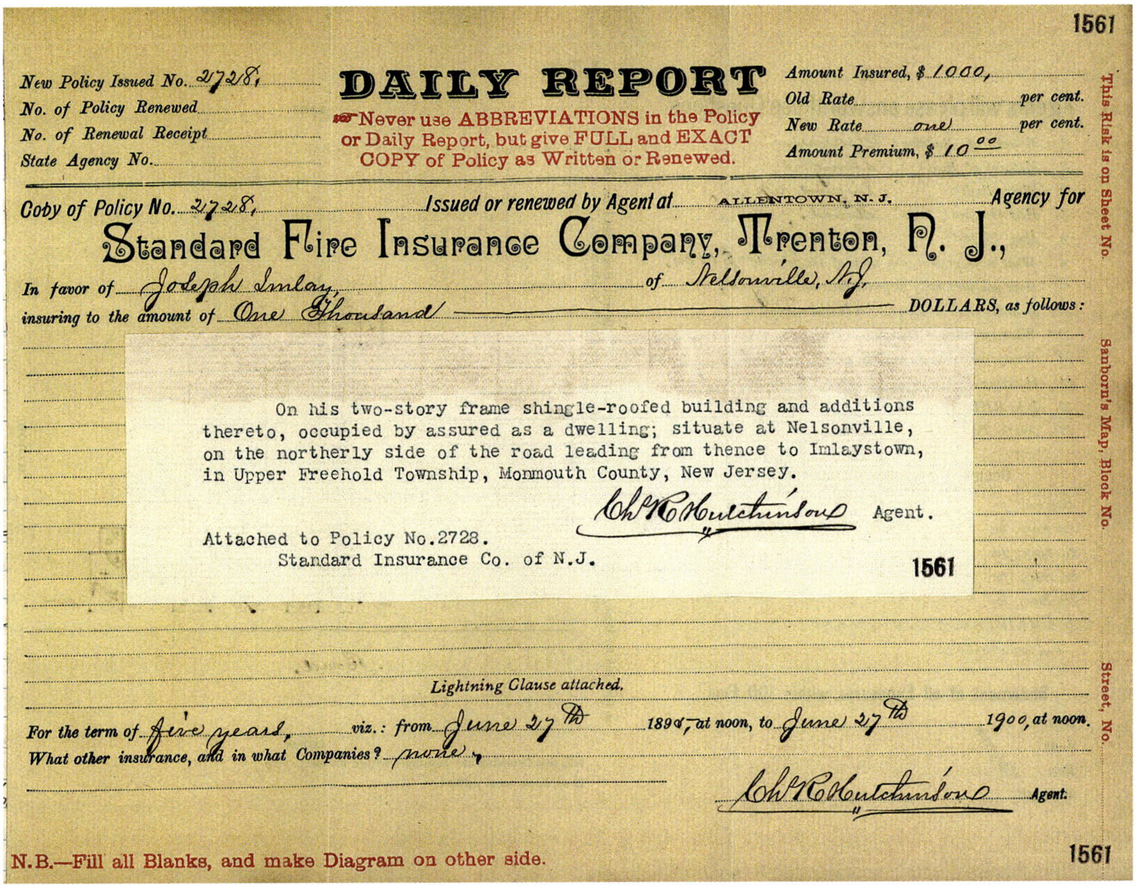
1561

New Policy Issued No. 2728,
No. of Policy Renewed
No. of Renewal Receipt
State Agency No.

DAILY REPORT

Never use ABBREVIATIONS in the Policy or Daily Report, but give FULL and EXACT COPY of Policy as Written or Renewed.

Amount Insured, $ 1000,
Old Rate ........ per cent.
New Rate one per cent.
Amount Premium, $ 10 00

Coby of Policy No. 2728, Issued or renewed by Agent at ALLENTOWN, N. J. Agency for

Standard Fire Insurance Company, Trenton, N. J.,

In favor of Joseph Imlay, of Nelsonville, N.J.
insuring to the amount of One Thousand ——— DOLLARS, as follows:

On his two-story frame shingle-roofed building and additions thereto, occupied by assured as a dwelling; situate at Nelsonville, on the northerly side of the road leading from thence to Imlaystown, in Upper Freehold Township, Monmouth County, New Jersey.

Ch. H. C. Hutchinson Agent.

Attached to Policy No.2728.
Standard Insurance Co. of N.J.

1561

Lightning Clause attached.

For the term of five years, viz.: from June 27th 1895, at noon, to June 27th 1900, at noon.
What other insurance, and in what Companies? none,

Ch. H. C. Hutchinson Agent.

N.B.—Fill all Blanks, and make Diagram on other side.

1561

This Risk is on Sheet No. Sanborn's Map, Block No. Street, No.

Figure 8. The face of a daily report form for the Standard Fire Insurance Company, 1900. Many insurance companies created their own versions of this form, all very similar. Agents were directed to mail a copy to the company on the day that a new policy or new coverage went into effect, hence the name. Collection no. 49, Monmouth County Historical Association, Freehold, N.J.

researchers about both individual sites and entire industries.

While many of the smaller companies refused to insure industrial properties at all, others did not observe a blanket prohibition. Industrial sites made up a relatively small portion of the business of the Salem County Mutual Insurance Company in the city of Salem, New Jersey, but the company had a conspicuous practice of insuring glass-manufacturing facilities. Glassmaking was an important industry in southern New Jersey, and Salem Mutual's applications for insurance—and the site plans that accompany them—form snapshots of the industry at different stages of its industrialization. Over time, its surveys show how glassmaking operations developed from sites organized in separate buildings, widely spaced for fire safety reasons, into singular larger buildings using fire-resistant construction for the sake of greater industrial efficiency. Anyone studying the glass industry in the mid-Atlantic region would do well to search this collection.

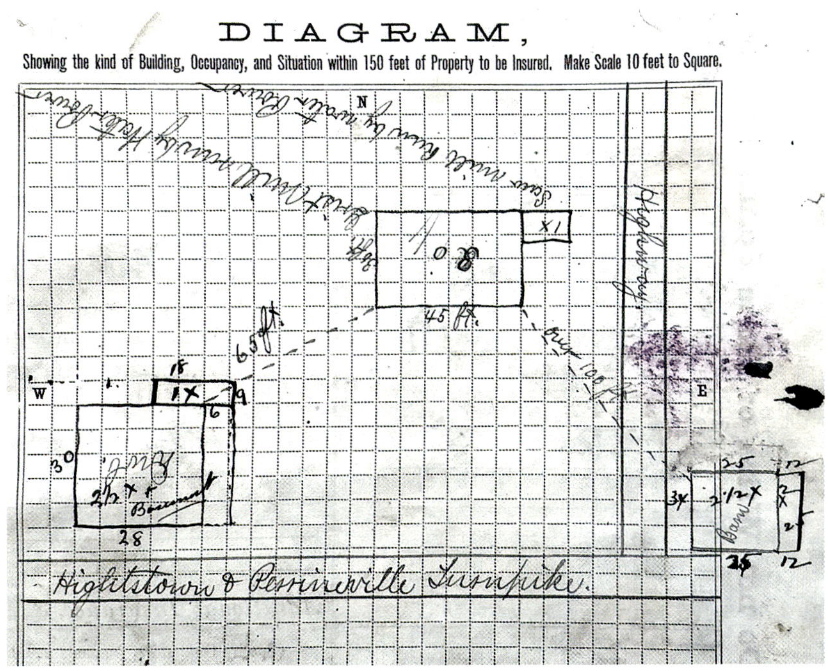


Figure 9. Detail of the reverse side of a daily report form, ca.1895. This document provides the only known representation of the gristmill shown here, which was built in 1773 and disappeared ca. 1900, and of the sawmill attached to it. From the Allen & Stults book of insurance surveys. Courtesy of the Allen & Stults Company.

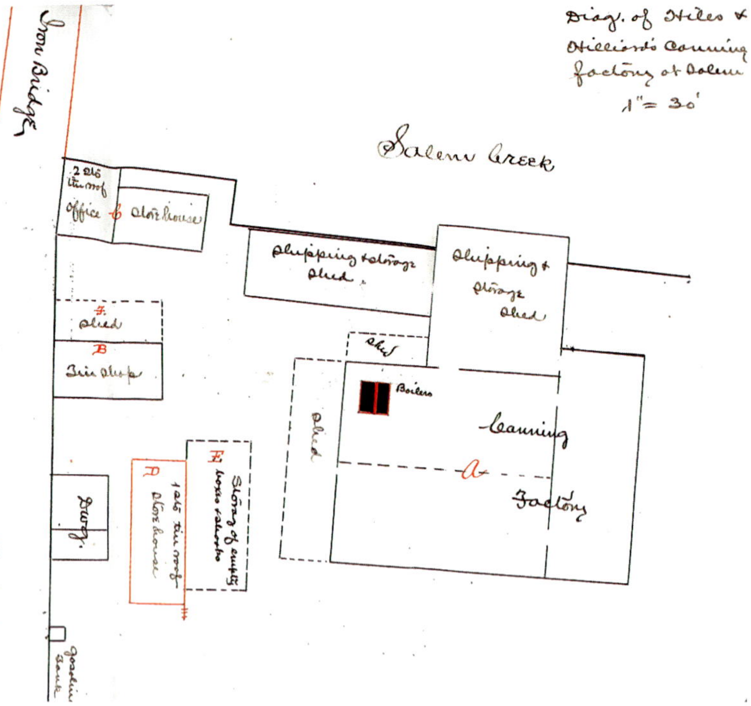


Figure 10. Site plan from the insurance survey for the Stiles & Hilliard Company canning factory, Salem City, 1880. Surveys prepared for small insurance companies often provide less detail than those for larger companies. This one was carefully drawn to scale. Salem County Mutual Fire Insurance Company Collection, Salem County Historical Society.

Salem Mutual evidently did not require that its surveys be as detailed as those of, for example, Franklin Fire. The 1880 plan of the Stiles & Hilliard Company's canning factory in Salem City is incapable of showing the interior layout of the factory in any detail but does convey the general arrangement of uses on the site and the spaces devoted to each (Figure 10). It also locates the boilers and a curious small building identified as a "gasoline bank," an early instance of the use of gasoline and a feature bound to grab the attention of a fire insurance underwriter. Note the distance it was placed from other buildings, but right along the edge of a street.

Specialized companies that produced insurance surveys of industrial properties emerged by the third quarter of the nineteenth century, developing a new kind of documentation: the axonometric or bird's-eye view. One of the first was the regional Hexamer Company of Philadelphia, which began producing industrial surveys and a few surveys for other large properties in 1866. Hexamer surveys may have been the first to feature an axonometric view of the properties surveyed, together with a plan view. The Free Library of Philadelphia holds the nearly three thousand hard-copy Hexamer General Surveys, but they can be more easily accessed online.[13]

Surveyed by Hexamer in 1875, the John Lucas Paint Works in Gibbsboro, New Jersey, was one of the first commercial paint factories in the United States (Figure 11). The site consisted of a single large factory adjacent to a pond from which it drew water, and was surrounded by small ancillary buildings. The level of detail shown in the axonometric drawing is representative of the Hexamer surveys and eventually became a standard for industrial insurance surveys. The Hexamer practice of coloring the buildings a pastel yellow for frame construction and a pastel pink for brick construction also became an industry standard when adopted for Sanborn maps. These innovations were believed to make it easier for insurance company personnel to visualize the risk and to properly judge the right premium to charge the factory owner.

In the fourth quarter of the nineteenth century, a group of more than twenty industrial insurers that came to be known as the Associated Factory Mutuals created an unprecedented collaboration to produce the Hexamer-type industrial survey. Beginning about 1878, their joint operation, called their Plan Division, created thousands of industrial site surveys during its first several decades and improved upon the example of the Hexamer surveys.[14] Drawn and reproduced upon larger sheets, they added more information about the processes used in the factories and paid greater attention to fire suppression capability and firefighting apparatus available on-site. Beginning in 1890, they continued the Hexamer practice of featuring a bird's-eye axonometric view of the entire factory. The geographic scope of the Plan Division surveys mirrored that of the associated companies, beginning in the Northeast where most of the constituent companies were located and spreading to the Midwest, and by the early twentieth century to the South.[15] The Plan Division supplied a copy of each survey to the insured factory, and sometimes one can still find them at these sites, often laminated for protection and durability, or framed under glass.[16]

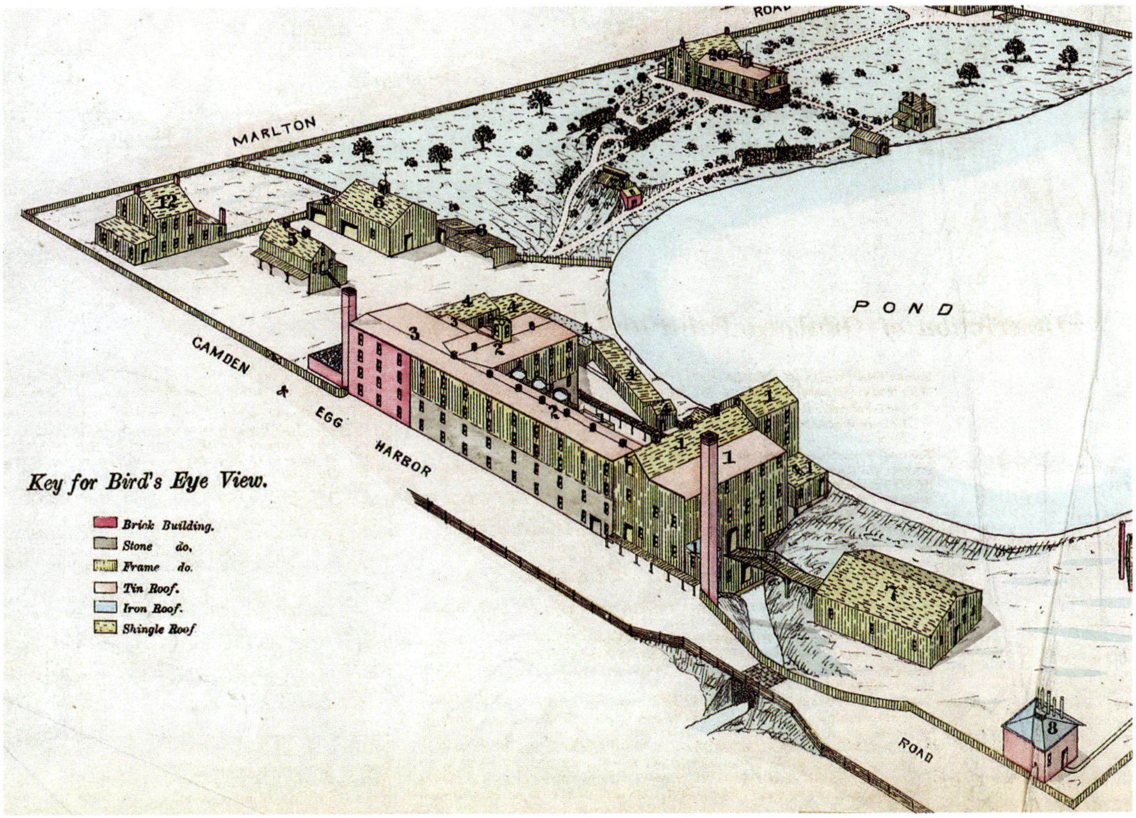


Figure 11. Detail of the Lucas Paint Works in Gibbsboro, N.J., 1875. Hexamer General Surveys, sheet 968. This image shows the level of detail provided in the axonometric views that the Hexamer Company helped pioneer. After 1890, drawings of this type also became a standard feature of industrial insurance surveys prepared for the Associated Factory Mutual companies. From the Hexamer General Surveys Collection. Courtesy of the Free Library of Philadelphia, Map Collection.

**Agents and Companies**

Understanding the basics of how insurance companies and their agents interacted will help modern historians match the needs of their inquiries to the records that will yield the most essential information. Companies varied widely in the size and scope of their operations. Some companies were purely local, serving individual towns. Somewhat larger companies were organized on the county level, usually headquartering in the county seat. Larger companies typically operated statewide as well as across state lines. Except for the very smallest insurance companies, which could conduct all operations from their own offices, the business of insurance companies was conducted through intermediary agents. Agents kept their own records for purposes that paralleled those of the companies, and often with the same content. Architectural historians should be mindful of this recordkeeping redundancy. Records no longer obtainable from one source may have been duplicated in another. One does not always need to look for a company's records. For locally focused studies, an individual agent's or agency's records may be more helpful.

The agent and the insurance company played different roles, but in some ways the agent played a more important role. It was the agent who "wrote" an insurance policy; the company merely "underwrote" it. The agent was also the coordinator of insurance coverage. Companies in the nineteenth and early twentieth centuries were rarely willing to accept the entire risk on a property, so the agent would cobble together policies from two to four insurance companies, which together would assume a risk totaling about 90 percent of the property's market value. These might include one local company, a county-based firm, another that operated on a statewide basis, and a subsidiary of a nationwide company. To do so not only spread the risk across multiple firms with deeper reserves but also geographically. This practice intensified the redundancy of these records. It meant, for example, that the agent might have kept entries for the same property in more than one policy register. This might explain why agents kept copies of the insurance surveys they prepared: the duplication offered a hedge against needing to supply the same survey to a different company in the future.

Researchers should always pay attention to the geographic spread of small insurance companies' risks, which were frequently wider than one might think. While some companies limited their business to the county in which they were domiciled, others were more ambitious. In the New Jersey collections thus far discovered, the risks insured spread far beyond the boundaries of the companies' home counties. The Mercer County Mutual Fire Insurance Company, for example, was insuring properties in about half of New Jersey's twenty-one counties by 1880.[17] The Salem County Mutual Insurance Company wrote insurance on numerous properties in the resort city of Cape May, two counties away, during the 1870s. Those predate that town's great fire of 1878, which consumed thirty-five acres of property in the heart of the city, including several of Cape May's large early hotels. No architectural historian has yet carefully examined these records, but they, and similar records from other companies or agencies, may one day become prime sources of information about the town's architecture before the great fire.[18]

### Rural Properties: Where Sanborns Do Not Reach

Insurance agencies in the Sanborn era certainly relied upon Sanborn maps—just like modern researchers. Sanborns covered both cities and towns large and small and even the occasional isolated industrial property, but they did not cover rural areas. Designed with wider and more inclusive geographic reach than Sanborns, insurance surveys and daily reports can yield important information about built environments outside of higher density settlements.

Agencies were responsible to insurance companies for surveys or daily reports that graphically showed a plan view of insured properties not covered by available insurance maps. The geographic spread of the surveys they produced probably mirrored the reach of their local business communities. In the case of the Allen & Stults agency in Hightstown, New Jersey—just one agency—its policies saturated a region of about two hundred square miles spread across parts of three counties. The agency produced about two thousand surveys, of which about half survive, including about eight hundred surveys of farmsteads between about 1895 and 1927, making possible many types of comparative study.

These surveys reveal different ways that these farms were spatially organized. Some show farmsteads laid out vertically, in which buildings were lined up behind the farmhouse and perpendicular to the road that the farmhouse faced, as if there was a desire to keep them from public view (Figure 12). Conversely, other farmsteads were arranged horizontally—or parallel to the public road—as if the owner were proud of his farm's physical plant and wanted to show it off (Figure 13). There also were different varieties of compact cluster arrangements. On still other farms, agricultural outbuildings stood hundreds of feet from the farm residence and its domestic outbuildings.

Insurance surveys of farmsteads can also aid the study of specific farm building types and the emergence of specialized farming. For example, many of the surveys indicate the presence of a "wood house" as one of the outbuildings nearest the farmhouse, nearer than even the privy or a smokehouse. Some indicate windmills for water pumping, while others document farm shops or powerhouses. One survey shows an early twentieth-century farmstead with an acetylene-fueled lighting system. A few surveys detail the layouts of cranberry farms in the northern reaches of the New Jersey pine barrens, while others reveal the emergence of egg-producing "chicken farms" that became a common sight in central New Jersey around World War II.

These surveys could also support the study of specific populations, especially in the early twentieth century as the New Jersey farmscape diversified. For example, an Allen & Stults survey records at least one of the farms of a group of farmers who immigrated to the Hightstown area in the years before World War I. Immigrants from this group later formed the American Czechoslovak Farmers Club a few miles south of Hightstown. Numerous surveys also document the emergence of a Jewish community in the years following 1900, as many families either leased or bought pre-existing farms. Some of these farms had been surveyed for their previous occupants and were later resurveyed for their Jewish owners, providing opportunities to chart the manner in which the later farmers transformed the property of their predecessors, as well as to document the functional changes to which surviving buildings were adapted. While the names of many of these families remain known today, the places where they lived would be very hard to document without the insurance surveys. Federal censuses of agriculture, state agricultural reports, oral histories, and items in local newspapers from the period could be brought together to enrich the information provided by the surveys.

The breadth of the collections discovered in New Jersey suggests what may be possible elsewhere in the nation in researching rural built environments. While insurance records have been found in all corners of the state in collections ranging greatly in size, my searches have borne more fruit in Mercer County, my home county, than elsewhere (Figure 14). While I have yet to find collections from Trenton's own companies or agencies, the county is nonetheless exceptionally well endowed with surviving insurance records. The early INA insurance blotters from the 1790s through 1805 contain written descriptions of several Trenton-area properties. A Pennsylvania company called the Bucks County Contributionship, founded in 1809 and modeled upon the Philadelphia Contributionship, has preserved policy registers from the years 1879–1902. Despite its name, 70 percent of its business in that period was insuring Trenton properties, and another 10 percent covered western Mercer and nearby parts of Burlington County: altogether about 2,700 properties.[19] The Franklin Fire Collection in Philadelphia also includes surveys for a few hundred Trenton properties, including the First Presbyterian Church of Trenton, and a few others sprinkled throughout the county (see Figures 2 and 3). The Bucks County Contributionship also insured First Presbyterian in the 1880s. In fact, it was only after I read in the Contributionship's policy register that Franklin Fire held a survey of this church that I contacted the Historical Society of Pennsylvania to see it.

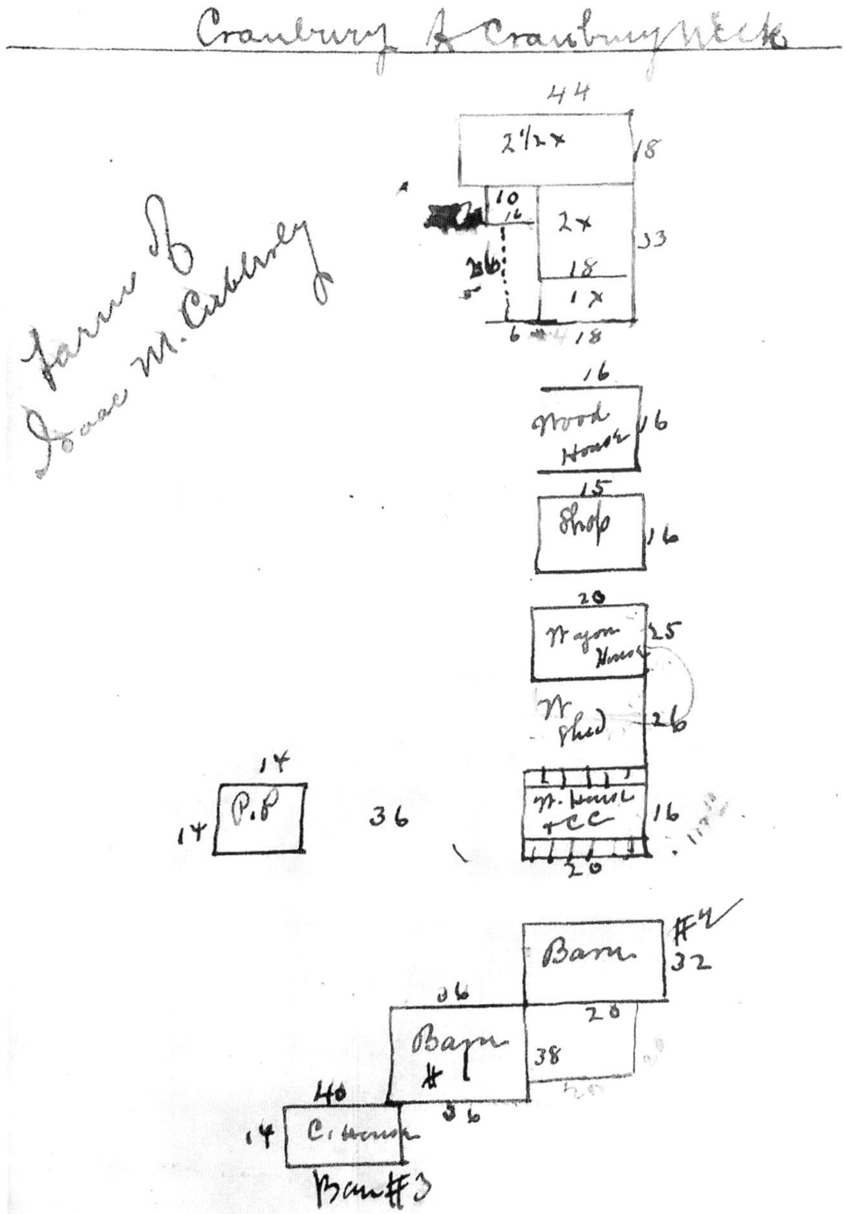


Figure 12. Allen & Stults Company early twentieth-century survey of a farmstead near Hightstown, N.J., exhibiting a "vertical" arrangement of the farm buildings behind the farm residence. Courtesy of the Allen & Stults Company.

Mercer County's eastern half is also well represented. A small company serving only West Windsor Township created records on about three hundred properties there, mostly farms, between 1857 and the early twentieth century.[20] Some of the surveys produced by an agent at Allentown, just across the line into Monmouth County, describe properties in the southeastern part of Mercer between 1885 and the 1890s.[21] A policy

Figure 13. Allen & Stults Company early twentieth-century survey of a farmstead near Hightstown, N.J., exhibiting a "horizontal" arrangement of the farm buildings parallel to the road. Courtesy of the Allen & Stults Company.

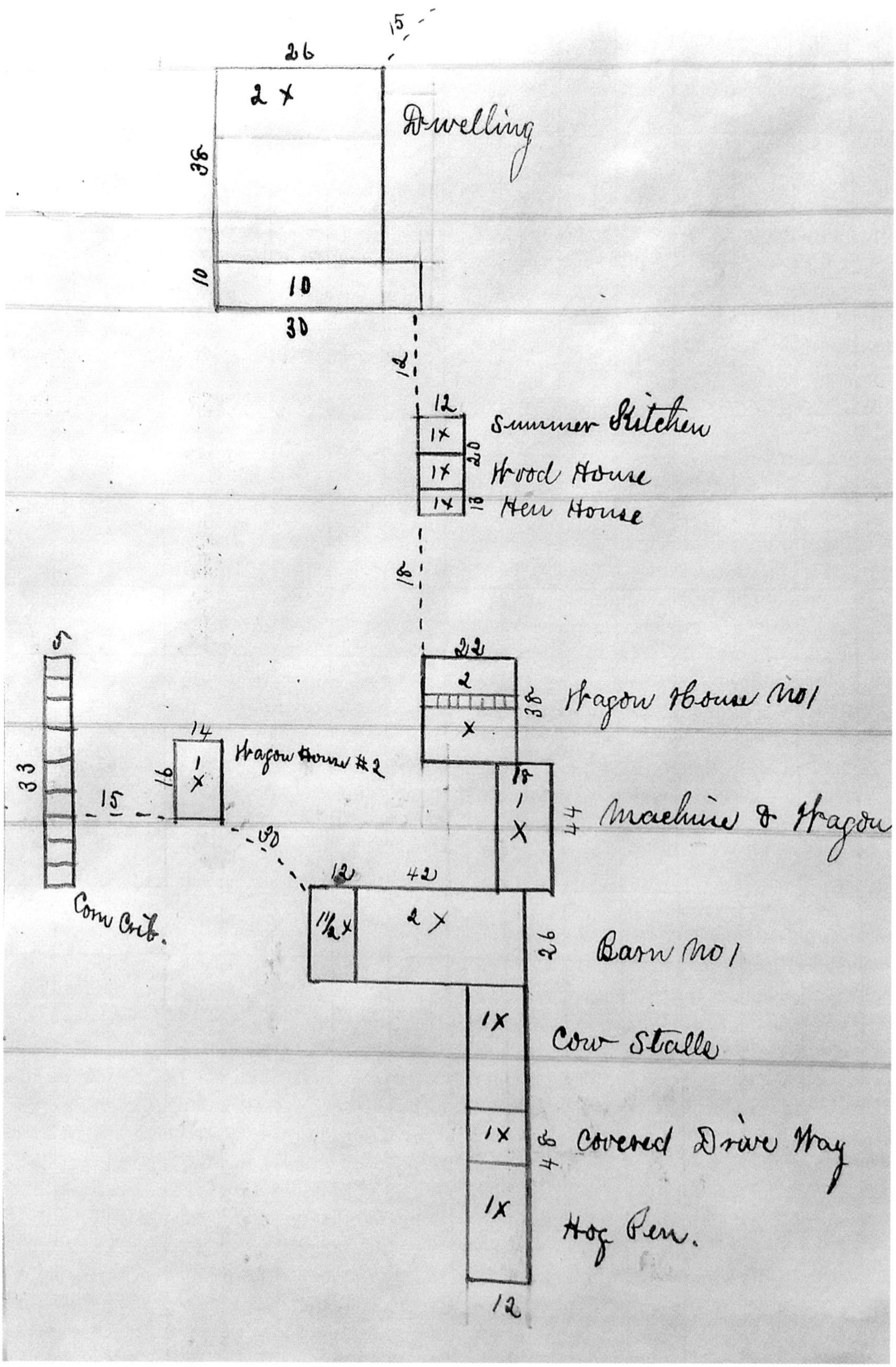

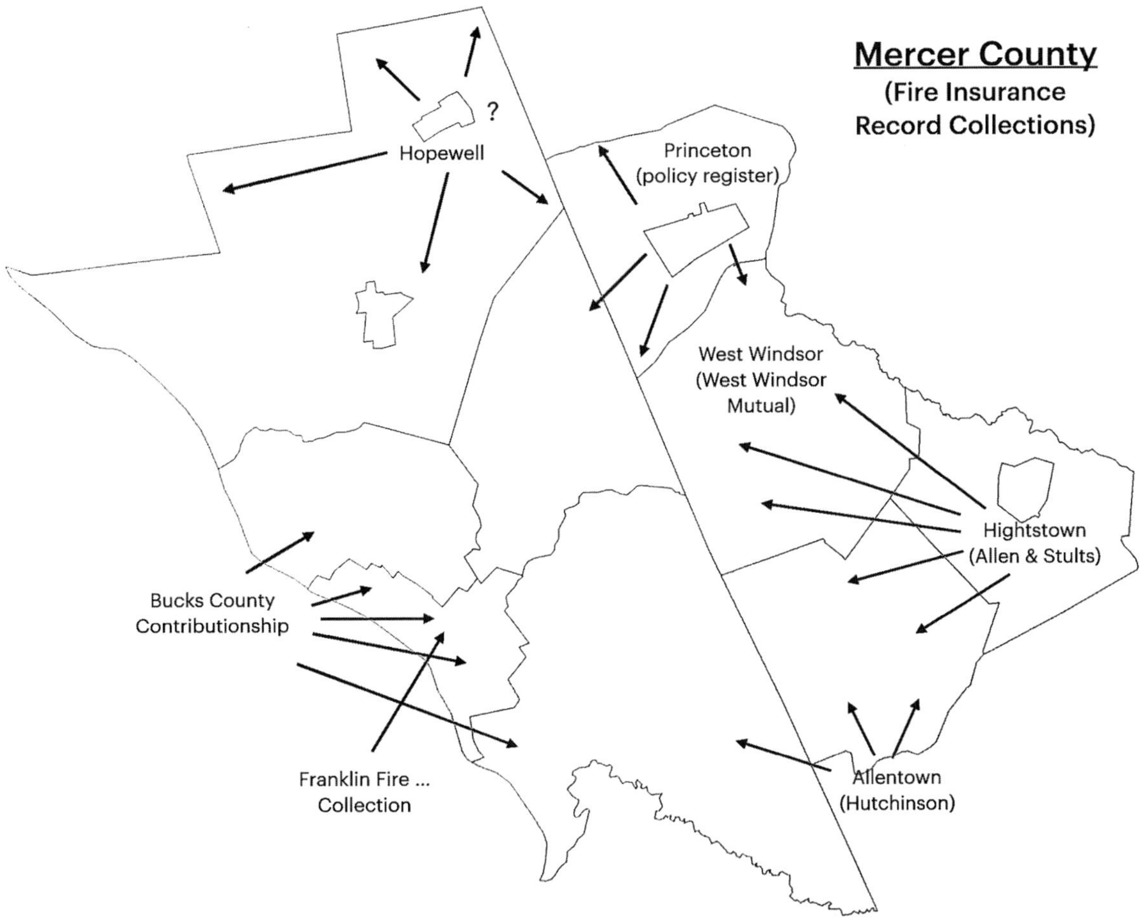


Figure 14. Map of Mercer County, N.J., showing the distribution of surviving collections of fire insurance records. Records for Hopewell exist although their identity and location are not publicly available. Graphic by Robert W. Craig.

register created by a Princeton insurance agent during the 1890s has also survived, describing perhaps five hundred properties. And the insurance surveys produced by the Allen & Stults agency in Hightstown cover the eastern half of Mercer County.[22] The existence of yet another collection of agency records from northwestern Mercer has also been confirmed, but it remains in private hands, a suggestion that many collections of insurance records across the country may remain at large. The example of Mercer County should convince architectural historians that there must be many jurisdictions in other states where several discrete collections may combine to reveal remarkably saturated coverage of rural and more urban properties.

### Finding Insurance Records and Making Them Usable

Finding collections of fire insurance records has been the work of decades. Perhaps the first systematic use of such records for architectural history and historic preservation purposes came in the 1950s and 1960s, when National Park Service historians and architects creating the Independence National Historical Park in Philadelphia discovered and extensively used the records of the Philadelphia Contributionship and those of the Mutual Assurance Company of Philadelphia.[23] These records provided strong support for their efforts to restore or reconstruct the park's eighteenth-century historic buildings.[24] I came upon this story in the early 1980s, when I helped conduct research for an administrative history of the park. Both insurance companies, however, had limited the scope of their underwriting to Philadelphia properties exclusively, which induced some to believe (myself included) that the existence of early insurance records was probably peculiar to Philadelphia, so the experience did not lead to a widespread search for similar records elsewhere.

Records of the Insurance Company of North

America (INA), founded in Philadelphia in 1792, have long been known to historians there, but they have been hard for architectural historians to access. INA began as a marine insurer but branched out to fire insurance in 1794.[25] Headquartered in Philadelphia, it insured risks well beyond Pennsylvania from the first. New York City, Boston, Baltimore, and Charleston all had insurance companies by the 1790s, but comparable collections of insurance surveys do not appear to have been reported for these cities.[26] The Mutual Assurance Society of Virginia, however, began issuing fire insurance policies in the mid-1790s, and its records now form a large collection at the Virginia State Library. Architectural historian Gary W. Stanton led an effort to index this material, and the index is available online today.[27]

Enumerating individual companies and citing surviving collections of their early records is not the best way to understand either the scale of the industry or the scale of the task that faces architectural historians who seek these records. In New Jersey alone, for example, the number of fire insurance companies exploded beginning in the second quarter of the nineteenth century. By 1875, more than 170 fire insurance companies were chartered by the state legislature, and an unknown number of additional companies were formed under a general incorporation act for insurance companies.[28] More than 120 of these companies remained active in New Jersey alone through the 1890s.[29] Other states faced a comparable proliferation of companies.[30] Researchers can expect that recharterings, name changes, and corporate reorganizations will further complicate the picture. Each of these companies and their many agents would have produced records comparable to those illustrated above. One of the leading writers on the American insurance industry estimated that there were 150,000 insurance agents in the United States by 1922.[31]

And yet finding the surviving collections is just the researcher's first task. The insurance industry was radically decentralized through the nineteenth and early twentieth centuries, spreading hundreds of agents across each state's cities and small towns. The dispersal of surviving records today reflects these realities. Researchers cannot expect that all surviving company or agency records have already been captured by collecting institutions. The companies that produced or collected them and remain in business may still own them. Some are held by successor firms. The INA archive, for example, is held today by the Chubb group of insurance companies, after a series of corporate mergers and divestitures. Yet the researcher is encouraged to tread carefully when attempting to access such privately-owned records. Delicate negotiation may be required. The first point of contact should be a company's corporate archivist, but keep in mind that they are not in the business of supporting scholarly researchers. Companies hire archivists to efficiently manage their record holdings for ongoing internal reasons and business purposes, not to curate their oldest materials.

Still, companies with the oldest records are likely either the industry's oldest companies or their corporate successors, and many maintain a pride in their company's longevity. One could easily fill a bookshelf with histories that these companies published about themselves. It will sometimes be the case that a company can be persuaded that the records most interesting to architectural historians are ones that no longer serve any ongoing business purposes. But beware: companies will eventually figure that out on their own. It will be essential to the survival of such collections that a company be convinced of their records' continuing importance and that an outside entity is prepared to receive them before a company determines that it can no longer house them. A sense of quiet urgency is needed. Otherwise, the dumpster awaits.

Researchers are encouraged to use a similar process to find agency records. Some may already have been donated to a local historical society. Like companies, agencies are notable for their own longevity. Some agencies may still be in possession of their old surveys and policy registers. About twenty years ago, I requested and received a list of the insurance agencies in New Jersey that were more than one hundred years old. The number was more than twenty. Even younger agencies may have swallowed up older ones and absorbed their archives in a process that I have termed the "genealogy of professional practice," which one can also sometimes see in architectural and civil engineering firms.

Still other agency records may have survived in the hands of an agency's last owners or their descendants. To find clues for such records, the researcher should first use city directories and statewide business directories to identify defunct insurance agencies and the names of their likely successor firms. Then the researcher could perhaps meet with the representative with the longest institutional memory in the oldest remaining insurance agency in the town to ask how one might proceed further. The researcher also should consult the local historical society to learn whether it has ever been approached by the holders of such material, and if so, how to contact that party. If the society is in active negotiations to acquire such material, it may not be forthcoming with information. If such records went to a different institution, however, or did not meet the requirements of the organization's collection policy, then the society may be more likely to reveal what it knows.

In any effort to find fire insurance records to support a research project focused on a small region, it may be wise to begin by searching for local agency records because their policy registers may indicate the identities of all or most of the companies for which they wrote insurance. Agency records may also include copies of the surveys supplied to the companies, and if not, may note the names of the companies that hold the surveys.

Researchers should be prepared to find agency and company records in any manner of archival disarrangement. Because time is always in short supply, most researchers will only be able to examine individual records that relate to particular buildings or properties. The indexes the agencies created for their own use will be important to recover for such efficient research. Existing indexes, each often limited to individual volumes, usually only provide the names of the policy holders. In the absence of any other information, these names can be very helpful, as persons studying individual buildings will often have a menu of names to be checked against that type of index. A researcher who finds a collection indexed in this way should try to obtain a copy of these indexes, and to place them in a location where they can become known to other researchers.

Because of their great volume and the diversity of fire insurance records, much of their latent value will only be realized once they can be studied comparatively. They hold the potential to revolutionize the study of many types of buildings by greatly expanding the volume of potential evidence. Many architectural historians will only find fire insurance records to be of great value when they have been indexed to foster discovery of groups of buildings related by type, construction, or use. Architectural historian Jeffrey Cohen set a good example when he worked with students to index the Franklin Fire Collection. He used database software to produce fields categorizing properties as residential, civic, commercial, educational, industrial, or religious, for example. The database also identifies taverns, hotels, dwellings, and shops, and the number of stories and the principal construction material are also provided. Cohen has acknowledged that such work can be incredibly tedious, but the breadth of his categories makes the collection much more valuable as a resource for study. Narrowly defined indexes that only provide property owners' names, important as they are, should be avoided when new indexes are made.

Opportunities may abound to find collections of agency and company records that can illuminate otherwise unknowable features of the historic built environment. The vastness of the insurance industry, however, means that only a deep commitment by the architectural history community will find and save these records and the irreplaceable information they contain. Time is short, and the clock is ticking.

### AUTHOR BIOGRAPHY

**Robert W. Craig** is a historian and architectural historian, and a recent winner of the Vernacular Architecture Forum's Paul E. Buchanan Award. He was the text editor of the 2014 VAF conference guidebook *Down Jersey: From Bayshore to Seashore*. An independent scholar and member of the Princeton [N.J.] Research Forum, he was for many years New Jersey's statewide coordinator for the National Register of Historic Places program. He works to promote the use of valuable, but generally overlooked, architectural records through his new consultancy, Advanced Old Building Research. This article is part of that effort.

ACKNOWLEDGMENTS

The author wishes to acknowledge help he has received over the years both from historian Paul W. Schopp of Richard Stockton University's South Jersey History and Culture Center, who has partnered in the discovery of surviving insurance record collections, and from architectural historian Janet Sheridan, who helped ensure the smooth transfer of the Salem County Mutual records.

NOTES

1. Throughout this essay I use the terms "agent" and "agency" (and their plurals) interchangeably. More properly, however, the agent was a person licensed to conduct business for one or more insurance companies, and the agency was a business that employed one or more agents.

2. Insurance Company of North America fire insurance blotters, 1794–1805, INA Records, Chubb Archives, Philadelphia.

3. J. Lewis Rowand Collection, policy register, vol. 3, p. 126, Historical Society of Haddonfield, N.J.

4. The fact that the policy number is given along with the register entry number indicates that the policy register was kept by an agent, not by the underwriting company. If kept by a company, the policy number would be the register entry number.

5. The Philadelphia Contributionship insurance surveys can be accessed online through the Philadelphia Architects and Buildings website, philadelphiabuildings.org, or directly through the Contributionship's website at www.1752.com.

6. William R. Tharp, "Roads, Race, and Retail: The Transformation of Short Pump, Virginia," *Buildings & Landscapes* 29, no. 2 (Fall 2022): 78–79.

7. For a discussion of this house and the full text of the description, see Robert W. Craig, ed., *Down Jersey: From Bayshore to Seashore,* unpublished guidebook for the Vernacular Architecture Forum Annual Conference, May 7–10, 2014, Galloway Township, N.J., 175–77.

8. First Presbyterian Church of Trenton, N.J., insurance survey, 1853. Survey no. 19407, Franklin Fire Insurance Company of Philadelphia Surveys Collection, Historical Society of Pennsylvania, Philadelphia.

9. Herbert J. Githens, *Historic Preservation Plan, Atsion Mansion and Store,* [. . .] *Shamong Township, October 14, 1999,* copy at N.J. Historic Preservation Office, Trenton.

10. Janet Sheridan, "Garwood House Revealed: A Departure from Plain Architecture," *Preservation Salem Newsletter* 12, no. 1 (Fall 2002): 4–5, 9–10.

11. The policy was discovered in the Clarke Family Collection, CO 402, Manuscripts and Special Collections Division, Firestone Library, Princeton University, Princeton, N.J.

12. In Allentown, New Jersey, agent Charles R. Hutchinson used daily report forms with very similar formats from the mid-1880s into the 1890s from INA, the Fire Association of Philadelphia, the Mount Holly Insurance Company, the Continental Insurance Co., the Standard Fire Insurance Co. of Trenton, and the Royal Insurance Co. [Liverpool, U.K.].

13. Search for "Hexamer General Surveys" at philageohistory.org. An earlier guide to this material is Joyce A. Post, *A Consolidated Name Index to the Hexamer General Surveys* (Philadelphia: n.p., 1974).

14. The firm is known today as FM Global, headquartered in Norwood, Mass.

15. This story is best told in *The Factory Mutuals, 1835–1935: Being Primarily a History of the Manufacturers Mutual Fire Insurance Company* [. . .]. (Providence, R.I.: Manufacturers Mutual Fire Insurance Company, 1935), 272, 275, et passim.

16. Several such documents have been found, sometimes within the insured premises itself. Some of them have been laminated; others were framed under glass. Some libraries devoted to industrial history have accumulated collections of such surveys.

17. See the Mercer County Mutual handbill inside the cover of the policy register in the J. Lewis Rowand Collection, Historical Society of Haddonfield, Haddonfield, N.J.

18. For more about the great fire in Cape May City, see Jeffrey M. Dorwart, *Cape May County, New Jersey: The Making of an American Resort Community* (New

Brunswick, N.J.: Rutgers University Press, 1992), 120; and George E. Thomas and Carl Doebley, *Cape May, Queen of the Seaside Resorts: Its History and Architecture* (Philadelphia: Art Alliance Press, 1976).

19. The surviving records of the Bucks County Contributionship also include two volumes of minutes from 1809 forward. The records are privately held and are not yet available to researchers. For more information, contact the Trentoniana Division, Trenton Public Library, N.J.

20. West Windsor Mutual Fire Insurance Association records, Division of Special Collections and University Archives, Rutgers University Libraries, New Brunswick, N.J.

21. Charles R. Hutchinson Collection, Monmouth County Historical Association, Freehold, N.J.

22. The Allen & Stults Company entered the insurance business in 1890. Its collection of surveys is on loan to the Hightstown-East Windsor Historical Society, Hightstown, N.J.

23. Anthony N. B. Garven et al., *The Architectural Surveys, 1784–94*, vol.1 (Philadelphia: Mutual Assurance Co., 1976).

24. Constance M. Greiff, *Independence: The Creation of a National Park* (Philadelphia: University of Pennsylvania Press, 1987).

25. Historian Hannah Farber has written an impressive new book, *Underwriters of the United States: How Insurance Shaped the American Founding* (Williamsburg, Va.: Omohundro Institute of Early American History and Culture, and University of North Carolina Press, 2021). Farber focuses almost exclusively on marine insurance, but she describes the early years of the INA.

26. Two insurance companies were founded in South Carolina in 1776, but they apparently were marine insurers. The Essex Fire and Marine Insurance Company was founded in Salem, Massachusetts, as early as 1776, and was incorporated in 1803. In New York City, a Mutual Assurance Society was founded in 1787 and incorporated in 1798. The Baltimore Equitable Society, founded in 1794, was the first insurance company in Maryland. In Boston, the Massachusetts Mutual Fire Assurance Society was incorporated in 1798. After admittedly cursory searching online, I have not found reports of collections of surveys or policy registers for any of these early companies.

27. For a guide to the Mutual Assurance Society of Virginia records at the Virginia State Library, see https://ead.lib.virginia.edu/vivaxtf/view?docid=lva/vi01257.xml. A link to the index to these records is provided on the same site, or at http://umwhispresc.wpengine.com/masidxsch.

28. John Hood, *Hood's Index to the Laws of the State of New Jersey, 1664–1903* (Camden, N.J.: Sinnickson & Chew, 1905), 573–81, provides a list of the incorporation statutes. For the general incorporation statute, see An Act to Provide for the Incorporation of Insurance Companies, ch. 74, 1852, *New Jersey Laws*, 159.

29. *Annual Report[s] of the New Jersey Department of Banking and Insurance*, 1891—, (Trenton: [state printer]).

30. [Charles C. Hine, comp.], *Insurance Blue-Book, 1876–1877: An Insurance Annual Containing Sketches of Representative Companies and Pictures of Their Home Offices*, Centennial Issue ([New York]: C.C. Hine, 1877).

31. Robert P. Barbour, *The Agents Key to Fire Insurance: Concise and Helpful Information for Agents, Brokers, and Field Men Regarding Essentials of the Business*, 3rd ed. (New York: Spectator Company, 1922), 10.

# Reviews

**Tara A. Dudley**

*Building Antebellum New Orleans: Free People of Color and Their Influence*

Austin: University of Texas, 2021

336 pages, 94 black-and-white and 22 color illustrations

ISBN: 9781477323021, $50.00 HB

ISBN: 9781477323045, $50.00 EB

Review by Charlette M. Caldwell

Engagement, as Tara A. Dudley defines it in *Building Antebellum New Orleans,* encapsulates the architectural and building histories of underrepresented communities, bringing to the fore the signification of commitment and conflict that faces a racialized group when acquiring property and asserting the right to build on their property. As Louisiana grew rapidly between the 1830s and the 1840s, the *gens de couleur libres* community—free people of color who were of mixed Black and European ancestry—prospered, engaging in building trades and property acquisitions that left an indelible mark on the built environment. As Dudley writes, these free people of color and their buildings have been unexplored fully in architectural history, leaving a crucial gap that she expertly fills to show these communities' influences on American architecture.

The free people of color in New Orleans trace their origins to informal relationships between White men and women of color. Laws were lenient regarding interracial relationships, which contributed naturally to the growth of a distinct mixed-race class. Two families in particular, the Dolliole family and the Soulié family, contributed significantly to the building industry in New Orleans, their work concentrated mostly in the Vieux Carré and Faubourg Tremé neighborhoods. And although the population numbers of the *gens de couleur libres* decreased in the city toward the end of the antebellum period, their presence nonetheless influenced the economic opportunities available for them.

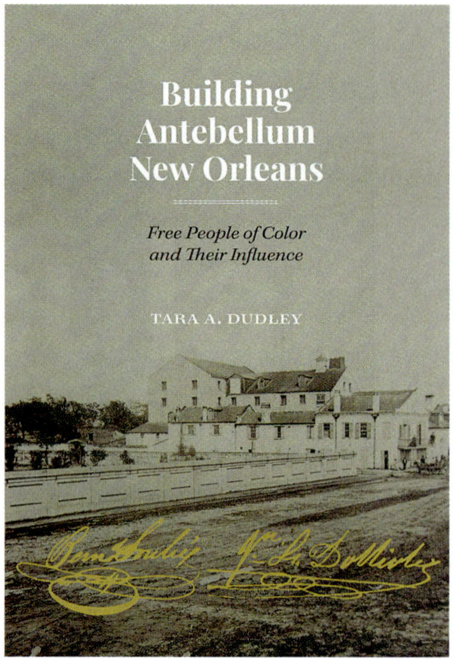


The book is divided into three parts. In the first, "Ownership: Possessing the Built Environment," Dudley uses the property histories of the Dolliole and the Soulié families as case studies to structure the book, delving first into a detailed history of their property acquisitions before exploring their ramifications. In chapter 1, "The *Gens de Couleur Libres'* Acquisition of Property," Dudley details how the ownership of property "was the first step in the architecture-driven identity-building process by which many builders and developers of color established their place in antebellum New Orleans" (25). Members of these families often used inter vivos (between living people) donations to transfer or gift property to relatives. This was often the case after a family member passed away or gifted the property to their offspring. Despite increasing limitations placed on people of color during this time, through donations and working with business associates, families like the Dollioles and the Souliés acquired a significant amount of property, establishing birthrights for their descendants.

In chapter 2, "The Ramifications of Use and Location," Dudley examines the building histories not only in the Vieux Carré and the Faubourg Tremé, but also in other suburbs and streets, demonstrating how the *gens de couleur libres* interacted and moved about the city of New Orleans from its origins as a European colony to an American city. These families took advantage of areas deemed unimportant by White Creoles and Americans, establishing a secure propertied foothold by people of color. As Dudley explains, "the *gens de couleur libres'* success as property owners and speculators presented a dichotomy in a city becoming more and more American culturally and racially segregated and attempting to keep free people of color in their 'proper place' in daily life. On the other hand, their reality underscored the parity they retained with White Creoles and many Americans" (71). The concentration of these properties was also significant due to their sheer size, and because their placement affected the racial demographics in the city long after the population size of the *gens de couleur libres* dwindled after the 1840s.

Part 2, "Engagement: Forming and Transforming the Built Environment," begins with chapter 3, "The Architecture of the Dolliole and the Soulié Families," which focuses on the uses of engagement, or how the *gens de couleur libres* formed and transformed the built environment in which they lived. This chapter is most significant to Dudley's argument, as she explores how members of each family demonstrated the ways in which builders and developers—through both informal and formal training—learned the building trades and incorporated distinct architectural forms in buildings erected on their properties. She writes that these builders' efforts "reflect the transitional nature of architectural forms and styles in the territorial and early antebellum periods" in New Orleans's history (79). Dudley remarks that the style most familiar to these builders would have been the creole cottage, as they learned their profession in the late eighteenth and early nineteenth centuries, when the style was most popular; she notes, however, that these builders adapted the style to their needs. In chapter 4, "Uncommon Industry," the author further elaborates on the building success of native *gens de couleur libres* and those seeking refuge in the city; she also emphasizes the work of individual builders who contributed to a brewing building culture that was supplemented by a larger collective effort within the community.

The fifth chapter, "Raised to the Trade," provides the context in which the *gens de couleur libres* conducted their business. This chapter is especially important to Dudley's contention that these communities have been excluded from dominant architectural histories because of their lack of physical plans and formal training in architecture. As Dudley writes, *gens de couleur libres* like the Dollioles and the Souliés learned the "business of building construction, property development, and real estate speculation from their parents, relatives, and other members" of their community (153). Yet during the 1830s, Irish and German immigrants began to displace the *gens de couleur libres* as craftsmen, with the trend becoming more apparent in the 1840s and 1850s. This is further explored in chapter 6, "The Status Quo," in which Dudley provides an in-depth analysis of how free Black builders were relegated to less lucrative and prominent projects because of the influx of French, White Creole, and Americans in the New Orleans building industry. These builders and architects were proficient in so-called "high" styles in demand at the time while the *gens de couleur libres* continued to build in styles comfortable to their trades and clientele.

Part 3, "Entrepreneurship," is made up only of chapter 7, "Money, Power, and Status in the Building Trades." The word "entrepreneur" was often used in trade documents to describe the work of both Black and Creole master builders and property owners. Dudley writes that the economic viability of the free Black community in New Orleans was based upon the "acquisition of marketable skill before and after being freed; the possession of a good reputation in the White community through kinship and patronage; and having access to freedom by being born free or having free kin" (197). She uses the example of François Lacroix, who was one of the wealthiest *hommes de couleur libres* during the antebellum period. His property dealings and those of the Dollioles and Souliés led to economic stability atypical for most people of color living at the time. This chapter supports the crux of Dudley's argument, which is presented most clearly in her conclusion: that *gens de couleur libres* were not only active in New Orleans building culture, but an integral key to its character. These communities established their own birthrights through deep engagement with the built environment, reflecting the conflict and commitment born from racialized identity and the hardships facing people of color before the Civil War. They claimed their privilege through building culture and made an impact on the landscape that is still visible today.

Dudley's work is an important addition to architectural history as it centers building narratives on underrepresented people rather than forcing their stories into widely accepted canonical narratives. The author utilizes an extensive array of primary sources to support her argument, which is especially critical when narrating and interpreting the architectural and building histories of underrepresented actors—falling in line with a rich tradition of historians of the vernacular, yet adding to recent scholarship that continues to diverge from so-called canonical narratives.

*Building Antebellum New Orleans* is an excellent study of the evolution of architectural practices and how styles are transformed and adapted over time rather than fixed in one period. Although some vernacular architectural histories break away from the tyranny of style that is often associated with "high-style" architecture, using style as a tool to discuss building histories is key in that it provides the historian a document of changing cultural values over time. In this regard, the author expertly uses historical and cultural contexts to ground the architectural and building histories of the numerous sites mentioned in her research.

Dudley, through these case studies, also creates an interesting, implicit conversation about race, class, and the competition for resources in the acquisition of property and funding for building projects. And while her analysis leans heavily on prominent families and individuals, this choice is understandable given the research constraints imposed due to the limited availability of building and trade documents as well as family records. In addition, Dudley's usage of the phrase "building culture" to describe the work of free people of color in New Orleans is an excellent way to interpret their relationship to the built environment. It adds to the fact that the study of vernacular architecture is the study of the building histories of communities and of the cultural values attached to places that evolve over time.

*Building Antebellum New Orleans* sets out to include within the historical record the important contributions of the *gens de couleur libres* to the built landscape of New Orleans, focusing upon their unique stories and patronage as responses to the changing trends around them, rather than as passive participants. This work is a crucial contribution to growing scholarship that seeks to re-center underrepresented communities and individuals by using standard tools of interpretation and narration, but also by incorporating primary sources and documents not typically considered "architectural."

AUTHOR BIOGRAPHY

**Charlette M. Caldwell**, a doctoral candidate in architectural history and theory at Columbia University, holds a fellowship at the Library Company of Philadelphia. Her dissertation examines the architectural history of the African Methodist Episcopal Church from the late eighteenth to the nineteenth centuries, and how perceptions of Blackness affected building practices of the Black church.

---

**Carolyn L. White**

*The Archaeology of Burning Man: The Rise and Fall of Black Rock City*

Albuquerque: University of New Mexico Press, 2020
xvi + 262 pages, 75 black-and-white figures, 6 tables
ISBN: 9780826361332, $75.00 HB
ISBN: 9780826363930, $34.95 PB
ISBN: 9780826361349, $75.00 EB

Review by Mark C. Childs

---

The boundaries of disciplines and professions are evolving cultural constructs.[1] Author Carolyn White—the Mamie Kleberg Chair in Historic Preservation, director of the Historic Preservation Program, and director of the Anthropology Research Museum at the University of Nevada—explicitly positions her own work within the ongoing construction of disciplines in *The Archaeology of Burning Man: The Rise and Fall of Black Rock City*. Following anthropologist James Deetz's view of "the fields of archaeology, history, and cultural anthropology as pursuing the same object,"[2] White participated in and studied the "mundane" aspects of the place called Black Rock City, the annual encampment of the Burning Man Festival in northern Nevada, each year from 2008 to 2016 (23). The framing of the book may be of particular interest to readers of *Buildings & Landscapes,* as three main themes weave throughout it: documenting daily life, attention to temporality, and reconsidering practices of archaeology.

Chapters 1 and 2 describe the framework for White's research. In chapter 1, White situates her work in a review of the emergence of the practices of contemporary archaeology as well as the history and literature of Burning Man. She focuses primarily upon "how people live on a daily basis in the city and how the mundane character of daily life takes place in this temporary place" (31). Chapter 2 describes her theoretical grounding. To structure her documentation and interpretation of the site, White uses Lefebvrian tripartite space (*conceived–perceived–lived*), de Certeau's *strategies* and *tactics,* Bataille's framework on the social expenditure of wealth (*the accursed share*), De Landa's *meshwork,* and Deleuze and Guattari's *smooth and striated space*.[3] There is a danger of overcomplication from such a conceptual toolkit, but White uses these concepts to clearly organize and ground her observations as she gives us the gritty details of building, inhabiting, and deconstructing the encampment.

Chapters 3 through 8 follow a narrative arc from construction, to occupation, to decamping. Much of this work could inform the practical parts of a travel guide; however, its directness causes these chapters to read somewhat like a checklist. Construction of the Man starts the event (the Man is a multistory wooden effigy at the center point of the urban form, and the hub of the event). "In cooperation with the BLM [Bureau of Land Management], the central point of the city, the location where the Man will stand, is pinpointed. . . . The Golden Spike ceremony formally kicks off the build cycle of Burning Man" (57). White documents the construction, inhabitation, and deconstruction practices not only of the Man but also of showers and greywater systems, furniture and food, community and private spaces, fuel and garbage systems, but even these "mundane" practices have extraordinary aspects. For example, the exceptional efforts the Burning Man community makes to limit and remediate MOOP ("matter out of place," or litter) are interwoven throughout these everyday practices. Materials such as glitter are banned; greywater is evaporated rather than poured out to avoid contaminating the playa; surfaces are built and removed to allow fires. After Exodus (people leaving the city), a highly planned clean-up takes place in three phases—teardown, playa restoration, and inspection.

Burning Man is a short-lived annual encampment whose parts are being decommissioned even as others are being constructed and inhabited. The same is true of all settlements on different time scales, but other festival grounds, markets, camps of seasonally migrating peoples, and pilgrimage sites share Burning Man's chronological pattern. Some of the earliest known settlements, the fourth-millennium BCE Trypillia megasites in Ukraine, also may have been seasonally occupied.[4] As White notes, Black Rock City "is a place where the rhythm of daily life is accelerated and where all archaeologists might imagine the role that similar elements may have played at other sites" (233). Changes arise from year to year both from the event's annual theme and from the diffusion of innovations. Formally selected themes shape the annual incarnations of art installations and institutions such as the Man and the Temple. (The Temple serves as "a place of contemplation, a place to rest, a place of reflection, a place of rituals, weddings, reunions, etc." and its burn closes Burning Man.)[5] Innovations such as hexayurts—sleeping quarters constructed of insulation panels—tend to spread by example; first introduced in 2003, there were more than 2,500 of these structures in 2016. Such social processes of change are apparent and can be investigated on an active site more readily than on unearthed archaeological sites.

The epilogue revisits the introduction's questions of discipline. As White describes it, active site archaeology "lives between archaeology and cultural anthropology and provokes methodological questions" (231). Because inhabitants are using and actively reshaping the place as it is studied, active site archaeology must incorporate research methods of cultural anthropology. For example, White interviews designers about the evolution of their plans, "rides along" with site inspectors, and lives in Black Rock City. Studying the present also provides perspective to consider traditional archaeological artifacts. The author suggests that archaeologists should imagine the temporality, complexity, and ongoing change of once-living places: "It is important for archaeologists to bring noise, disruption, and movement into their interpretations of their sites" (233). Understanding the dynamics of prosaic practices such as the multiple uses of spaces and the flipping of a space between public and private modes can enrich the interpretation of sites. Studying the present also may suggest what might be missing from archaeological records. Burning Man's commitment to eliminating MOOP from the site, for example, effectively removes much of the material that potentially would provide significant evidence in classic archaeology.

The practice of active site archaeology highlights another question of disciplinary boundaries. Translational research, the study of how to translate research into practice, has blossomed in the medical fields.[6] Analogous work in the built environment would entail developing best practices for translating the findings of studies on "what was" and "what is" into tools for designing future places. Architects, landscape architects, urban planners, and the broader range of people who shape the built environment are informed by the work of historians and archaeologists. How can our current practices of translating research into practice be improved? As a community event of designers and artists actively engaged in work, Burning Man offers a distinct opportunity to study the intermeshing of research and practice. Have White's interviews, discussions, or lectures at Burning Man itself helped to shape the place? What will "burners" do with the gift of reflection that this book offers?

A population and its experts' conceptions of urban and architectural practice also drive urban form. Active site study, particularly at a site dedicated to art and design such as Black Rock City, could be enriched by a review of the active, contested, and dominant conceptions of placemaking its creators espouse, and potentially how changes in the conceptual dialog are reflected in changes in the built environment. It would be useful to know if the concepts of Lefebvre, de Certeau, Bataille, and others employed by White are also used by the makers of Black Rock City, and what other urban design concepts are part of the active dialog.

Quoting Lefebvre, the author concludes that "Black Rock City offers a fine example of the construction of social space; it 'is a tool of thought and action, means of production, means of control and domination, of power' " (222).[7] Carolyn White's *The Archaeology of Burning Man* offers a fine example of the construction of a disciplinary practice.

AUTHOR BIOGRAPHY

Architect, urban designer, and poet, professor emeritus **Mark C. Childs** is the author of eight books, including *Foresight and Design* (2022), *The Zeon Files* with Ellen Babcock (2016, New Mexico Heritage Preservation Award 2017), and *Urban Composition* (2012, EDRA Book Award 2013).

NOTES

1. See Eliot Freidson, *Professionalism Reborn* (Chicago: University of Chicago Press, 1994); Eliot Freidson, *Professional Powers* (Chicago: University of Chicago Press, 1986); and Thomas Bender, *Intellect and the Public Life* (Baltimore: Johns Hopkins University Press, 1993).

2. James Deetz, "History and Architectural Theory: Walter Taylor Revisited," *American Antiquity* 53, no. 1 (1988): 13–22.

3. See Henri Lefebvre, *The Production of Space*, trans. Donald Nicholson-Smith (London: Wiley Blackwell, 1974); Michel de Certeau, Luce Giard, and Pierre Mayol, *The Practice of Everyday Life*, Steven Rendall, trans. (Berkeley: University of California Press, 1984); Georges Bataille, *The Accursed Share: An Essay on General Economy*, vol. 1, trans. Robert Hurley (1967; repr., New York: Zone Books, 1988); and Manuel De Landa, *A Thousand Years of Nonlinear History* (1997, repr., New York: Swerve, 2000); Gilles Deleuze and Félix Guattari, *A Thousand Plateaus: Capitalism and Schizophrenia*, Brian Masumi, trans. (1980; repr., Minneapolis: University of Minnesota Press, 1987).

4. John Chapman, "The Standard Model, the Maximalists and the Minimalists: New Interpretations of Trypillia Mega-Sites," *Journal of World Prehistory* 30 (2017): 221–37.

5. Temple Guardians, "What is the temple?" https://templeguardians.burningman.org/about-the-temples/.

6. S. H. Woolf, "The Meaning of Translational Research and Why It Matters," *JAMA* 299, no. 2 (2008): 211–13.

7. Quotation from Lefebvre, *The Production of Space*, 126.

**Claire W. Herbert**
*A Detroit Story: Urban Decline and the Rise of Property Informality*
Oakland: University of California Press, 2021
ix + 340 pages, 16 color plates, 32 black-and-white illustrations
ISBN: 9780520340084, $29.95 PB
ISBN: 9780520340077, $85.00 HB
ISBN: 9780520974487, $29.95 EB

Review by Kelley Lemon

In her book *A Detroit Story: Urban Decline and the Rise of Property Informality*, author Claire W. Herbert, an assistant professor in the Department of Sociology at the University of Oregon, examines Detroit through the lens of occupied space to document the conditions that spur the decline of urban centers, and to understand how those conditions promote informal practices within vacant and abandoned spaces. Her study also seeks to determine who participates and who ultimately benefits (and concurrently suffers) when such practices are recognized and formalized through rules. Property informality, as Herbert defines the term, encompasses the "informal practices that arise from the transgression of laws regulating real property—land, houses, buildings" (5).

*A Detroit Story* is organized into three parts: "Social and Spatial Context," "Informality in Everyday Life," and "Informal Plans and Formal Policies," with a total of nine chapters, plus a preface, introduction, and conclusion. Herbert's preface primes the reader and essentially addresses the questions/assumptions the reader may have about her position as a White researcher studying a primarily Black community, as she acknowledges how her presence resembled elements of gentrification—a process often characterized as young, highly educated, and resourced Whites moving into and displacing communities of color and considered an undesirable effect of neighborhood and

city investments. Herbert moved to Detroit with her family, and they lived in a neighborhood called Piety Hill from 2011 to 2016. Her observations, interviews, and documentation of people illegally using property (squatting, salvaging, homesteading, demolishing) in the neighborhood would become the foundation of her research and this book.

In her introduction, Herbert tells the story of a resident named Jerome, who shows her his garden in a nearby lot and describes his experiences with the site. He observed the city's lack of response to typical maintenance and infrastructural issues and then began identifying opportunities to improve conditions for himself and his neighborhood, including cleaning and growing food on vacant lots and clearing sewer grates of trash. The vacant lots on his block were owned by the city or Bank of America, but such ownership did not deter him, he said, because "nobody minds" (2). Jerome's story is important because it represents the underpinning of Herbert's research questions in Detroit. How is it possible to appropriate property informally or illegally in the city without consequences? Perhaps more importantly, why are these practices often supported and encouraged by those tasked to enforce the rules? Jerome, and other residents like him, channel their energy and efforts into improving the community around them, and they are not the exception. Herbert frames the conditions that make such practices possible and shows how they allow for Jerome and many others to manage their daily living in the city.

In part 1, "Social and Spatial Context," Herbert outlines how informal practices of property thrive, particularly in areas experiencing urban decline. Chapter 1 describes what the process of urban decline looks like in Detroit and discusses how many factors beyond the collapse of the auto industry contributed to its present state. The author argues that these factors are not unique to Detroit, but are occurring and will occur in cities around the world; she references places like Rio de Janeiro and Peru to contextualize similar informal practices and demonstrate that property informality is not just relegated to the poor. Chapter 2 helps the reader understand how these precise conditions allow informal practices to proliferate. Detroiters assume informality of vacant and abandoned property with little risk, particularly with the very real opportunity to meet their immediate and future needs. Factors such as declining city tax revenues impair the enforcement of rules for informal transgressions, often forcing cities like Detroit to concentrate remaining resources in areas typically more affluent and established—a decision that could easily be construed as economically and racially motivated. Further, vacancies and blight in neighborhoods become burdensome to maintain and surveil, which allows for informal practices to commence. The third chapter details how the illicit activity of property informality becomes legitimized and accepted by neighborhood residents and city officials and regulators alike. Property informality and appropriation can provide many positive benefits to neighborhoods, such as cleanup and demolition of dangerous, run-down buildings and structures while encouraging squatters to occupy vacant houses. It may also have the effect of discouraging socially unacceptable (and illegal) practices, such as drug houses.

Herbert states that illegality does not always mean illicit or harmful, despite the violation of rules or laws. This social acceptance of informal use and improvement is referred to as an "ethos of care" in their informal practices—the "ideological adherence to a loose set of normative ideals about how one ought to relate to property and the community, which characterizes and guides their responses to illegal property use in their neighborhoods" (59).

Part 2, "Informality in Everyday Life" (chapters 4 through 7), describes property informality practices through three types of appropriators and defines each one. Necessity Appropriators are poor, predominantly Black residents of Detroit who rely upon informal appropriation for meeting daily needs. Lifestyle Appropriators are predominately younger White newcomers to the city, who call their illegal occupation "Homesteading." Routine Appropriators are more stable, longtime residents—typically African Americans—who are frustrated over time by the lack of resources and responses from the city or appropriate property to resolve their immediate issues. Herbert identifies and organizes these individuals based upon their appropriation of vacant houses and parcels in the city and their motives as they use their method of appropriation to seize opportunities, options they navigate largely through Detroit's structural shortcomings. All the interviewees described in the book participated in the ethos of care.

The focus of chapter 5, Necessity Appropriators (NAs), are those who practice property informality in ways that help them navigate and survive the city. Appropriations of necessity include squatting in and scrapping vacant homes and buildings across the city, actions that serve the appropriators' immediate needs, respectively, for shelter and cash. Herbert found that NAs, unlike Routine Appropriators and Lifestyle Appropriators, did not participate in any gardening or urban farming as a means of securing food sources, because these activities often require additional resources, including knowledge, skills, financial capital, and, perhaps most significantly, time. Most NAs described their appropriation practices as actions they were not proud of and did not want to pursue, but because of their circumstances and the poor quality or lack of services available to them, see them as their only survival solution. Appropriating out of necessity often places individuals in precarious and temporary situations at best, and in dangerous situations at worst.

In contrast to NAs, Lifestyle Appropriators (LAs) typically appropriate vacant and abandoned property by choice. In chapter 6, Herbert identifies LAs as those who tend to engage in appropriation through homesteading, urban farming/agriculture, and scrapping. Unlike NAs, LAs actively seek these conditions as a change from their current daily lives and traditional employment, and they look to cities such as Detroit for these opportunities. LAs also have access to other resources and privileges in the form of people, money, and social connections that afford them the option to take big risks with few consequences.

In chapter 7, Routine Appropriators, or RAs, are classified somewhere between the NAs and LAs. RAs tend to be long-term Detroit residents who, frustrated or disillusioned with the [lack of] systems of the city, take charge of improving their community on their own terms. RAs generally are property (home) owners who often cycle between NA and LA status—whether they are scrapping to make ends meet, squatting in homes they used to rent or own (a practice that Herbert calls "holdover squatting"), or farming vacant lots to improve their aesthetic value and dissuade dumping. RAs also work to deter the establishment of drug houses and other illicit activity in their neighborhood blocks by cleaning and painting houses, or by tearing down those houses that are too dilapidated and unsafe. All of the RAs whom Herbert interviewed expressed sincere justification in their motives for appropriating, despite it being unlawful.

Part 3 of *A Detroit Story,* aptly named "Informal Plans and Formal Policies," illustrates how the residents' informal practices of property and the city's official planning and regulation mechanisms often clash, conflict, and resolve in ways that are unequal. In chapter 8, "Surviving or Settling the City," Herbert writes that Detroit's future will be determined not only through top-down planning efforts, but also by bottom-up, informal practices such as those utilized by NAs, LAs, and RAs. Through her narrative analysis, the author attempts to tease out how NAs, LAs, and RAs understand their formal practices within the context of city laws, and how their improvisations allow them to navigate life in the city, shaping Detroit in the ways they think it should be. NAs and RAs often justify their practices as survival in a city that has failed them on multiple fronts, whereas LAs commonly justify their actions as settling land or pioneering a vast new frontier with an abundance of possibilities. It is here that Herbert carefully notes the word choices of each appropriator type to better understand how they view the city and their relationship within it.

Whose vision of the city of Detroit will be galvanized in new rules and regulations? In chapter 9, "Regulating Informality, Reproducing Inequality," Herbert writes that revitalization efforts are well underway in the city, and she documents which informal practices already have been formalized and celebrated, and which others criminalized and rejected. Here Herbert introduces two new terms, "co-optative formalization" and "suppressive formalization," to describe the processes that occur at the city level to reestablish policy. Real examples of policy and legal changes include anti-scrapping laws (suppressive formalization) designed to deter the practice of removing materials from buildings and prohibit selling such materials to scrapyards by punishment (fines, jail time, or both), versus a program called Salvaging Detroit (co-optative formalization), which creates a marketplace around salvaged materials, often from deconstructed buildings, for purchase at very low costs. Both practices entail the deconstruction of property that NAs, RAs, and LAs do not legally own, yet the policies created around them are either punitive or rewarding. Co-optative formalization tends to support the informal practices of LAs, whereas suppressive formalization negatively impacts NAs. And depending upon which informal practice they utilize, RAs could be either helped or harmed by newly established policies. As Chuck, a White, lifelong Detroit resident and Routine Appropriator, said:

> I have no problem with squatters. None whatsoever. First thing you have to realize in the city of Detroit and a lot of cities now—you leave a house vacant long enough and it's gonna get destroyed and now you have nothing. So I personally have no problem with it as long as the tenants are acting like neighbors and not idiots. You're cutting your grass, you're taking out your trash, you're protecting the property. So no, I have no issue; matter of fact, I encourage it (64).

*A Detroit Story* is a compelling book that encourages readers to see Detroit through the lens of informal property use, and it is a great reference to use in understanding cities in decline and how residents find new ways to relate to space to address their needs. Herbert writes their narratives in a style that allows the reader to feel present with her during the interviews, fully immersed in the stories and the daily lives of the appropriators. As practitioners and scholars of the built environment—especially those of us who focus upon community engagement and environmental justice—Herbert's study offers further opportunity to reflect upon other places deep in the work of revitalization and renewal, and it challenges us to consider how our own design work can contribute to the future of cities.

AUTHOR BIOGRAPHY

**Kelley Lemon** is a registered professional landscape architect and an assistant professor in the Department of Landscape Architecture at the University of Illinois at Urbana-Champaign.

---

**Irvin J. Hunt**

*Dreaming the Present: Time, Aesthetics, and the Black Cooperative Movement*

Chapel Hill: University of North Carolina Press, 2022
288 pages, 21 black-and-white illustrations, 1 map
ISBN: 9781469667942, $23.99 EB
ISBN: 9781469667928, $95.00 HB
ISBN: 9781469667935, $29.95 PB

**Monica M. White**

*Freedom Farmers: Agricultural Resistance and the Black Freedom Movement*

Chapel Hill: University of North Carolina Press
xiii + 208 pages, 11 black-and-white illustrations
ISBN: 9781469643700, $14.99 EB (2018)
ISBN: 9781469663890, $19.95 PB (2021)

Review by Jennifer Nardone

---

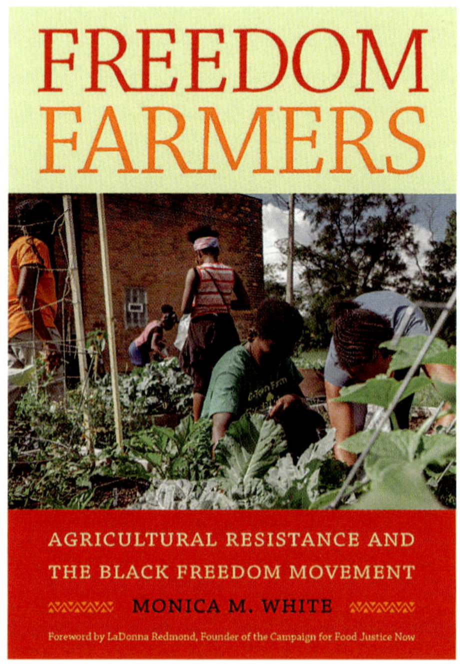


Over the last two decades, researchers and scholars have begun the complicated process of untangling the colonial landscape. These efforts are not confined to the colonial landscape of seventeenth-century wood-frame houses in greater Boston or the eighteenth-century plantation fields along the James River, many of which have been preserved over centuries and are now open for public tours and events. Those sites, even when there is no remaining structure visible—a plantation, a church, a cemetery—are forged in the settler-colonial imagination. Much like vernacularism encouraged architectural historians to look beyond monumental structures, settler colonialism as a methodology demands accountability for the White supremacy embedded in both vernacular and monumental spaces. "The vernacular" certainly expands our understanding of how space and place are defined by diverse groups of people. Settler colonialism, however, rejects the presumption that everyone envisions a landscape as a defined—or even liminal—space. What if disorder and impermanence are the only meaningful acts of resistance against ubiquitous White supremacy? Are those legible spaces in the vernacular landscape? As Irvin J. Hunt asks in his new book, when talking about spaces, places, and race, can we "unravel Blackness from *property*?" (95).

Two recent books—neither one written by historians, architectural or otherwise—grapple with what it means to interpret architecture and landscapes intended to be indecipherable to anyone who is initially viewing or scrutinizing such sites. In his book *Dreaming the Present: Time, Aesthetics, and the Black Cooperative Movement,* Irvin J. Hunt, an assistant professor of English and African American Studies at the University of Illinois at Urbana-Champaign, considers architecture as temporal rather than spatial. Hunt focuses on Black cooperatives and other efforts to build systems of mutual aid as anti-places rather than as ephemeral, vernacular spaces. To that end, Hunt focuses his study upon three cooperative efforts: the Negro Cooperative, founded by W. E. B. Du Bois in 1918; the Young Negroes' Cooperative League (YNCL), organized by George Schuyler and Ella Baker in the early years of the Great Depression; and Fannie Lou Hamer's Freedom Farm, in operation from 1969–76.

Cooperatives aim to disrupt capitalist economies, including the economics of place (i.e., who owns a cooperative?). Hunt argues that Du Bois, Baker, Hamer, and their allies viewed cooperatives as a moment in time rather than as the foundation for a permanent alternative to the capitalist economy. That, after all, would require codifying a different kind of (sustainable) economy—a variation on the historicized concept that certain institutions can be "of but not in" a dominant economic system. Black cooperative movements "had no interest in going anywhere, only taking place," Hunt surmises. "They indeed had a destination: new locations in a present heretofore unseen" (5). Hence, Du Bois, Baker, and Hamer never intended to establish permanence, only to persist in the present.

While vernacularism often includes a consideration of temporal and impermanent spaces, Hunt's book encourages a different reading of space altogether. Scholars often see "subversive space" within a racialized landscape. African Americans may find safety and meaning in the ephemeral, where they are able to counter White surveillance and violence. Often such places look innocuous to White people: churches, family gatherings, parades, juke joints; these spaces come and go, they were never meant to be permanent.[1] African Americans found ways to subvert segregation and White supremacy through impermanence and codification of conceptual space, rather than through architectural planning.

Defining the Black vernacular landscape as a series of "racially subversive spaces" or "ephemeral realities" seems flat and one dimensional as compared to Hunt's vision of space as movement—not just physical movement but a resistance movement, possible only in an imagined space. The "freedom" found within these spaces does not rely upon some version of magical realism, however. Freedom, Hunt argues, is derived from the absence of a strategic plan in pursuit of longevity. The Black cooperative movement was, in fact, not about movement. These movements focused on the moment, not momentum. Hunt identifies three variations on his theme: "sustained insipience," or a movement that continuously begins without a clear ending; a kind of "planned failure" (18) practiced by Schuyler and Baker; and, in the case of Fannie Lou Hamer's Freedom Farm, a "pluripresent" (19) movement that happened in a place that does not exist—a nowhere place.

To Hunt, Du Bois's Negro Cooperative Movement represents "sustained insipience," or a movement that continuously returns to a beginning without an exact end goal (17). Here, the author goes deep into an analysis of Du Bois's cooperative efforts. He sees an almost supernatural force behind Du Bois's work, what he calls "necro-power" which results in "death worlds," or "the inability to forget what we don't remember" (61). This is the imprint of collective generational trauma and loss caused by slavery, segregation, and systems of White supremacy. Loss shapes the Negro Cooperatives. With no end to the beginnings, however, what really can be lost? Perpetual beginnings cannot result in loss, but they can conjure a sense of what never was.

Schuyler and Baker, on the other hand, envisioned their YNCL as a "planned failure," untethered to the traditional movement goal of longevity. Schuyler opened the first YNCL in New York City in 1930, and within a few years, over two dozen chapters were open around the country. YNCL members established buying clubs, grocery stores, and other cooperatives. Schuyler only allowed members aged sixteen to thirty-six years old into the YNCL in order to avoid stagnation, or what Hunt calls "the codification of strategic anarchy" (92). As part of a network of grassroots activists during the civil rights movement, Baker frequently criticized groups like the National Association for the Advancement of Colored People (NAACP) and Southern Christian Leadership Conference (SCLC) for their institutionalism. Hunt calls Baker a "hidden influence" on YNCL, while Schuyler represented the public face of the movement as cooperatives opened around the country during the 1920s and '30s (79). Unlike Marcus Garvey's United Negro Improvement Association of the same era, the YNCL served as a site of anti-capitalist resistance. We assume any economic resistance and activist movement has a goal—in this case, to create some sort of sustainable alternative economy outside of capitalism. However, creating a space for anti-capitalist resistance intended to fail, Hunt argues, "unsettles prevailing conceptions of what it means to succeed at anti-capitalist resistance" (95).

For Hunt, Fannie Lou Hamer's Freedom Farm Cooperative, founded in Sunflower County, Mississippi, in 1967, represents "pluripresence," a place for people who have nowhere to go. Freedom Farm was that nowhere, or what Hunt refers to as a "reclamation of nowhere," an idea without geography, a physical manifestation of nowhere (138). Of course, Freedom Farm was "a somewhere"; it was deeded, legally owned property. Hunt argues that Hamer represents the intersection of collective and individual property ownership. By 1970, the cooperative owned close to seven hundred acres of land and ran a "pig bank" that produced thousands of pigs to feed impoverished families in the Delta. Hunt draws upon Walter Benjamin's notion of "the dialectic," John Locke's definition of rights in property, Karl Marx's axiom that people cannot be separated from property, and, when considering black-and-white photographs of Freedom Farm, references Roland Barthes's description of an image as "an expected flash" (169). At times, the intellectual cascade of cultural and rhetorical references and asides seems incongruent with this subject matter. Perhaps Hunt would argue that incongruence is his goal.

Hunt dedicates more text to the physical landscape of Freedom Farm than to Du Bois's Negro Cooperative or to Schuyler and Baker's Young Negroes Cooperative League, despite his assertion that the Freedom Farm represented a nowhere, or at least served as the "nowhere" for people who otherwise had nowhere to go. There are no measured floor plans or narrative descriptions of spatial relationships in *Dreaming the Present*. Rather, in order to envision shared Black spaces, Hunt removes the physical space altogether; if maintained, then Hunt's book would be yet another attempt to elevate subversive Black spaces from within a colonial landscape. Hunt argues that this simply cannot be done on the landscape itself, even within the vernacular environment. Hunt reimagines these real spaces as something that might have been, or never were. It is Afrofuturism on the landscape, where the Black past is not engulfed by the White colonial landscape, and a reimagining of what space and landscape might mean without the constraints of the dominant (racist) paradigm.

Sociologist Monica M. White considers some of the same broad issues as Hunt in her book, *Freedom Farmers: Agricultural Resistance and the Black Freedom Movement*, published as part of the Justice, Power, and Politics series from the University of North Carolina Press.[2] While Hunt emphasizes the intentional impermanence of many Black cooperative movements, White connects historical cooperative movements like Hamer's Freedom Farm with the food justice and urban farming movements of today. White considers herself "an activist and urban ethnographer" of the food justice movement in Detroit, thus situating herself as a participant-observer with a particular interest in "connect[ing] contemporary urban farmer-activists to an earlier time when African Americans turned to agriculture as a strategy for building sustainable communities" (6).

White defines her theoretical framework as "collective agency and community resilience," or CACR, and situates this framework within the emerging field of Reliance Science (7), an interesting counter-perspective to Hunt's consideration of Black cooperatives as temporary spaces, both literally and figuratively. The Black cooperative efforts of Du Bois and Hamer, White argues, were constructive movements, not necessarily efforts to dismantle or destroy segregation and capitalism. She identifies three key strategies of CARC endeavors: commons as praxis, prefigurative politics, and economic autonomy (8).

Hunt saw Du Bois's Negro Cooperative movement as a "sustained incipience" or a continual beginning without an end, as a "practice of democratizing time" (Hunt, 21). White, on the other hand, argues that Du Bois "was convinced that cooperatives were the key way to obtain freedom," implying there is an end goal—freedom—and it is, in fact, attainable (White, 50). Du Bois's goals of Black economic autonomy aligned with other efforts of the era. Beginning in the 1890s, Booker T. Washington and George Washington Carver introduced the Tuskegee College and Agricultural Experiment Station, as well as the Jesup Agricultural Wagon, a horse-drawn truck that served as a "movable school" for the impoverished Black farming communities of rural Alabama (44). Washington promoted a nascent version of Black capitalism, emphasizing the importance of property ownership to social and political equality. Marcus Garvey, too, promoted similar goals of Black property ownership—not as a bridge to social equality, but as a means of escaping the White political economy altogether. White situates Du Bois within these competing (or complimentary) movements in search of economic autonomy. His Negro Cooperative "enact(ed) commons as praxis as they provide frameworks for sharing resources for the collective good," or what Du Bois described as a "partially segregated Negro economy" (60–61).

Whereas Hunt's *Dreaming the Present* considers Hamer's Freedom Farm as a "nowhere" pluripresence, White identifies three material objectives of Freedom Farm in her book: 1) building affordable, safe housing; 2) creating an entrepreneurial clearinghouse and small business incubator; and 3) developing an agricultural cooperative that would meet the food and nutritional needs of African Americans in Sunflower County. The author also connects Freedom Farm to a similar effort in neighboring Bolivar County, Mississippi: the North Bolivar County Farm Cooperative (NBCFC). The NBCFC was founded in 1967 as a resource for African Americans who did not leave as part of the Great Migration—"the holdouts," as White describes them. White views both of these Mississippi cooperatives as places of resistance to food deprivation and malnutrition, but also as sites of Black autonomy and of CACR, which are living conditions.

Both authors address the presence of ecological grief in their books. Slavery, sharecropping, and later urban renewal policies and programs have resulted in a painful, often traumatic, relationship between African Americans and the land. Enslaved and free African Americans have been deeply connected to agriculture and resource management in the Americas since Europeans arrived, yet the legacy of slavery and sharecropping has stigmatized farming among many African American communities. That history, combined with decades—centuries—of environmental racism and manufactured poverty have kept African Americans living in urban areas without access to gardens in which to cultivate nutritious foods. White dedicates the last chapter of *Freedom Farmers* to current urban farming efforts like the Detroit Black Community Food Security Network, where she works alongside other activists who "re-enact many of the same strategies" as earlier cooperative efforts like Du Bois's Negro Cooperative and Hamer's Freedom Farm (118).

While at first glance Hunt's *Dreaming the Present* and White's *Freedom Farmers* may seem far afield from architectural studies, they each provide a distinctive insight into what constitutes "the vernacular," especially as related to re-envisioning Black spaces of the past, empowering Black spaces of the present, and imagining Black spaces of the future.

AUTHOR BIOGRAPHY

**Jennifer Nardone**, PhD, is a professor of U.S. and African American History at Columbus State Community College in Columbus, Ohio.

NOTES

1. On surveillance, freedom, and the ephemerality of architecture in the Mississippi Delta, see Jennifer Nardone, "Roomful of Blues: Jukejoints and the Cultural Landscape of the Mississippi Delta," in Alison K. Hoagland and Kenneth A. Breisch, eds., *Perspectives in Vernacular Architecture, IX: Constructing Image, Identity, and Place* (Knoxville: University of Tennessee Press, 2003), 166–75.

2. Monica M. White, PhD, is Distinguished Chair of Integrated Environmental Studies (2021–25) and associate professor of Environmental Justice at the University of Wisconsin–Madison; she also holds a joint appointment in the Department of Community and Environmental Sociology and the Nelson Institute of Environmental Studies. Dr. White is the founding director of the Office of Environmental Justice and Engagement at UW–Madison, and she is the first Black woman to earn tenure in both the College of Agricultural Life Sciences (established 1889) and the Nelson Institute (established 1970).

---

**C. J. Alvarez**

*Border Land, Border Water: A History of Construction on the US-Mexico Divide*

Austin: University of Texas Press, 2019

301 pages, 34 black-and-white illustrations, 21 maps

ISBN: 9781477319000, $54.00 HB

ISBN: 9781477319024, $35.94 PB

ISBN: 9781477319031, $29.95 EB

Review by Germán Pallares-Avitia

---

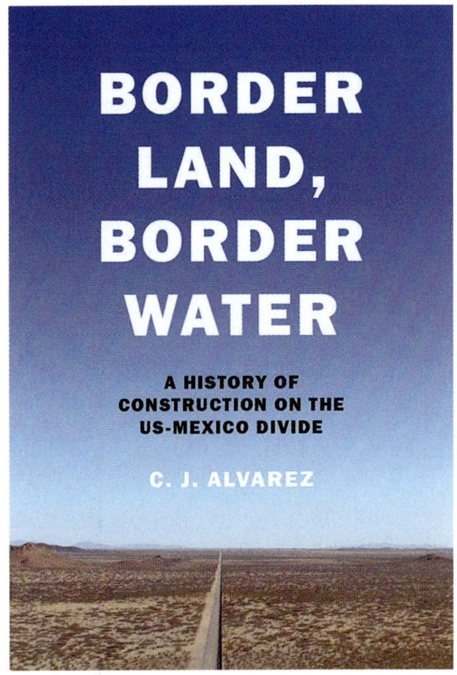


During the past few years, a proliferation of publications around border issues were inspired by the racist, anti-immigrant discourse surrounding the United States' border with México. Scholars, designers, planners, and architects focused on finding solutions to the "border problem"; these solutions typically simplified the México/U.S. border into a line, and the border problems into the figure of the immigrant. Revisions of a border history that focused on the political delineation of the borderline supported the design solution proposed for the border. Although social, political, and anthropological histories of the México/U.S. border have been produced, few books focusing on the history of its built environment have been published. *Border Land, Border Water: A History of Construction on the US-Mexico Divide* by C. J. Alvarez, an associate professor of Mexican American and Latina/o Studies at the University of Texas at Austin, offers one of the first approaches to the history of construction along the border, emphasizing the infrastructure that helped to define, transform, and secure it.

Alvarez's book, winner of the Vernacular Architecture Forum's Abbott Lowell Cummings Award in 2020 for the book that made the most significant contribution to the study of vernacular architecture and cultural landscapes, examines the American and Mexican governments' efforts to build infrastructure along the border, with a primary focus on the American side. These projects, intended to control and modify nature, were seen as modernizing agents. Controlling the unruly and unpredictable nature of rivers, deserts, plains, and mountains symbolized dominance of the colonialist nation-state over the uncivilized natural environment. Over time, these projects led to the development of infrastructure that varied from divisive to transformative and connective.

*Border Land, Border Water* brings into perspective the politics of the binational negotiations that these projects demanded. It explores how, in the construction of the borderline, both countries constructed infrastructure that reflected the different foreign policies of the historical periods when they were built. Alvarez especially focuses on bringing to light the American political apparatus behind the infrastructural projects for water works, dams, bridges, and highways that delineated the border. By acknowledging the borderline as a capitalist colonial structure that is anchored in land grabbing, private property, and control, Alvarez historicizes its mechanisms for controlling the flow of nature, people, and merchandise.

Instead of organizing the chapters of this book by the typology of its built projects or by the institutions that participated in their conception and construction, Alvarez organizes chapters chronologically. This strategy helps the reader to better understand the evolution of the built environment around the border. It narrates a historical account of the border from geographical and political perspectives: from the tracing of the border line resulting from the 1836 Texan independence and the 1848 Treaty of Guadalupe Hidalgo to the final settling of the actual borderline in 1963 when the territory of El Chamizal was returned to México, and the project for the channeling of the Rio Grande was executed.

The exhaustive research in *Border Land, Border Water* can be divided into three main sections. The first section consists of an account of the projects that were executed in order to delineate and demarcate the border. The book's second section deals mainly with infrastructural projects—those designed to control the flow of nature, border water, and the flow of people—dams, river straightening, fence building, and the first attempts to militarize the border. In the last section, Alvarez explores projects that he defines as "compensatory building" that were intended to "mitigate the unsustainable results of the previous" building projects, as well as to what degree the political forces behind them disturbed and radically altered the inherently systemic territorial landscapes of the transborder areas (4).

In recounting the history of how the border became demarcated, the author not only narrates the political efforts behind delineating it on paper, but also expands upon the strenuous physical efforts involved in the task of marking it on the ground, offering a perspective on the binational project of building the first border monuments. These obelisks, built to mark the borderline where a natural border did not exist, were intended to reorganize and control nature and peoples, both indigenous populations and citizens of both states. This monument project survey not only brought to the collective imagination the prejudices and stigma of marginality to border people, flora, and fauna, but it also offered surrealist descriptions of the arid desert landscape. These descriptions of animals, plants, and buildings, distorted in shape and form by the heat mirages, surprised and frightened the geographers and engineers working on the projects.

Alvarez dedicates a whole chapter to the effects that the Mexican Revolution brought to the border landscape. Although accounts of this period's history have been extensively recorded in other books like David Dorado Romo's *Ringside Seat to a Revolution,* a microhistory of the Juárez-El Paso region, Alvarez's book focuses on the built environment as a historical character.[1] He identifies this period as a time of destruction instead of construction, where the connective infrastructure, like the one laid out by the international railroads, was under attack. Alvarez also explores how the safeguarding and reconstruction of this infrastructure brought militarization and securement of the borderlands. The borderland, specifically its desert landscape, becomes a military training camp for the American armed forces. Used to train the army into enduring harsh climate conditions, the borderlands desert then becomes a model for future interventions elsewhere.[2]

The military surveys brought a renewed intention to control nature, but this time the rivers and the flow of water were targeted in the control efforts of the government. Infrastructural waterworks like dams and the strengthening of the Rio Grande characterized this post–Mexican Revolution/post–WWI period. With the farming crisis of the 1920s, special efforts were made to bring resources to the agricultural industries in the United States. Water securement brought a need and appreciation of Mexican labor, as Alvarez spotlights. At the same time, protection from animal diseases ignited the construction of dividing fences at the border.

As the midcentury period arrived after WWII, the borderlands suffered their greatest transformations: the border became a space of division and the expression of nationalism. Everlasting infrastructure would come to symbolize both the connections and divisions between the two countries. Alvarez here expands upon the history of the return of the El Chamizal territory, an area between Juárez and El Paso that by its dimensions could be deemed insignificant but that gained international importance as a successful diplomatic affair. This section also explores the infrastructural projects derived from this agreement, primarily the channeling of the Río Bravo/Rio Grande, which marked the final and current state of the borderline. At the same time that he explains how water control brought new problems to the borderland ecosystems, like salinity due to water flow differentials, Alvarez provides a perspective on solutions such as "compensatory building" projects (4).

By the 1970s relations between both countries changed and the border became less porous, criminalizing the border crosser. These compensatory building projects turned into infrastructure that would facilitate policing as well as border trade: bridges and fences were the main typologies constructed. Military technology was brought to the border to serve in the "war against drugs," and the built environment had to comply with this type of surveillance. A de-naturing of the borderlands would ensure easier control, and almost no length of the river remained unchanged by construction at the end of the 1970s. Fences were built to harm people, not merely to prevent their movement, as Alvarez shows in construction documents. Plans and drawings of sections and elevations of the fences, as well as descriptions of their materials and construction methods, reveal how they were designed to move people outside of major urban sites and push those immigrants to places where life is untenable.

By revising the political history that formed

the México/U.S. border—from the U.S. expansionism of the early 1800s, to Texas independence, the Mexican–American War, and the border policing projects of the mid-twentieth century—Alvarez helps his readers to more fully comprehend the political climate at the border to this day. His book uses the built environment to illustrate how binational enterprises provide local responses to global conflicts, as it brings a new perspective that reveals how infrastructure contributes to the complex, interrelated political and economic systems that exist between México and the United States.

What Alvarez accomplishes is telling a story of these infrastructure projects and the tremendous changes they brought to the built environment; however, he misses on their effects upon the border dwellers. Readers do not learn about changes to the daily lives of the *fronterizos,* other than a brief mention of how the inhabitants of the Chamizal and Isla de Cordova regions were affected by the channeling of the river, or how the construction of a dam, the Falcon International Reservoir, affected the towns of Zapata, Texas, and Ciudad Guerrero, Tamaulipas. By using the same lens of the man-made landscape, the author could have offered a perspective on the ways in which the built environment contributes to the unification or separation of border-dwelling people.

Alvarez makes clear to the reader the vital fact that the border is not "a single place, a single thing," but a series of ecosystems, geographies, and climates (1). He also acknowledges, importantly, that rivers are not simply natural demarcations of political boundaries but are also important construction sites that have endured spatial controls and modifications by the state and private institutions. The author illustrates how these modifications to the natural environment were paradoxically designed to impede the movement of humans, vehicles, and animals while also ensuring the transit of merchandise. In that sense, the argument of the book centers around building the borderline, and not building around that line. As Alvarez states, the book is not focused on border city development; rather, it is a unilateral history, from the American perspective, of how politics are reflected in the built environment. As someone who has experienced the border firsthand, and as someone who views the border at ground level, Alvarez's treatment of this topic is much more nuanced and includes complexities that other histories have failed to appreciate, a perspective that should be more prevalent in border studies.

AUTHOR BIOGRAPHY

**Germán Pallares-Avitia** is assistant professor at the Rhode Island School of Design, where he teaches courses on the history and theory of architecture. He is currently working on developing the manuscript of his book *Life on the Border: Constructing the México/US Borderlands, 1961–1971.*

NOTES

1. David Dorado Romo, *Ringside Seat to a Revolution: An Underground Cultural History of El Paso and Juárez, 1893–1923* (El Paso, Texas: Cinco Puntos Press, 2005), 11.

2. Ersela Kripa and Stephen Mueller, *Fronts: Military Urbanisms in the Developing World* (Novato, Calif.: Applied Research + Design Publishing, 2020), expands upon this practice.

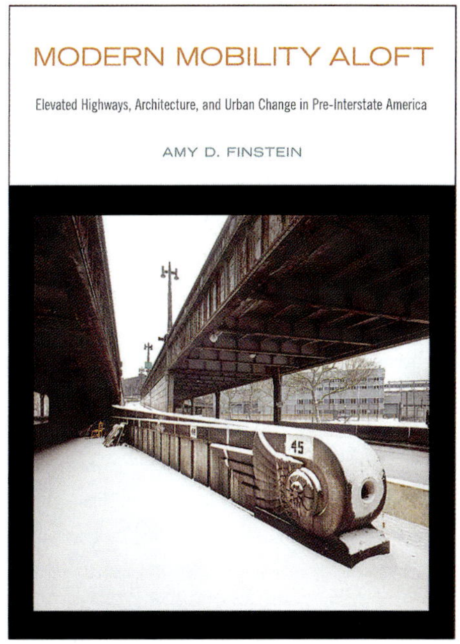


**Amy D. Finstein**

*Modern Mobility Aloft: Elevated Highways, Architecture, and Urban Change in Pre-Interstate America*

Philadelphia: Temple University Press, 2020

xi + 289 pages, 114 black-and-white illustrations

ISBN: 9781439919187, $29.95 PB

ISBN: 9781439919170, $115.50 HB

ISBN: 9781439919194, $29.95 EB

Review by Robin B. Williams

Amy D. Finstein's *Modern Mobility Aloft: Elevated Highways, Architecture, and Urban Change in Pre-Interstate America* is a welcome addition to the growing body of literature on the impact of automobiles on the American built environment that includes suburbanization and large-scale highway systems.[1] Instead of the broad national scope of most studies, Finstein offers a doubly focused approach, analyzing a specific type of automobile infrastructure—the elevated urban highway—through three early examples: Wacker Drive in Chicago, the West Side (or

Miller) Highway in New York, and the Central Artery in Boston. Her sharper focus allows her to unpack the complexities of urban highway construction at the local level. Yet, by exploring the topic across three different cities spanning roughly sixty years, she adeptly reveals the diversity of challenges and responses to accommodating the automobile. Most refreshing is her analysis of the highways as built form and their relationship to contemporaneous trends in architecture.

Finstein draws on the methodology employed by Leo Marx in *The Machine in the Garden,* which analyzed how the intrusion of the railroad onto the American frontier served as an expression of modernity that shaped the public's view and use of the American landscape. As she notes, "This book builds on Marx's pivotal model by positioning the rise of the automobile and its representation of machined progress as the twentieth-century equivalent of his paradigm" (11). Her study enriches the understanding of elevated urban highways as more than engineering projects to address their civic and social objectives and ramifications. Organized into three sections, the book achieves a successful balance between surveying the broader context of the emerging technologies reshaping cities, including automobiles, and providing a focused analysis of the three elevated highway case studies.

The first section involves a thorough discussion of "three innovations that radically and successively altered the basis of urban life and urban form"—the railroad, the skyscraper, and the automobile—and that responded to the growing desire for technology, speed, and privatization (15). Finstein insightfully connects the desire for speed in nineteenth-century rail-based transit systems to the rapid evolution of technologies relating to business recordkeeping, telecommunications, and commerce that drove demand for office buildings. Facilitating their upward growth and more rapid internal movement, the elevator allowed skyscrapers to dominate urban skylines, a visible expression of the privatization of the public realm that anticipated the impact of the private automobile. Of the various forms of new technology addressed in the first chapter, her discussion of automobiles, surprisingly, was most problematic in oversimplifying the degree to which private property owners controlled street pavement work and in neglecting to mention the impact of street-use legislation such as jaywalking laws that set an important precedent for the exclusive use of elevated highways by private vehicles.

Those omissions are amply compensated by her highly detailed second chapter examining the range of proposed solutions to the growing crisis of automobile congestion that emerged by the 1920s. Here Finstein provides a fascinating back history on four categories of proposals, ranging from stop-gap regulatory practices (such as one-way streets and parking bans) and small-scale engineering solutions to large-scale engineering and beautification plans and utopian visions of futuristic car-based urbanism, with elevated highways drawing from all four. With this last topic of utopian visions, Finstein establishes the linkages between architects and automobility—addressing Le Corbusier, Hugh Ferriss, Harvey Wiley Corbett, Frank Lloyd Wright, and Norman Bel Geddes—that distinguish her book from other studies of highways and roads. With its focus on the technological challenges facing cities during the late nineteenth and early twentieth centuries, this first section offers great value and perspective on topics far broader than the declared topic of the book and could easily be a standalone reading.

The second and third sections are more straightforward in their deep analysis of the three case studies. Section 2 (cheekily entitled "Elevated Expectations") explores the roles played by politicians, engineers, and architects in the promotion and design of each of these projects. All three projects grew out of similar circumstances: long-standing transportation proposals focused on waterfront areas of congestion that combined issues of shipping and freight with growing transportation needs. They also all drew on the precedent and, paradoxically, the unpopularity of elevated railroads as an argument in favor of an alternative form of elevated infrastructure. As Finstein notes, "despite some differences, these projects developed from parallel problems, shared hopes for urban revitalization and a common belief in elevated highways as visible, efficient and modern responses to these conditions" (79). Section 2 anchors each project to the prevailing architectural culture of their respective city and era—beaux arts Chicago, art deco New York, and streamlined Boston—reinforcing their architectonic quality.

Finstein gives excellent attention to the governmental institutions and people responsible for each project, while providing detailed discussions of the debates and disagreements that shaped them. In the case of Wacker Drive, the original vision for a multilevel roadway grew out of Daniel Burnham and Edward H. Bennett's famous 1909 Plan of Chicago. Wacker Drive illustrates the early variability of how an elevated roadway could be achieved, involving the elevation of a whole section of downtown Chicago in the two blocks south of the highway, rendering its elevated nature invisible from the Loop area; facing the Chicago River to its north, however, the multilevel nature of the road is starkly apparent. Following Burnham's premature death in 1912, Bennett shepherded the project, which had been delayed by legal battles until 1918, through to its completion in 1926.

Legal challenges also delayed development of the West Side Highway in New York, which grew out of proposals for grade-separated solutions to the problems posed by at-grade private railway lines as early as 1908, with the highway being realized only in the 1930s. Concerns over the highway's aesthetic impact led to the hiring of architects Sloan and Robertson, whose firm specialized in skyscraper design, to embellish the highway, including the on and off ramps, railings, and light standards. Among the decorative motifs were winged wheels. Curiously, Finstein does not note their resemblance to the more famous contemporaneous appearance of this motif on the Chrysler Building.

Of the three projects, the Central Artery in Boston experienced the longest gestation period, being rooted in proposals dating back as far as 1902, with construction beginning in 1950, initially as a municipal project but realized under state government control. Principally designed by engineers, architect Harold C. Knight authored the sign bridges (structures above the roadway holding signs), light standards, ramps, and the highway's overall profile. Although this project materialized during the late 1940s when "streamlined" architecture was in vogue, the finished product (and title of the chapter) would be more accurately called modernist or even international style Boston.

In charting the evolution of each project, Finstein thoroughly illustrates proposals, design details, and construction photos that provide a clear sense of their respective features. The images of the numerous precedents and proposals are especially valuable. While several maps of proposed routes are included, more detailed maps showing how the three highways in their final form related to their surrounding contexts would have been helpful.

The final chapter, entitled "Aftershocks," addresses the legacy and fate of each highway following their completion. Of the three, only Wacker Drive remains in place, largely because it least conformed to the physical norm of elevated highways. The growing scale and scope of highway construction nationwide, especially after passage of the Federal-Aid Highway Act of 1956 that funded the U.S. Interstate Highway System, also witnessed growing opposition to the disruptive and destructive nature of highways passing through cities. Within a few decades of their respective completions, the West Side Highway and the Central Artery faced mounting calls for their removal. The former was replaced by an at-grade roadway between 1973 and the 1990s, while the latter was replaced by an underground highway—the infamous Big Dig project—from 1991 to 2007.

Feinstein's writing is highly accessible and ably marshals numerous historic images to support her argument. At the beginning of each chapter, she outlines a series of numbered points that are then successively addressed through the chapter. The technique, though somewhat formulaic, provides a clear framework that facilitates an even treatment of each project. The analysis is underpinned by an impressive body of research communicated through numerous and often highly detailed footnotes. Even more impressive and an excellent resource for readers is the extensive bibliography, which outlines the many archival repositories and even the specific collections that she consulted. Additionally, she lists the many primary source reports, books, and journal and newspaper articles relating to the topic.

With its inclusion of the role of architects as part of the design team of elevated highways and their connection to the visionary projects authored by architects in the 1920s and '30s, *Modern Mobility Aloft* effectively broadens and deepens our understanding of highways as built form. Finstein introduces numerous prominent figures who will be unfamiliar to many readers, while offering a broadened context for understanding familiar designers in architectural history, such as Le Corbusier, Hugh Ferriss, and Norman Bel Geddes. Yet her analysis also synthesizes in a compact and highly digestible way the technical, economic, social, and political complexities that also shaped urban highways. The unpacking of this complicated evolution of urban highway infrastructure prior to the more familiar development of the U.S. Interstate Highway System should be valuable to anyone interested in the history of modern cities, the history of urban design, civic infrastructures, and the cultural landscapes associated with automobiles.


AUTHOR BIOGRAPHY

**Robin B. Williams** chairs the Architectural History Department at the Savannah College of Art and Design. He is the lead author of *Buildings of Savannah* (2016) and coauthor of a forthcoming book on the history of Savannah's urban plan and how it shaped the city's architecture (University of Georgia Press).


NOTES

1. On suburbanization see Kenneth T. Jackson's *Crabgrass Frontier: The Suburbanization of the United States* (New York: Oxford University Press, 1985); Robert Fishman, *Bourgeois Utopias: The Rise and Fall of Suburbia* (New York: Basic Books, 1987); Roger Silverstone, ed., *Visions of Suburbia* (London: Routledge, 1997); Dolores Hayden, *Building Suburbia: Green Fields and Urban Growth, 1820–2000* (New York: Vintage Books, 2003); and Robert Bruegmann, *Sprawl: A Compact History* (Chicago: University of Chicago Press, 2005). On the impact of automobiles on cities, see Clay McShane, *Down the Asphalt Path: The Automobile and the American City* (New York: Columbia University Press, 1994); and Jane Holtz Kay, *Asphalt Nation: How the Automobile Took Over America and How We Can Take It Back* (Berkeley: University of California Press, 1997). On the development of highways, see Thomas L. Karnes, *Asphalt and Politics: A History of the American Highway System* (Jefferson, N.C.: McFarland & Company, 2009); Tom Lewis, *Divided Highways: Building the Interstate Highways, Transforming American Life* (New York: Viking Penguin, 1997); and Earl Swift, *The Big Roads: The Untold Story of the Engineers, Visionaries, and Trailblazers who Created the American Superhighways* (Boston: Mariner Books, 2012).

# List of Editors: *Perspectives in Vernacular Architecture* and *Buildings & Landscapes*

*Perspectives in Vernacular Architecture* (1982); *Perspectives in Vernacular Architecture, II* (1986)

EDITOR: Camille Wells

*Perspectives in Vernacular Architecture, III* (1989); *Perspectives in Vernacular Architecture, IV* (1991)

EDITORS: Thomas Carter and Bernard L. Herman

*Gender, Class, and Shelter: Perspectives in Vernacular Architecture, V* (1995); *Shaping Communities: Perspectives in Vernacular Architecture, VI* (1997)

EDITORS: Elizabeth Collins Cromley and Carter L. Hudgins

*Exploring Everyday Landscapes: Perspectives in Vernacular Architecture, VII* (1997); *People, Power, Places: Perspectives in Vernacular Architecture, VIII* (2000)

EDITORS: Annmarie Adams and Sally McMurry

*Constructing Image, Identity, and Place: Perspectives in Vernacular Architecture, IX* (2003); *Building Environments: Perspectives in Vernacular Architecture, X* (2005)

EDITORS: Alison K. Hoagland and Kenneth A. Breisch

*Perspectives in Vernacular Architecture: The Journal of the Vernacular Architecture Forum* 11 (2004); *Perspectives in Vernacular Architecture: The Journal of the Vernacular Architecture Forum* 12 (2005); *Perspectives in Vernacular Architecture: The Journal of the Vernacular Architecture Forum* 13.1 (2006)

EDITORS: Jan Jennings and Pamela Simpson

*Perspectives in Vernacular Architecture: The Journal of the Vernacular Architecture Forum* 13.2 (2006/2007), Special 25th Anniversary Issue

EDITORS: Warren Hofstra and Camille Wells

*Buildings & Landscapes: Journal of the Vernacular Architecture Forum* 14 (Fall 2007); 15 (Fall 2008); 16.1 (Spring 2009); 16.2 (Fall 2009)

EDITORS: Howard Davis and Louis P. Nelson
REVIEW EDITOR: Marilyn Castro

*Buildings & Landscapes: Journal of the Vernacular Architecture Forum* 17.1 (Spring 2010); 17.2 (Fall 2010); 18.1 (Spring 2011); 18.2 (Fall 2011); 19.1 (Spring 2012); 19.2 (Fall 2012)

EDITORS: Marta Gutman and Louis P. Nelson
REVIEW EDITOR: Andrew K. Sandoval-Strausz

*Buildings & Landscapes: Journal of the Vernacular Architecture Forum* 20.1 (Spring 2013); 20.2 (Fall 2013); 21.1 (Spring 2014); 21.2 (Fall 2014); 22.1 (Spring 2015); 22.2 (Fall 2015)

EDITORS: Cynthia G. Falk and Marta Gutman
REVIEW EDITOR: Andrew K. Sandoval-Strausz

*Buildings & Landscapes: Journal of the Vernacular Architecture Forum* 23.1 (Spring 2016); 23.2 (Fall 2016); 24.1 (Spring 2017); 24.2 (Fall 2017)

EDITORS: Anna Vemer Andrzejewski and Cynthia G. Falk
REVIEW EDITOR: Matthew Lasner

*Buildings & Landscapes: Journal of the Vernacular Architecture Forum* 25.1 (Spring 2018); 25.2 (Fall 2018); 26.1 (Spring 2019); 26.2 (Fall 2019)

EDITORS: Anna Vemer Andrzejewski and Carl Lounsbury
REVIEW EDITORS: Andrew Johnston and Jessica Ellen Sewell

*Buildings & Landscapes: Journal of the Vernacular Architecture Forum* 27.1 (Spring 2020); 27.2, Environmental Issue, Michael J. Chiarappa, Guest Editor (Fall 2020)

EDITORS: Lydia Mattice Brandt and Carl Lounsbury
REVIEW EDITORS: Andrew Johnston and Jessica Ellen Sewell

*Buildings & Landscapes: Journal of the Vernacular Architecture Forum* 28.1 (Spring 2021)

EDITORS: Lydia Mattice Brandt and Carl Lounsbury
EDITOR DESIGNATE: Michael J. Chiarappa
REVIEW EDITORS: Andrew Johnston and Jessica Ellen Sewell

*Buildings & Landscapes: Journal of the Vernacular Architecture Forum* 28.2 (Fall 2021)

EDITORS: Lydia Mattice Brandt and Carl Lounsbury
EDITOR DESIGNATE: Michael J. Chiarappa
REVIEW EDITOR: Rachel Leibowitz

*Buildings & Landscapes: Journal of the Vernacular Architecture Forum* 29.1 (Spring 2022); 29.2 (Fall 2022)

EDITORS: Lydia Mattice Brandt and Michael J. Chiarappa
REVIEW EDITOR: Rachel Leibowitz

*Buildings & Landscapes: Journal of the Vernacular Architecture Forum* 30.1/2 (Spring/Fall 2023)

EDITORS: Lydia Mattice Brandt and Michael J. Chiarappa
EDITOR DESIGNATE: Margaret M. Grubiak
REVIEW EDITORS: Rachel Leibowitz and Amanda C. Roth Clark

# Enjoyed *Buildings & Landscapes?*

## Join the VAF!

Become a part of this active community of architectural historians, urban planners, preservationists, historians, art historians, landscape historians, geographers, curators, folklorists, archeologists, and designers at:

**http://vafweb.org/join**

The Vernacular Architecture Forum is the premier organization in North America dedicated to the study of common buildings and landscapes. Founded in 1979, the VAF draws scholars and professionals from across complementary disciplines who approach the everyday built environment as a window into history, life, and culture.

Membership benefits include:

- A paper and electronic (via JSTOR) subscription to the VAF's journal, *Buildings & Landscapes,* the leading source for scholarly work on vernacular architecture within and beyond North America.
- Direct receipt of the quarterly Vernacular Architecture Newsletter
- Registration discounts for the VAF annual conference and sponsored events
- Access to the VAF member forums.

**Student, institutional, and lifetime membership rates are available.**

# University of Minnesota Press

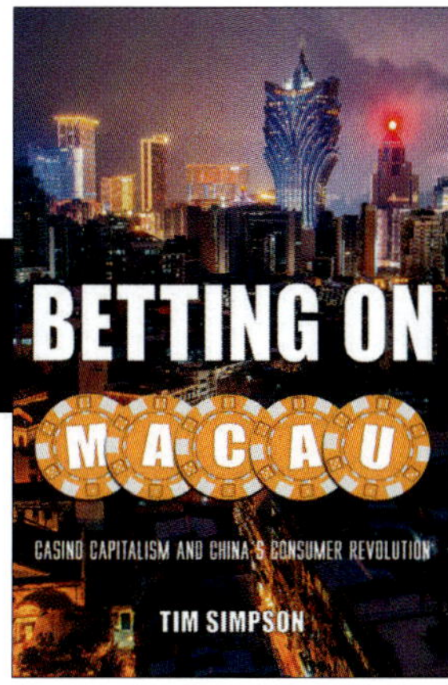

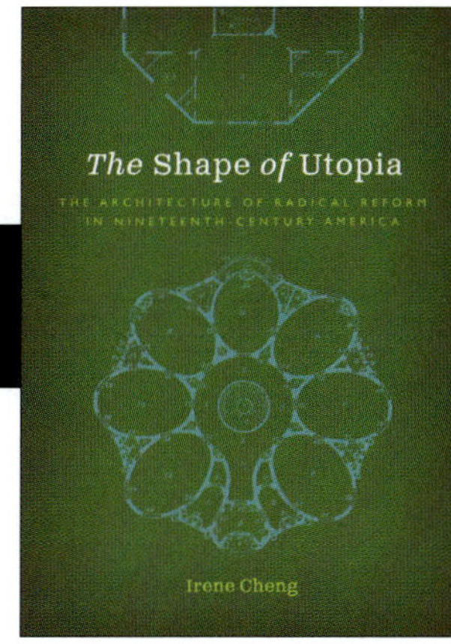


## Horror in Architecture
***The Reanimated Edition***
Joshua Comaroff and Ong Ker-Shing

"Deeply researched, packed with detail, and bold in scope and imagination." —**Achille Mbembe**, philosopher, author of *On the Postcolony*

$24.95 paperback | 264 pages | 142 images
Available January 2024

## Betting on Macau
***Casino Capitalism and China's Consumer Revolution***
Tim Simpson

"A must-read for scholars and practitioners of urban planning and architecture." —**Miodrag Mitrašinović**, coeditor of *The Emerging Public Realm of the Greater Bay Area*

$30.00 paperback | 388 pages | 39 images
Globalization and Community Series

## The Architecture of Disability
***Buildings, Cities, and Landscapes beyond Access***
David Gissen

"An urgent and exhilarating manifesto that calls for nothing less than a complete rethinking of architecture." —**Beatriz Colomina**, author of *X-Ray Architecture*

$24.95 paperback | 216 pages | 26 images

## Nothing Permanent
***Modern Architecture in California***
Todd Cronan

"A brilliant reinterpretation of the divergent strains of twentieth-century modern architecture in Southern California." —**Judith Sheine**, author of *R. M. Schindler*

$39.95 paperback | 400 pages | 165 images

## The Shape of Utopia
***The Architecture of Radical Reform in Nineteenth-Century America***
Irene Cheng

"Combines architectural and social analysis to offer a deeply informed interpretation of the complex interactions between political ideals and geometric form." —**Margaret Crawford**, University of California, Berkeley

$35.00 paperback | 360 pages | 140 images
Buell Center Books in the History and Theory of American Architecture Series

## Against the Commons
***A Radical History of Urban Planning***
Álvaro Sevilla-Buitrago

"One of the most important, original, and radical contributions to planning theory and history in the past fifty years." —**Neil Brenner**, University of Chicago

$29.00 paperback | 318 pages | 26 images

University of Minnesota Press • 800-621-2736 • www.upress.umn.edu

MINNESOTA